MASCULINITIES
IN SIXTEENTH-CENTURY FRANCE

MASCULINITIES
IN SIXTEENTH-CENTURY FRANCE

PROCEEDINGS OF THE EIGHTH
CAMBRIDGE FRENCH RENAISSANCE COLLOQUIUM
5–7 JULY 2003

edited by

Philip Ford and Paul White

CAMBRIDGE FRENCH COLLOQUIA
CAMBRIDGE 2006

CONTENTS

Illustrations   vi
Acknowledgements   viii
Introduction   ix

1   A Prototype of the Modern Man:
    Saint Joseph in France, *c.* 1400–1650
    GARY FERGUSON, University of Delaware   1

2   Feminising the Warrior at Francis I's Fontainebleau
    KATHLEEN WILSON-CHEVALIER, American University of Paris   23

3   Situating the Masculine: Gender, Identity, and the Cosmos,
    in Maurice Scève's *Délie*, Marsilio Ficino's *De amore*, and
    Leone Ebreo's *Dialoghi*
    KATHRYN BANKS, University of Durham   61

4   Rhetoric and Virility in Ronsard's *Folastries*
    CATHY YANDELL, Carleton College   85

5   Re-Reading Platonic Sexuality Sceptically in
    Montaigne's 'Apologie de Raimond Sebond'
    TODD W. REESER, University of Pittsburgh   103

6   Betwixt and Between: Hermaphroditism and Masculinity
    JOHN O'BRIEN, Royal Holloway, University of London   127

7   Masculinité et virilité: récits d'un roi sans enfants
    GUY POIRIER, University of Waterloo   147

8   Men are from Mars: Jean de Sponde's Homeric Heroes
    and Vision of Just French Leaders
    MARC BIZER, University of Texas, Austin   167

9   Éros masqué: figures mythiques de l'homosexualité
    GISÈLE MATHIEU-CASTELLANI, Université de Paris 7   181

INDEX   199

ILLUSTRATIONS

Fig. 1   Léon Davent after Francesco Primaticcio, *Hercules, Omphale and Pan* (engraving, Paris, Bibliothèque nationale de France)   46

Fig. 2   Rosso Fiorentino (?), *Bacchus, Venus and Cupid* (oil on canvas, Collection Musée national d'histoire et d'art, Luxembourg)   47

Fig. 3   Tapestry after *The Battle of Centaurs and Lapiths* bay of the Galerie François Ier, 1540s (Vienna, Kunsthistorisches Museum)   48

Fig. 4   Rosso Fiorentino, *The Education of Achilles* bay, 1530s (Galerie François Ier, château de Fontainebleau)   49

Fig. 5   Tapestry after *The Loss of Perpetual Youth* bay of the Galerie François Ier, 1540s (Vienna, Kunsthistorisches Museum)   50

Fig. 6   Rosso Fiorentino, *The Punishment of Attis* bay, 1530s (Galerie François Ier, château de Fontainebleau)   51

Fig. 7   Léon Davent after Francesco Primaticcio, *Jupiter and Semele*, etching (Vienna, Albertina)   52

Fig. 8   Anonymous seventeenth-century drawing of a tondo by Rosso for the Cabinet du roi, Fontainebleau, *Constantine burning the heretical books* (location unknown)   53

Fig. 9   Tapestry after the *Danäe* bay of the Galerie François Ier, 1540s (Vienna, Kunsthistorisches Museum)   54

Fig. 10   Rosso Fiorentino, *The Fire of Catania/Troy* bay, 1530s (Galerie François Ier, château de Fontainebleau)   55

Fig. 11   Rosso Fiorentino, *The Cleobis and Biton* bay, 1530s (Galerie François Ier, château de Fontainebleau)   56

Fig. 12   Tapestry after *The Unity of the State* bay of the Galerie François Ier, 1540s (Vienna, Kunsthistorisches Museum)   57

Fig. 13   Francesco Primaticcio, *The Antipodes*, early 1540s
            (Paris, Louvre, Département des Arts Graphiques, Inv.
            8512)   58

Fig. 14   Francesco Primaticcio, *Jupiter as Diana*, early 1540s
            (Paris, École des Beaux-Arts, M1155)   58

Fig. 15   'Portrait satyrique d'Henry III', in [Artus Thomas], *Isle
            des hermaphrodites* (1605)   144

Fig. 16   Niccolò Bellin, *François Ier*, Cliché Bibliothèque natio-
            nale de France, Paris   145

Fig. 17   'Portrait monstrüeux et allegorique d'Henri III'   146

ACKNOWLEDGEMENTS

We should like to express our sincere gratitude to the following institutions, whose continued support made the Colloquium possible: the Institut Français du Royaume-Uni; Cambridge University Department of French; Clare College, Cambridge; and Trinity College, Cambridge. We are also grateful to Gary Ferguson, Liz Guild, Gillian Jondorf, and Neil Kenny for their help as members of the Steering Committee, and to Elizabeth Kenny and Richard Wistreich for the colloquium concert, 'Real Basses, Real Men'. Finally, we should like to record our considerable thanks to Wendy Bennett, Head of the French Department at the time of the colloquium, and to the present Head of Department, Emma Wilson, for their encouragement, support, and enthusiasm.

INTRODUCTION

If the Renaissance has traditionally been associated with the ascendancy of the individual and the importance of self-representation and self-fashioning, this general tendency may also be observed more particularly in the area of gender stereotypes and performance in the early modern period. While the preceding age had offered a limited number of male role models for which there continued to be a certain nostalgia in popular culture — the chivalric knight–lover being only the most obvious of these — Renaissance society developed a wider range of male exemplars. Following the lead of François Ier, the nobleman was expected to have a humanist education as well as a chivalric one, to be able to combine rhetoric with the martial arts. The greater emphasis on a personal form of religion in the early decades of the century had its impact on male conduct outside the religious sphere, while the influence of Ficinian neo-Platonism, particularly in the visual arts, justified the presence of sensual male as well as female figures in Mannerist art, presented to the viewer as objects of desire. The newly decorated royal palaces abounded in mythological scenes which celebrated the male body. The Masculinities Colloquium, held in Clare College in July 2003, set out to explore these often destabilising new models of male representation, focusing on issues such as the survival of the chivalric ideal, homosexuality and neo-Platonism, the role of mythology, and the changing attitudes towards male performativity at court.

A number of the papers in this collection focus on the feminising of the male stereotype, in both positive and negative ways. Gary Ferguson, for example, through the study of the figure of Saint Joseph, shows how a saint who had often been a figure of fun in medieval literature, where he could be presented as an aging cuckold, became a figure of devotion, especially revered for his nurturing qualities, and offering a more caring, personal model to the urban *paterfamilias* than the more authoritarian figures of earlier times. Similarly, Kathleen Wilson-Chevalier explores the way in which François Ier set out to tame his bellicose and unruly *noblesse d'épée* by a feminising of male conduct, reflected in the art of the newly refurbished and extended palace of Fontainebleau. As the King showed his visitors around the famous gallery which bears his name, he would have presented them with a sermon on the dangers of uncontrolled male aggression in contrast to the more desirable feminine qualities of unity, spirituality, and reconciliation. Nor is it just in the early years of the six-teenth century that this message was felt to be desirable. Marc Bizer's analysis of Jean de Sponde's commentary on Homer, dedicated to the man who would be the first of the Bourbon kings, Henri de Navarre, shows how the young scholar particularly recommends the more peaceful quality of *prudentia* to the king, as opposed to the more male *fortitudo*, as a way of combating the tendency towards violence and wrath which was such a baleful legacy of the wars of religion.

If Henri de Navarre is treated with respect by Sponde, his predecessor, Henri III, often fell foul of other writers of the period. His frequently scandalous behaviour, the position and influence of his *mignons* at court, his failure to produce an heir all provided reasons for his stigmatisation, not just in Protestant circles but also amongst the ultra-Catholic supporters of the *Ligue*. At the same time, just like the readers of the tabloid press in our own days, there was no lack of an audience willing to be at once shocked and titillated by the King's private life. John O'Brien explores the gender ambiguity which characterised Henri III by investigating the figure of the hermaphrodite in sixteenth-century society. Feminisation of the male as a civilising force is seen to have gone too far in his case, leading to a terminal erosion of royal authority. The failure of the royal couple to produce an heir only added to Henri's problems, which are considered, amongst other things, from a medical point of view by Guy Poirier. The King's attempts, through both religious/superstitious practice and surgical intervention, to produce a son were chronicled by Pierre de L'Estoile, who also recorded various satirical verses about the monarch's sexual practices, but it is Agrippa d'Aubigné who produced one of the more devastating portraits of Henri III in the *Tragiques* and in the *Histoire universelle*. In particular, his progression from being an active to a passive homosexual is linked by D'Aubigné to the King's loss of courage and character.

However, homosexuality is not always treated so harshly in French Renaissance texts, even if the prevailing legal and social climate repressed not only sodomy but also transvestism. Gisèle Mathieu-Castellani pro-vides a broad range of literary examples to show the way in which French writers, particularly through the use of mythology or of more general allu-sions to Greek texts, negotiated the expression in their works of the love that dared not speak its name. While this might be expressed somewhat covertly in writers such as Pontus de Tyard or Marc-Antoine Muret, other authors are more open. The Epicurean Cyrano de Bergerac, in particular, appeals to examples of ancient homosexual practice to justify its place in

INTRODUCTION

his created worlds of the Moon and the Sun, where it can act to subvert many of the accepted religious and political dogmas of his day. Even writers like Ronsard, known popularly for their robust heterosexuality, can produce works in which male beauty or same-sex relations are celebrated, or in which male stereotypes are called into question. Cathy Yandell discusses this second question in relation to Ronsard's *Folastries*, first published anonymously in 1553. Despite the highly sexualised content of the collection, she demonstrates the way in which there is a blurring of gender and sexual behaviour in these frequently explicit poems, and a rejection of a univocal approach to both writing and sexuality. Todd Reesser too explores the relation between the reading act and sexual identity in Montaigne's sceptical manifesto, the 'Apologie de Raimond Sebond', where he shows that the social relativism for which the essayist is renowned means that he refuses to allow sexual alterity in Plato to be glossed over and effaced by the reader.

Kathryn Banks also reads a Renaissance writer, Maurice Scève, in relation to earlier writers, in this instance the neo-Platonists Marsilio Ficino and Leone Ebreo, though in her case the gender issues have less to do with sex, and more to do with the philosophical notion of a gendered universe, in which male is associated with giving and female with receiving. Focusing on light imagery in the *Délie*, she explores the fragmentation of the darkened male subject. The lover in this collection presents himself as uniquely incapable of enlightenment by the celestial sun of the beloved, thus suggesting a world where men can no longer be sure of the presence of a benign cosmic order.

Thus, for the sixteenth-century male, masculinity is constantly being problematised and challenged. Religious diversity, humanist syncretism, Italian cultural, philosophical, and artistic influence all helped to call into question the simple binary differences between male and female which had largely gone unchallenged in previous centuries. At the same time, this clearly had a liberating effect on a number of men, who were able to give expression to a more nuanced representation of what it is to be male through the appropriation of models from other times and cultures. The papers in this collection all reflect on these important issues, which have important echoes in our own pluralistic but frequently fractured society.

A Prototype of the Modern Man:
Saint Joseph in France, c. 1400–1650

Gary Ferguson

Few ancient figures in late medieval and early modern France can have known the success of Joseph of Nazareth. The extent of the development of the saint's cult is reflected in three large international conferences organised between 1970 and 1980 and the major volumes to which they gave rise: while the first covers discussions of Joseph during the first fifteen hundred years of the Christian era, the second and third deal exclusively with his treatment in the Renaissance and in the seventeenth century.[1] The feast of Saint Joseph was introduced in Rome only in 1479; a little less than a century and a half later, in 1621, it was extended to the entire Catholic Church as a holy day of obligation. Writing in 1639, the Jesuit Paul de Barry looked back on Joseph's meteoric rise to prominence, even speculating on the reasons why it should have occurred only in recent times, and why, formerly, the saint should apparently have been so neglected.[2] Barry also salutes those he identifies as the saint's principal

---

[1] *Saint Joseph durant les quinze premiers siècles de l'Église*, Cahiers de Joséphologie, XIX (Montréal: Centre de Recherche et de Documentation Oratoire Saint-Joseph, 1971); *Saint Joseph à l'époque de la Renaissance (1450–1600)*, Cahiers de Joséphologie, XXV (Montréal: Centre de Recherche et de Documentation Oratoire Saint-Joseph, 1977); *Saint Joseph au XVIIᵉ siècle*, Cahiers de Joséphologie, XXIX (Montréal: Centre de Recherche et de Documentation Oratoire Saint-Joseph, 1981). These volumes, which have been extremely useful for the present study, will henceforth be referred to, respectively, as *SJQ*, *SJR*, and *SJXVII*.

[2] Paul de Barry, S. *Joseph, le plus aymé, et le plus aymable de tous les saincts, apres Jesus et Marie*, 4th ed. (Lyon: Pierre and Claude Rigaud, 1646), ch. 4, pp. 40–56. As a number of contributors to *SJQ* point out, however, it would be misleading to suggest that Joseph was never discussed by Patristic and medieval theologians; on the contrary, many of the ideas developed by the writers studied here can be traced back to earlier authorities. For a survey of these, see also Joseph Dusserre, *Les Origines de la dévotion à saint Joseph*, Extrait des Cahiers de Joséphologie, 1953–1954 (Montréal: Centre de Recherches et de Documentation Oratoire Saint-Joseph). Nevertheless, Joseph was normally treated in the context of biblical exegesis or dogmatic exposition

devotees: after Christ himself and the Virgin Mary, come, in order of importance, Teresa of Avila (1515–1582), the Minim, Gaspar de Bono (1530–1604), and François de Sales (1567–1622) (op. cit., pp. 57–93). The trajectory that leads in the seventeenth century to François de Sales, Barry, Jean Jacquinot, and many others, begins in the fifteenth with such noted churchmen and scholars as Pierre d'Ailly and Jean Gerson. The former wrote a *Tractatus de duodecim honoribus Sancti Joseph* that was published around 1482.[3] Gerson, who will figure prominently in this study and whom Barry designates as Joseph's ninth most ardent admirer, composed numerous works in the saint's honour, including a series of *Considérations sur saint Joseph*, parts of an office for the Betrothal (*desponsatio*) of Our Lady, and the *Josephina*, a poem comprising almost three thousand Latin verses. He also preached two sermons on the saint to the Council of Constance in 1416 and 1418.[4]

While the chronological parameters of this study cover the period of the initial development and establishment in France of the cult of Saint Joseph, it is not my purpose here to rehearse this history.[5] Rather, I shall be concerned with a number of didactic and devotional texts — sermons, meditations, treatises, and the like — concentrating, to the extent possible, and on the assumption that they would have been susceptible of reaching the widest audience, on those written in the vernacular and made available to contemporaries in print. Nevertheless, some of the sermons of François de Sales were not initially published, and the same is true of the works of Gerson, both French and Latin, though this did not prevent them from ex-

---

relating to the incarnation or the Virgin Mary. Only from the fifteenth century on did he become the principal focus of a rapidly expanding body of theological and devotional writing, and the object of an increasingly widespread cult.

[3]   D'Ailly died in 1420. His *Tractatus et sermones* were published around 1482 and again in 1490. The treatise on Saint Joseph was published separately for the first time around 1499.

[4]   For a summary of Gerson's works on Saint Joseph, see Mgr P. Glorieux, 'Saint Joseph dans l'œuvre de Gerson', in *SJQ*, pp. 414–28.

[5]   The reader is referred to the three volumes listed in note 1 above. A useful summary and bibliography are also provided in the introduction to Francis de Sales, *Sermon Texts on Saint Joseph*, trans. and ed. Joseph F. Chorpenning, OSFS (Toronto: Peregrina, 1999), pp. 11–62. On the development of devotion to Joseph in France in the first half of the seventeenth century, and especially on the leading role played in the process by members of various religious orders, see Bernard Dompnier, 'Les Religieux et saint Joseph dans la France de la première moitié du XVIIème siècle', in *Religieux, saints et dévotions: France et Pologne, XIIIème–XVIIIème siècles*, Siècles: Cahiers du Centre d'Histoire 'Espaces et Cultures', 16 (Clermont-Ferrand: Presses Universitaires Blaise-Pascal, 2003), pp. 57–75.

ercising a major influence on later writers.[6] My aim will be to examine the principal aspects of the character of Saint Joseph as it emerges from these works, the functions that the figure of Joseph seems to have served, and some of the reasons that might explain his rise to prominence in this particular form at this particular time.

* * *

At the outset, it is worth noting that the task facing Joseph's promoters was not only that of bringing the object of their veneration out from the shadows; it also required the rehabilitation of his popular image. Medieval theatre frequently portrayed the patriarch as excessively old and somewhat comic; as his wife gave birth to a son he had not fathered, he verged at times on the figure of the cuckold.[7] Joseph needed, therefore, to be rejuvenated and rendered more serious — a man whose faith was tested but remained intact. Jean Gerson led the way, stressing that, at the time of his marriage, Joseph must have been in the prime of his manhood ('jouvence') and probably about thirty-six, since this is the best age at which to marry, according to Aristotle.[8] The argument is taken up by a number of sixteenth-century preachers and writers, such as Jean Raulin and Olivier Conrard, who variously allege that Joseph must have been young enough to have been considered capable of fathering a child in order to have appeared a viable husband for the Virgin, and so to have served as a plausible guarantor of her reputation once she was pregnant. Moreover, he must have been able to support Mary and Jesus through his labour as a carpenter, and to protect and provide for them during their ar-

---

[6]   Gerson died in 1429. Although many of his works were published following the introduction of the printing press, this was not the case, as far as I have been able to determine, with those that will be examined here. Four sermons on Joseph preached by François de Sales are extant in either complete or outline form; I will quote most extensively from the last of these. This sermon, in French, was published in 1629 as the nineteenth of the *Entretiens spirituels*. Of the other three sermons, which date from 1612, 1614, and 1621, the first two are in Latin, the last is in Latin and French. All four sermons were published together in English translation with an introduction by Chorpenning (see the previous note).

[7]   According to Aimé Trottier, however, Joseph was less a figure of fun in French theatre than in German. For the most part, he was not presented as suspecting Mary of adultery, though his age might be a source of humour (see 'Saint Joseph dans le drame religieux de langue française au Moyen Age et durant la Renaissance', in *SJR*, pp. 633–52).

[8]   Jean Gerson, *Considérations sur saint Joseph*, in *Œuvres complètes*, ed. Mgr P. Glorieux, 10 vols in 11 (Paris: Desclée, 1961–1973), VII. 63–94 (p. 75).

3

duous flight into Egypt.[9] Joseph's youth at the time of his marriage is defended also by Lefèvre d'Étaples, and both he and Erasmus are concerned to demonstrate that Joseph never suspected his future wife of adultery.[10]

Saint Joseph receives much more than a face-lift and a character 'make-over', however. Elevating him above all other saints, his promoters set him alongside the Virgin Mary and present him as sharing many of her traditional privileges. Gerson again leads the way, asserting that Joseph was sanctified or consecrated in his mother's womb, like John the Baptist, Jeremiah and, most notably of course, Mary. The same is maintained by Jean Raulin, Quentin Rabineau, Olivier Conrard, and Christophe de Cheffontaines.[11] To anyone without formal theological training it might well have seemed that Joseph was believed, like Mary, to have been immaculately conceived, that is, to have been preserved from original sin from the moment of conception. While most writers stop short of affirming this, the possibility had been raised by Gerson in his 1416 sermon to the Council of Constance, and others like Conrard follow him in leaving the question open: while Joseph was, at the least, purified in the womb, whether he was preserved from sin in the same way as the Virgin, only God can know.[12] Since Joseph entered the world sinless, it is also to be believed that he remained free from mortal sin throughout his life, and that, after death, he was taken up into heaven. While all agree that Joseph's soul was received into heaven, some teach that, again like Mary, he was assumed also in body. Since Joseph died before Christ, however, it was necessary that he wait in Limbo until Christ's own resurrection and ascension. This idea, found in Gerson and repeated by Rabineau and Conrard, is developed with particular force by François de Sales.[13] The Bishop of Geneva

---

[9]   Cf. *SJR*, pp. 380–81 and 513, discussing Raulin, Sermon for Christmas Eve, in *Sermones de sanctis* (Venice: J. B. Somaschus, 1576), I. 89–95, and Conrard, *La Vie et louenge du benoist sainct Joseph* (Lyon: en vente chez O. Arnoullet, *c.* 1535).

[10]   See Georges Bavaud, 'La Figure de saint Joseph dans l'œuvre d'Érasme et de Lefèvre d'Étaples', in *SJR*, pp. 141–55 (pp. 142–6 and 150–2).

[11]   See Gerson, *Considérations*, p. 67, and *SJR*, pp. 287, 381, 504, and 517–18, discussing Raulin, Sermon; [Rabineau?], *Ung notable sermon contenant l'excellence et saincteté du pur et saint vierge Joseph* (Rouen: Martin Morin, [1507]); Conrard, *La Vie*; Cheffontaines, *Perpetuae Mariae Virginis, ac Joseph sponsi ejus virginitatis, catholica defensio* (Lyon: M. Jovium and J. Pillehotte, 1578).

[12]   Gerson, *Œuvres*, V. 349; Conrard, op. cit., f. h ii^{r-v}.

[13]   Gerson leaves open the question of bodily assumption; see 1416 sermon to the Council of Constance, *Œuvres*, V. 356. Rabineau and Conrard are both less hesitant, as is François de Sales. See *Notable sermon*, f. b iii^{r-v}, and *La Vie*, f. i i^r and i ii^v–iii^r, which both present Joseph visiting Mary with Jesus after the resurrection; François de

4

goes so far as to imagine a dialogue between Christ and his foster-father in Limbo, in which the latter recalls all that he did for Jesus when he was a small child, and for which he invites Christ to show his gratitude.[14] Liturgically, also, Saint Joseph was set up alongside Mary. Barry published an office in his honour that he encouraged his readers to recite on Saturdays, a day traditionally devoted to Mary but which, according to Barry, is appropriate for celebrating both the Blessed Virgin and her spouse. New joint feasts were also proposed, such as that of the Betrothal, for which, as has been noted, Gerson composed office texts, as later in the sixteenth century did the Dominican Pierre Doré.[15]

One particular characteristic that Joseph shares with Mary receives more attention than any other, however: his virginity. The chaste nature of Joseph and Mary's marriage is a recurrent theme in almost all writers of the period, from Gerson, through Erasmus and Lefèvre, to François de Sales, Barry, and Jacquinot. In addition, many refute the idea that Joseph had children from a previous marriage, so that his virginity, like that of his spouse, was 'perpetual'. Most notable among these writers is Christophe de Cheffontaines, who defended this position in a lengthy treatise

---

Sales, 1622 sermon, *Entretiens spirituels*, *Œuvres*, Annecy edition, 27 vols (Annecy: J. Niérat, 1892–1964), VI. 352–70 (pp. 369–70).

[14] This dialogue recalls those traditionally imagined between Christ and the souls in Limbo collectively (patriarchs, prophets, and so on), when he comes to lead them to freedom, beginning with Adam, the first man. Cf. Jacques de Voragine, *La Légende dorée*, ed. J.-B. M. Roze, 2 vols (Paris: GF–Flammarion, 1967), I. 278–81. This restriction of the dialogue from the Fathers to the Father fits well with the argument that will be developed in this paper. A similar description of the death of Saint Joseph is found in François's *Traité de l'amour de Dieu*, in *Œuvres*, ed. André Ravier with Roger Devos, Bibliothèque de la Pléiade (Paris: Gallimard, 1969), pp 319–972 (pp. 702–3).

[15] On the history of this feast, see the *Dictionnaire de spiritualité ascétique et mystique, doctrine et histoire*, 17 vols (Paris: Beauchesne, 1937–1995), III, cols 1641–5. On its early promotion by Henri Chicot and Jean Gerson, see Max Lieberman, 'Henri Chicot et le culte de saint Joseph', in *SJQ*, pp. 409–13. For Gerson's Office, which comprises lessons for matins and propers for the Mass, see *Œuvres*, VIII. 55–61; for Doré's Office, see *La Premiere Partie des Collations royalles... La Seconde Partie... Avec ung nouvel office de la Desponsation de la B. vierge Marie* (Paris: Jehan André, 1546), pt 2, pp. 277–306. Anne de Marquets's *Sonets spirituels* contain a number of poems in honour of the feast, suggesting that the devotion was established liturgically at the Dominican priory of Poissy in the late sixteenth century; see the edition by Gary Ferguson (Geneva: Droz, 1997), pp. 297–300. It is also worth noting here that François de Sales, in a sermon preached on the Feast of the Purification in 1620, states that it is more likely that Joseph presented the Christ-child to Simeon in the Temple, rather than Mary (*Œuvres*, Annecy ed., IX. 261).

published in Latin in 1578.[16] Many consider, moreover, that the holy couple formalised their intention to remain chaste throughout their marriage by taking vows.[17] François de Sales preaches on the virginal marriage of Mary and Joseph using the analogy of the palm tree in a way that combines the introit from the Mass of Saint Joseph's day, 'justus ut palma florebit' (Psalm 91. 13/92. 12), and a passage from Pliny's *Natural History*, on the basis of which he affirms that the female palm bears fruit without the introduction of any substance from the male tree, but only when planted in its shade.[18]

Joseph's chastity, moreover, involves not only abstinence from all sexual activity, but a complete victory over all movements of sexual desire. In the words of Gerson: 'c'est bien de croire que saint Joseph ot en son corps et en sa char estraint ou amoins reprimé, refroidis et afebloy le nourrissement de pechié qui vient en nous par le pechié originel, lequel nourrissement de pechié est appele par l'Apostre concupiscence'; and again: 'son cuer n'estoit point occupé ou travaillé ou ars et bruis par l'aspre et furieuse passion de vil charnel desir.' This is important, given that the Virgin Mary was the most beautiful of women ever to have existed (many writers stress also the physical beauty of Joseph himself and of Christ), so that if he had been subject to 'male et forte concupiscence charnele', his life would have been one of endless torment.[19]

Saint Joseph is not only promoted as sharing Mary's virtues and privileges; in a particular way, he is accorded precedence over her. While Mary is the foremost of the saints and closest to Christ by virtue of being his mother, in the historic disposition, Joseph is set in authority over both. As husband of Mary, he is the legal possessor of her body, and by that same right, he becomes not only the guardian of her child but his legal

[16]   Cheffontaines, op. cit.; cf. Georges Ponton, 'Saint Joseph selon Christophe de Cheffontaines', in *SJR*, pp. 283–93. To refute the idea of an earlier marriage, Gerson appeals to Saint Jerome (*Considérations*, p. 76). On Conrard, following Gerson and Jerome, see *SJR*, p. 513; cf. pp. 639–41.
[17]   The idea is supported, for example, by Lefèvre d'Étaples, but not by Erasmus; cf. *SJR*, pp. 151 and 154–5.
[18]   1622 sermon, *Œuvres*, Annecy ed., VI. 353–5; cf. 1621 sermon, Annecy ed., VIII. 397–402 (pp. 400–1). The reference to the *Natural History* is to Book XIII, ch. 7 (or 4).
[19]   *Considérations*, pp. 68–9 and 77. Gerson specifies that concupiscence was extinguished in Joseph as a result of the strengthening of his reason by grace, through his fleeing idleness and the occasions of sin, and through the salutary occupations of prayer, fasting, and work.

father. Jesus is thus particularly indebted to Joseph, who, although he was not his genitor, nevertheless willingly and generously assumed the role of father to him.[20] Moreover, it is to be believed that the authority that Joseph enjoyed over the Son of God on earth continues in heaven, since, as Gerson reminds his readers, glory does not destroy nature, it perfects it.[21] For this reason, he is such a powerful intercessor.

At the same time, Joseph's authority over his family was exercised through responsibility and accompanied by reciprocal affection. Thus, he is constantly described as protector and provider: he supports his wife and child through his labour; he assures their safety during their flight into Egypt. Gerson calls him not only Christ's father, but also 'son nutriteur, son conduiseur et deffenseur, son docteur et instructeur', and portrays him holding, carrying, and embracing the Christ-child: 'Joseph... estoit esleu de Dieu a converser continuelment en la compaignie du tres bel et tres avenant et delicieux enfant Jhesus, a le porter, a le nourrir, a le baisier par licence et amitié paternelle.'[22] The title 'nutritius' or 'nutriteur' applied to Joseph and the image of him carrying, nursing, and kissing Jesus are not wholly without precedent, being found notably, though fleetingly, in Saint Bernard of Clairvaux.[23] Gerson, however, begins the development of a

---

[20] Gerson, *Considérations*, pp. 64–7. See also Georges Ponton, art. cit., pp. 287 and 290–1; Henri-Paul Bergeron, 'Saint Joseph selon les prédicateurs français de la Renaissance', in *SJR*, pp. 371–85, esp. pp. 383–4 on Olivier Maillard, François Le Picart and others; Marcel Lalonde, 'Deux ouvrages de frères mineurs français sur saint Joseph', in *SJR*, pp. 501–22, esp. p. 505 on Quentin Rabineau drawing on D'Ailly, and p. 518 on Olivier Conrard drawing on Gerson, cf. also p. 511; François de Sales, sermon outline of 1612, *Œuvres*, Annecy ed., VIII. 86–8; Barry, op. cit., pp. 60–9.

[21] *Considérations*, p. 73; cf., on Conrard, *SJR*, p. 520.

[22] *Considérations*, pp. 66 and 68; cf. pp. 67 and 72–3.

[23] One of Bernard's most notable passages referring to Joseph is the following: 'cui denique datum est quod multi reges et prophetae, cum vellent videre, non viderunt; audire, et non audierunt; non solum videre et audire, sed etiam portare, deducere, amplecti, deosculari, nutrire et custodire' ('Homilia II super *Missus est*', in *Patrologia Latina*, ed. J. P. Migne et al., 221 vols in 223 (Paris: Garnier, 1844–1890), CLXXXIII (1854), col. 70); cf. 'Hic est Joseph, locum quidem obtinens sponsi, re autem vera servus et dispensator, qui sane pater vocatur, magis autem nutritius est' (Sermon for the Circumcision, ibid., col. 134). Clearly, such descriptions are not out of character for a writer known both for the affective, even passionate tenor of his piety, and for his emphasis on Jesus's humanity. Nevertheless, this is not a subject on which Bernard dwells. The Latin term 'nutritius' is re-used by Gerson, cf. his 1416 Constance sermon (*Œuvres*, V. 357–8). Slightly before Gerson, images of Joseph as loving father had also been developed by Italian Franciscans, notably Ubertino of Casale and Bartholomew of Pisa (see Dusserre, op. cit., pp. 49–58). Rosemary Drage Hale also points out that the nursing/nurturing Joseph was not without precedent in medieval German cra-

theme that will be taken up in ever more effusive and affective terms —
by Conrard, François de Sales, Barry, and Jacquinot — as the 'nutritius
domini' becomes the 'père nourricier'.[24] Jacquinot, for example, addresses
the saint in the following exclamatory terms: 'De quels feux ne brûloit pas
votre ame, quand il vous arrivoit de coucher ou de lever, d'habiller ou de
deshabiller, de promener, de servir, de caresser, ou de porter sur votre giron, Jesus, votre Isaac, votre Benjamin, votre tout, et que ce Divin poupon
pour se revancher de vos caresses, vous rendoit mille baisers, vous flatoit
avec ses petites mains, vous soûrioit amoureusement, et s'attachoit à votre
col, aussi étroitement qu'aux tetins de sa Mere.'[25] The dialogue that François de Sales imagines between Jesus and Joseph in Limbo, referred to
above, is less lyrical, but no less affective, as the latter appeals to the former: 'Je vous ay porté entre mes bras, maintenant prenez-moy sur les
vostres; et comme j'ay eu soin de vous nourrir et conduire durant le cours
de vostre vie mortelle, prenez soin de moy et de me conduire en la vie
immortelle.' How can we doubt that this prayer was granted, the bishop
concludes, when Christ as a child gave his father so many kisses to repay
all his toil on his behalf?[26] While the Christ-child's kisses are here pledges
of future salvation, they are also simple expressions of gratitude and reciprocal human affection. As François notes elsewhere, commenting on
the parable of the prodigal son, 'son bon pere neanmoins l'embrasse, le
bayse amoureusement et pleure dessus luy parce qu'il estoit son pere et le
cœur des peres est tendre sur celuy des enfans'.[27] At the same time, Joseph's authority becomes explicitly patriarchal for François de Sales,
through a sustained comparison between the saint and his Old Testament
counterpart. As the latter ruled over the house of Israel, the former ruled

---

dle-rocking plays and rituals, but that formerly he was a purely comic figure ('Joseph
as Mother: Adaptation and Appropriation in the Construction of Male Virtue', in *Medieval Mothering*, ed. John Carmi Parsons and Bonnie Wheeler (New York and London: Garland, 1996), pp. 101–16).

[24] On Conrard, see *SJR*, pp. 518–19. For the term 'père nourricier', see François de
Sales, *Traité de l'amour de Dieu*, book 7, ch. 13 (Pléiade ed., p. 702) and Barry, op.
cit., p. 62.

[25] Jean Jacquinot, *La Gloire de S. Joseph representée dans ses principales
grandeurs* (Dijon: Pierre Palliot, 1644), p. 35. Cf. p. 540: 'le bien-heureux Joseph eut
droit de s'approcher de la personne adorable de son cher nourrisson, de manier sa tres-
sainte humanité, de le baiser et d'en être reciproquement baisé, non pas d'un seul
baiser, mais de mille et mille baisers de sa bouche sacrée.' At other points for
Jacquinot, the love between father and step-son takes on mystical accents, cf. pp. 125–
6.

[26] 1622 sermon, *Œuvres*, Annecy ed., VI. 370.

[27] *Avertissements aux confesseurs*, *Œuvres*, Annecy ed., XXIII. 279–97 (p. 281).

over Christ and his mother as God's vicar and lieutenant.[28] This dual nature is expressed by François in a striking formula: Joseph is an 'amabil[is] Patriarch[a]', 'aimable Patriarche'.[29]

Saint Joseph, as elaborated between the fifteenth and seventeenth centuries, is thus a figure of authority and a focus of affectivity.[30] He is a model of many Christian virtues that include humility, patience, justice, obedience to the will of God, and so on. Of all these virtues, however, that which receives by far the most emphasis is his chastity, his complete mastery of the body and its unruly desires. Having delineated the salient features of the saint's character, let me now begin to situate him in relation to a number of contemporary social and cultural developments.

* * *

First, the figure of Saint Joseph allowed Catholic writers to treat the subject of marriage and the role of men as husbands and fathers. From the early sixteenth century on, this would have been useful as a vehicle for responding to the challenge posed by the Protestant promotion of married life. By holding up the example of the virginal marriage of Joseph and Mary, Catholics were paradoxically able to praise marriage, stress the necessity within it of chastity, and maintain the traditional primacy accorded to celibacy. While this may have been important to writers in the wake of the Reformers, however, it clearly cannot explain the attraction of the subject for earlier theologians like Gerson. The phenomenon must therefore be set within a larger context.

---

[28]   See the 1612 sermon outline, *Œuvres*, Annecy ed., VIII. 86–8.

[29]   1621 sermon, *Œuvres*, Annecy ed., VIII. 397.

[30]   While Saint Bernard had also compared the New Testament Joseph to the Old Testament Patriarch, the Abbot is far from according him authority over Mary, and does not consider their marriage to be real. Joseph guards and protects Mary, his mistress ('domina sua'), and Christ is subject to him on her account ('Deus... subditus erat Mariae, nec tantum Mariae, sed etiam Joseph propter Mariam'). See *Patrologia Latina*, ibid., cols 60 and 69; cf. Dusserre, op. cit., pp. 29–30. On the other hand, as Caroline Walker Bynum has shown, Saint Bernard and a number of twelfth-century Cistercian writers employed images of nursing and motherhood in their descriptions of God, the apostles or Church leaders, in order to express an image of authority exercised nurturingly (*Jesus as Mother: Studies in the Spirituality of the High Middle Ages* (Berkeley, Los Angeles and London: University of California Press, 1982), p. 149 and chapter 4 in general). While the early modern Joseph evinces a similar duality, he must be situated within his own particular socio-historical context.

9

Historians of late medieval and early modern France have traced, among a number of parallel socio-political developments, the gradual but ineluctable rise of royal power under the Valois and the Bourbons, and the eventual triumph of the absolute monarchy. After the splintering of the Reformation, a similar reaffirmation of central authority and enforcement of discipline occurred within the post-Tridentine Catholic Church. While this vision of royal and Catholic hegemony might be associated most obviously with a monarch like Louis XIV, it was also embraced — albeit with less belligerence and less immediate success — by one like Henri III. When the Jesuits of the collège de Clermont offered Henri a volume of translated meditations for Lent in 1578, they included a dedicatory letter that praised the king's piety as a means to 'ramener à l'obeissance du Prince, et au giron de l'Eglise nostre Mere, ceux qui par mauvais exemples s'en pourroient estre separez'.[31] Both the absolute monarchy and the Counter-Reformation Church, however, were built on the ruins of the recent past — the fractured monarchy of the Hundred Years War and the divided Church not only of the Reformation but also of the Great Schism. And it is precisely in this earlier chaotic context that Saint Joseph was initially promoted — proleptically, if not prophetically — by Gerson, D'Ailly and others. According to Mgr Glorieux, it is highly probable that Gerson's devotion to Joseph dates to 1413, the year that saw the death of his friend Henri Chicot, also a tireless supporter of Saint Joseph, as well as the Cabochien crisis, with the riots that forced Gerson to take refuge in the cathedral of Notre-Dame while his house was looted. The resolution of this crisis, which was finally brought about peacefully, seemed to Gerson nothing short of miraculous, and he attributed it to the intervention of Saint Joseph, whose aid and protection, in all likelihood, he had invoked.[32] Later that same year, he penned both his sermon on the 'Desponsation' and the *Considérations sur saint Joseph*. It was thus to a country ruled by a king increasingly prone to bouts of madness, a country at war not only with England, but torn by internecine conflicts between Armagnacs and Bourguignons, in which the queen herself played an often notorious role, that Gerson first offered the image of Joseph the

---

[31]   Gaspar Loarte, *Les Meditations de la Passion de nostre Seigneur Jesus Christ, Avec l'Art de mediter* (Paris: Thomas Brumen, 1578), f. 2ᵛ. On the subject of Henri III's piety and its political dimensions, see Bruno Petey-Girard, '1574–1589: Littérature de spiritualité et "commandement du roy"', *Nouvelle Revue du Seizième Siècle*, 20/2 (2002), pp. 73–86.
[32]   *SJQ*, pp. 423–4.

authoritative and loving father.[33] Those to whom he addressed his exhortations included members of the nobility and the royal family, since Mary and Joseph themselves were of royal lineage.[34] Indeed, in the context of the conflict with England, this last consideration was of vital political importance, for the English had argued that Jesus's royalty, his claim to be King of the Jews, was inherited through his mother. Biblical precedent would thus discredit the French appeal to Salic law in order to proscribe succession through the female line. Gerson admits that Mary was indeed of both priestly and royal lineage, yet expresses doubt that this in itself would have given her son the right to rule temporally over the people of Israel. At the same time, he stresses that Joseph, who was descended from the house of David, must be considered Christ's real father because he was so according to law.[35] Thus, as women were being excluded in France from the right to transmit any claim to the throne, Joseph appears as a biblical example emphasising paternal prerogative, even when paternity is legal rather than natural.[36]

As the monarchy was fragmented in Gerson's day, so too was the Church, there being, in 1416, three different claimants to the papal throne. Just as Joseph was an important figure for Gerson in relation to the French monarchy, so also the theologian associated the saint explicitly with the reunification of the Church. In his sermon to the Council of Constance, preached on the feast of the Nativity of the Blessed Virgin in 1416, Gerson urged the assembly to institute a feast in honour of Joseph, who would

---

[33] Carolyn C. Wilson notes that in fifteenth- and sixteenth-century Italy, Joseph was promoted as a heavenly protector in a similar climate of political instability. See *St. Joseph in Italian Renaissance Society and Art: New Directions and Interpretations* (Philadelphia: Saint Joseph's University Press, 2001), pp. 12–20.

[34] For example, *Considérations*, p. 71, and the sermon for the Feast of the Betrothal (*Œuvres*, VII. 13).

[35] *Considérations*, pp. 69–70; cf. the sermon delivered to the Council of Constance in 1416 (*Œuvres*, V. 347).

[36] The principle of women's exclusion from succession was affirmed in 1317. As John Milton Potter notes, however, it was only after Agincourt that 'the French seriously undertook the extended definition of their doctrine of royal inheritance' ('The Development and Significance of the Salic Law of the French', *The English Historical Review*, LII (1937), pp. 235–53 (p. 238)). One of the major treatises was written by Jean de Montreuil, an opponent of Gerson and Christine de Pisan in the *Querelle de la rose*. Of relevance to my own argument is Potter's thesis that the Salic Law became 'one of the most convenient vehicles' for royal absolutism, as 'the dignities of the crown itself, the authority of the king, in short, the essential properties of the absolute monarchy of the Renaissance, were made to appear naturally and logically consequent' upon it (ibid., p. 252).

11

pray to Mary that the Church, for the sake of Christ, might be returned *'unico viro vero et certo*, Summo Pontifici sponso suo' — to the one, true, sure, man, the husband, the pope.[37] Two years later, preaching again to the Council, but now after the election of a single pontiff, Gerson made a similar appeal, urging that the Church institute a feast celebrating the marriage of Joseph and Mary, the type of that between the Church and the pope.[38]

Concomitant with the reinforcement of authority within the Church and the State, a strengthening of patriarchal authority has also been documented at what might be termed the microcosmic level, that of the *paterfamilias*, a development that Robert Muchembled relates to changing patterns of youth socialisation and control of the marriage market. In the Middle Ages, unmarried men tended to leave the family domain early and socialise in groups of their own age, known variously as 'royaumes de jeunesse', 'abbayes de Maugouvert' or 'bachelleries'. During the time these younger men were waiting to be married, they were accorded a fair degree of licence in their conduct, benefiting in this way from a socially sanctioned mechanism for letting off steam. The restriction of these younger men's access to marriageable women was thus enforced as much collectively as by the individual father of any given young man or woman. These patterns of collective socialisation gradually broke down, Mulchembled argues, owing to a number of factors, such as the firmer exercise of royal justice, the moralising campaign of the Church, population growth, and the expansion of the early modern city. As a result, individual families were thrown back increasingly on their separate resources and the nuclear family emerged as the primary unit of social life. As a corollary of the focusing of life within the family, authority came to reside increasingly in the head of the household, and, at the same time, the family became the principal, if not the quasi-exclusive, forum for the expression of affectivity — the home, as it were, of the emotions: 'le rôle du père de famille, qui n'était pourtant nullement négligeable, acquiert des dimensions nouvelles et impérieuses. Il se définit, plus vite dans certains milieux que dans d'autres, comme le pôle d'équilibre familial par excellence. Sacralisé par l'Église tridentine, investi d'une efficacité nouvelle par la volonté royale, il brise l'équilibre ancien des groupes d'âge et repa-

---

[37] *Œuvres*, V. 362, my italics.

[38] *Œuvres*, V. 542. On this and other traditional interpretations of the marriage of Mary and Joseph, see Marcel Lalonde, 'La Signification mystique du mariage de Joseph et de Marie', in *SJQ*, pp. 548–63. In the early modern period, however, this kind of reading became less common.

trie vers l'unité domestique, autant que faire se peut, des intérêts, des sentiments, des attitudes s'exprimant souvent ailleurs par le passé.'[39] Muchembled's argument clearly owes a debt (that the writer acknowledges) to the work of Philippe Ariès on the pre-modern family; yet Muchembled is careful to avoid Ariès's more immoderate formulations concerning the absence of affection between pre-modern parents and children that have elicited so much scholarly resistance.[40] While the writing of the history of sentiment is notoriously fraught with problems, there nevertheless exists a fair degree of consensus that, beginning in the cities of the Renaissance, the nuclear family withdrew increasingly into the intimacy of the private home, and life began to be conceptualised less in terms of clan and community. In the words of Jacques Gélis: 'A un statut où "public" et "privé" jouaient leur rôle dans la formation de l'enfant en a succédé un autre qui majore les droits de la mère et surtout du père sur leur enfant.... Au modèle rural a succédé un modèle urbain, et le désir d'avoir des enfants non plus pour assurer la permanence du cycle, mais simplement pour les aimer, et en être aimé.'[41] The period that sees the invention of Saint Joseph as loving patriarch, in other words, is precisely that which sees the emergence and consolidation of the nuclear family, and of royal, ecclesiastical, and paternal authority.

---

[39]   Robert Muchembled, *L'Invention de l'homme moderne: sensibilités, mœurs et comportements collectifs sous l'Ancien Régime*, 2nd ed. (Paris: Fayard, 1994; first pub. 1988), p. 338. For the foregoing argument, see chapter 5, pp. 291–366. It is interesting to note, in this connection, that paternal authority would often appeal directly to and be confirmed by that of the king through the *lettre de cachet*, which effectively bypassed other instances of justice (cf. pp. 339–40).

[40]   Philippe Ariès, *L'Enfant et la vie familiale sous l'Ancien Régime* (Paris: Plon, 1960). The particular argument concerning the lack of affective bonds between premodern parents and children received support from Lawrence Stone, *The Family, Sex and Marriage in England 1500–1800* (New York: Harper and Row, 1977), but has been vigorously refuted by, among others, David Herlihy for the Middle Ages and Steven Ozment for the sixteenth century. See Herlihy, 'The Making of the Medieval Family: Symmetry, Structure, and Sentiment', *Journal of Family History*, VIII (1983), pp. 116–30; *Medieval Households* (Cambridge, MA and London: Harvard University Press, 1985), especially pp. 112–30; 'The Family and Religious Ideologies in Medieval Europe', *Journal of Family History*, XII (1987), pp. 3–17; and Ozment, *When Fathers Ruled: Family Life in Reformation Europe* (Cambridge, MA and London: Harvard University Press, 1983).

[41]   Jacques Gélis, 'L'Individualisation de l'enfant', in *Histoire de la vie privée*, ed. Philippe Ariès and Georges Duby, vol. 3, 'De la Renaissance aux Lumières', ed. Roger Chartier (Paris: Seuil, 1986), pp. 311–29 (p. 328; see also pp. 319–20).

In a further parallel development, moreover, early modern parents increasingly sent their children to schools, frequently run by the Church. Children's education was thus entrusted to specialised professionals and institutions that, in their turn, became primary vehicles for ensuring the development and transmission of new ideals and values of family, as well as for the inculcation of new codes of public comportment, described famously by Norbert Elias as the 'civilizing process'.[42] The development of civility operated at the most basic level through a taking charge of the body and its functions, which, as many historians of the early modern period have noted, were increasingly regarded with suspicion and approached with circumspection. This was certainly no less the case within the domain of religious thought and practice than elsewhere. A recent study of the representation of Mary in published sermons, for example, discovers a shift of emphasis from the Virgin's corporality (her flesh, blood, and milk, her physical motherhood) to the qualities of her soul (her graces, moral virtues, her spiritual motherhood).[43] Such a change encourages a devotion in which all are invited to 'conceive', 'bear', and 'nurture' Christ in their soul. Saint Joseph, who was able to hold Christ physically, becomes, in this light, the foremost of these surrogate spiritual mothers. We saw above how Jacquinot portrayed Jesus clinging with equal tenacity to his father's bosom and to his mother's breast. Yet more strikingly, François de Sales begins his 1621 sermon by addressing Joseph as follows: 'O Sancte Joseph, "quibus te laudibus efferam nescio, quia quem cæli capere non poterant" tuis brachiis conclusisti.'[44] The bishop's listeners in the newly opened church of the Jesuit novitiate in Lyon would have recognised at once that most of the preacher's apostrophe to their titular

---

[42] Norbert Elias, *The Civilizing Process: The Development of Manners. Changes in the Code of Conduct and Feeling in Early Modern Times*, trans. Edmund Jephcott, vol. 1 (New York: Urizen Books, 1978; first published in German in 1939). On the subject of schooling and the early modern family, see Gélis, art. cit., pp. 322–5, and Ariès, op. cit. The crucial role played by schools in the inculcation and dissemination of codes of comportment is also demonstrated by Dilwyn Knox, '*Disciplina*: The Monastic and Clerical Origins of European Civility', in *Renaissance Society and Culture: Essays in Honor of Eugene F. Rice, Jr*, ed. John Monfasani and Ronald G. Musto (New York: Italica Press, 1991), pp. 107–35 (pp. 122–9). As his title indicates, Knox also argues for the importance of monastic and clerical precepts — and not simply courtly ideals — in the elaboration of codes of civility. This study of Saint Joseph would corroborate such a conclusion.

[43] Donna Spivey Ellington, *From Sacred Body to Angelic Soul: Understanding Mary in Late Medieval and Early Modern Europe* (Washington, DC: Catholic University of America Press, 2001).

[44] *Œuvres*, Annecy ed., VIII. 397.

A PROTOTYPE OF THE MODERN MAN

saint was in fact a quotation from the breviary. The respond in question, however, addresses not Joseph but the Virgin, opening with the words 'Sancta et immaculata virginitas'. Mary is praised because he whom the heavens cannot contain she bore in her womb — 'tuo gremio contulisti'.[45] Suppressing the opening and concluding words of the respond, François substitutes Joseph for Mary and the paternal arms for the maternal womb, the careful choice of verb (*contulisti* → *conclusisti*) being surely intended to underscore the parallel between the two. The bishop is clearly playing with his listener's expectations, frustrating them in a rather audacious way that would no doubt have been highly effective and, ultimately, all the more satisfying.

The 'civilising' of behaviour involved not only the regulation of exterior gestures, of course; the passions too were mastered and interiorised, social regulation becoming increasingly self-control. As Muchembled notes, 'les sujets des rois Bourbons apprirent lentement à contrôler leurs pulsions par des mécanismes intériorisés d'interdiction et de censure'.[46] Medieval society's regulation of behaviour through a system of externally determined honour/shame thus slowly gave way to regulation by means of interiorised guilt, inculcated by a heightened policing of morals by Church and State. While Elias's account of the development of civility accords particular prominence to Erasmus's 1530 treatise *De civilitate morum puerilium*, Gerson had already affirmed, over a century earlier, the necessity of speaking of sexual matters with discretion and circumspection. He did so by launching an attack on one of his perennial targets, the *Roman de la rose* — and this in the context of a discussion of Saint Joseph and the overcoming of concupiscence.[47]

Here again, then, Joseph can be seen as a focus for the preoccupations of the age, for if a poster-boy were needed for the interiorised, self-disciplined subject, surely there could be few candidates better qualified than the saint whose virtues were so exemplary, who was not only chaste,

---

[45] The text of the respond is as follows: 'Sancta et immaculata virginitas, quibus te laudibus efferam nescio: Quia quem caeli capere non poterant, tuo gremio contulisti.' It is followed by the verse: 'Benedicta tu in mulieribus et benedictus fructus ventris tui.' It was sung at matins on Christmas day and on other days in the Christmas season; it also formed part of the office of the Virgin on Saturdays. See *Breviarum Romanum* (1568), ed. Manlio Sodi and Achille Maria Triacca (Vatican City: Libreria Editrice Vaticana, 1999).
[46] Muchembled, op. cit., p. iii (Préface à la deuxième édition).
[47] *Autres Considérations sur saint Joseph*, in *Œuvres*, VII. 94–9 (p. 97).

15

but within whom sexual desire itself had been utterly vanquished?[48] When this model of chastity and self-control is also the 'amiable patriarch', simultaneously provider for his wife and child and representative of God set over them, Joseph appears as nothing less than an iconic representation of the paradoxes of the modern man — disciplined and disciplining, offering and seeking love. Although I have avoided addressing the issue thus far, this modern man is also paradoxical to the extent that as a figure of affection he is unquestionably the beneficiary of the traditional woman, taking on characteristics, especially those of nursing and nurturing, conventionally viewed as feminine.[49] Joseph valorises these 'female' characteristics, yet, at the same time, weakens their unique association with women, integrating them within the masculine and the patriarchal. Again, it is not surprising that this should have happened over a period of time that saw, on the one hand, many feminist initiatives and developments, but, on the other hand, fierce debate about the 'woman question', and a heightened regulation and restriction of women's autonomy and power. At the time when Gerson was first promoting Saint Joseph, Christine de Pisan was writing her defences of the female sex, and she and Gerson were involved in the *Querelle de la rose*; as we have seen, this was also the time at which women were being excluded from the right to pass on royal succession. The fifteenth and sixteenth centuries saw many challenges to traditional misogyny in the context of the *Querelle des femmes*; the sixteenth and seventeenth centuries saw the greater involvement of women in religious life, a 'feminisation' of religious discourse, the establishing of *salons*, the *précieux* movement, and so on. As has been noted, the period also witnessed, and especially after the Fronde, the increasing subordination of women to male authority, and the consolidation of both royal and ecclesiastical hegemony.

* * *

---

[48]   As has been mentioned, Joseph's virtues included charity, patience, humility, devotion, obedience, and so on. Cf., for example, Jacquinot, op. cit., pp. 400–78, and Barry, op. cit., esp. p. 31. Dompnier also argues that, within the context of the promotion of new modes of behaviour by the post-Tridentine Church, Joseph was presented as an example of self-discipline and the cultivation of an interior spiritual life (art. cit., pp. 72–4). Dompnier's analysis remains strictly within a religious framework, however, stressing the saint's function as a model of various individual moral virtues.

[49]   The appropriation of feminine traits to the figure of Saint Joseph has been noted by Hale, art. cit.

What, finally, can be said about Joseph's reception in late medieval and early modern France? How widely was this figure diffused? To what extent was it successful and with whom? I can do no more here than touch upon these questions. Joseph was certainly held up to men, women, and children as an exemplary husband and father. To some extent, married men were invited to identify with and to imitate him in particular; women and children were encouraged to adopt the attitudes of the Virgin and Christ — essentially loving and trusting obedience.[50] To the extent that the development of the nuclear family was associated with the city, Saint Joseph may have held particular appeal for an urban population, includeing, but certainly not limited to, merchants, tradesmen, and members of the robe nobility.[51] What I have not found to any significant degree in the texts I have examined is an explicit association of Joseph with the king, the pope, or bishops. Gerson's reading of the marriage of Mary and Joseph as a type of that between the Church and the pope is found in the works of a number of earlier theologians, but is not prominent in those of the later period. In the sixteenth century, allegorical (i.e. ecclesiological) interpretations of marriage seem to belong rather to the domain of com-

---

[50] Cf. Gerson, 'Desponsation' sermon, Œuvres, VII. 12–13. In the Introduction à la vie dévote, François de Sales prescribes precisely these roles for married people in the 'Avis pour les gens mariés' (Introduction, part III, ch. 38). Although Joseph and Mary are not mentioned here, husbands are exhorted to love and command, wives to love and obey (Œuvres, Pléiade ed., p. 235). Henri-M. Guindon discusses the use made of Joseph in one seventeenth-century marriage manual ('Saint Joseph, prototype des bons mariés, selon Charles d'Abbeville', in SJXVII, pp. 344–55).

[51] Hale argues, though without offering much in the way of evidence, that 'the new Joseph was constructed to resemble members of an emerging burgher class of merchants, artisans, and tradesmen now more actively involved in the economic and devotional life of the Church' (art. cit., p. 107). In her discussion of Joseph in Italy, Wilson cautions against assuming a restriction of the saint's appeal based on class: 'That St Joseph's patronage was embraced and sponsored by heads of Church and State, civic governments, and members of the patriciate also indicates that critical caution should be exercised in the degree to which it should be assumed that the saint was understood at this time as exponent of the humble working, family man' (op. cit., p. 75). Likewise, Dompnier notes that while the oldest French confraternities had largely been made up of carpenters and builders, this professional bias disappeared in later foundations in favour of a diversified membership. Moreover, many early seventeenth-century writers promoted devotion to Joseph as being appropriate to all social classes (art. cit., pp. 62–4). The same is true much earlier of Gerson, who had urged devotion to the marriage of Joseph and Mary upon people of all estates: kings, queens, nobles, popes, prelates, clerics, those who labour, the young who wish to make a good marriage, and those who wish to remain virgins ('Desponsation' sermon, Œuvres, V. 13–14).

mentaries on the Song of Songs.[52] The relationship between Joseph and secular and religious authority is mediated essentially by the figure of the father as head of the family. It is this figure that Joseph sanctioned and on which, in their turn, discourses of royal and ecclesiastical hegemony drew so extensively.[53]

In addition, it appears that Joseph played a particularly important role in institutional settings, and notably educational establishments. This is not surprising, perhaps, given the link, discussed above, between the rise of the nuclear family and the increase in schooling, and the crucial role played by schools in the dissemination of the ideals of civility. The Jesuits, for example, who were in the forefront of this project, were also great promoters of Saint Joseph, regularly dedicating their colleges and churches to him.[54] In the 1580s in Paris, one of their pupils was François de Sales, who remained not only devoted to Joseph but also close to the Society throughout his life. In 1621, for example, François preached twice on the saint's feast day in Lyon, both in the church of the Carmelites and in that of the Jesuit novitiate. The latter, which had been newly built and dedicated to Saint Joseph, was celebrating its patronal festival for the first time.[55] Significantly for my general argument, moreover, Ariès has argued that the Jesuit *Ratio studiorum* represents the culmination of a progressive reinforcement of educational discipline that had begun with the reforms of the colleges of the University of Paris in the fifteenth century. Gerson's role in this process is apparent in his reorganisation of the grammar school of Notre-Dame.[56] His interest in controlling more specifically the sexuality of young boys may be seen in his tract *De confessione mollitiei*,

---

[52]   Joseph as spouse of the Church signifying pastors, bishops, or the pope, is found, for example, in Saint Ambrose, the Venerable Bede, and Peter Cantor. See Marcel Lalonde, 'La Signification mystique'. On ecclesiological readings of the Song of Songs, see Max Engammare, *'Qu'il me baise des baisers de sa bouche': Le Cantique des Cantiques à la Renaissance* (Geneva: Droz, 1993), esp. chapter 7, pp. 251–318.
[53]   On the king as 'super-père', see Muchembled, op. cit., pp. 341–2.
[54]   The Society itself, indeed, was often considered to be under the special patronage of Saint Joseph. See Georges Bottereau, 'Saint Joseph et les jésuites français de la première moitié du XVIIᵉ siècle', in *SJXVII*, pp. 793–813.
[55]   See Barry, op. cit., pp. 78–9. The following year, François's death would occur in the same Jesuit house, an account again being given by Barry, the Provincial, op. cit., pp. 77–8. Cf. *Sermon Texts*, pp. 32–5 and 82.
[56]   See Ariès, op. cit., pp. 164–87, esp. pp. 168 and 179–80; cf. pp. 368–70.

which offers priests advice on eliciting confessions of the sin of masturbation.[57]

There is also evidence of Saint Joseph's popularity with religious women, especially members of some of the new congregations. François de Sales strove to ensure that devotion to the saint would be integral to the spiritual life of the Order of the Visitation, which he founded with Jeanne de Chantal. François's death occurred in 1622; this was also the year in which the feast of Saint Joseph was celebrated for the first time throughout the Catholic Church as a holy day of obligation. The last sermon that François preached on Saint Joseph's day was addressed to the sisters of the mother house of the Visitation in Annecy.[58] Teresa of Avila instilled a similar devotion to Joseph in the members of her reformed Carmelite order, many of whose convents were placed under the Saint's patronage. Teresa had adopted Joseph as her 'advocate', 'lord', and 'father', and the order she founded subsequently did much to propagate his cult.[59] Similarly, Olivier Conrard states that he wrote his treatise *La Vie et louenge du benoist sainct Joseph* at the request of the 'devotes religieuses du sainct convent de L'anonciade à Bourges'.[60] The hypothesis that the figure of the amiable patriarch held a certain appeal for religious women would tend to underscore the danger of assuming that women in history must necessarily have identified in particular with female figures.[61] Nevertheless, it must also be recognised that devotion to a male

---

[57] *De confessione mollitiei*, attributed to Gerson, *Œuvres*, VIII. 71–5. Cf. Thomas N. Tentler, *Sin and Confession on the Eve of the Reformation* (Princeton: Princeton University Press, 1977), pp. 91–3, and Jeremy Tambling, *Confession: Sexuality, Sin, the Subject* (Manchester and New York: Manchester University Press, 1990), pp. 43–4.

[58] Cf. Barry, op. cit., pp. 79–80. See also *Sermon Texts*, pp. 35–41.

[59] Teresa of Avila, *Life*, chapter 6, in *Complete Works*, trans. and ed. E. Allison Peers, 3 vols (London: Sheed and Ward, 1946), I. 34–5. For an account of the Carmelites' association with the cult, see Pierre Sérouet, 'Le Culte de saint Joseph dans le Carmel de France au XVIIe siècle', in *SJXVII*, pp. 770–92, and *Sermon Texts*, pp. 30–2.

[60] *La Vie*, f. i iiiiᵛ.

[61] Cf. Bynum, *Jesus as Mother*, esp. pp. 110–69, and eadem, *Fragmentation and Redemption: Essays on Gender and the Human Body in Medieval Religion* (New York: Zone Books, 1991), esp. pp. 151–179. In a perhaps related development, the seventeenth century also witnessed the flourishing of the cult of the Sacred Heart of Jesus. This was again promoted in particular by the Jesuits, and by François de Sales and the Order of the Visitation. In the thirteenth century, the devotion had been popular with women mystics (see Bynum, *Jesus as Mother*, pp. 18 and 170–262); in the

saint like Joseph would have represented a very safe and approved course for these women. This would be especially true if, as a contemplative nun, one were to assume the active and itinerant role of reformer and foundress. It would also be true in general, however, in a climate in which women's religious enthusiasm was often greeted with anything from caution to hostility on the part of the ecclesiastical authorities.

* * *

In conclusion, Joseph in the Gospels is notable for his lack of precise features. He is at one and the same time a vital and a peripheral figure in the story of the incarnation; his actions in the early years of Jesus's life are essential to the Son of God's survival, yet no words of his are recorded, and he disappears from the narrative as soon as he is no longer strictly necessary. In France and other Catholic countries of late medieval and early modern Europe, the contours of the figure of Joseph are firmed up, the colours filled in. A number of historians of religion have sought to account for Gerson's initial enthusiasm for Saint Joseph with reference to the troubled socio-political climate of fifteenth-century France.[62] While such arguments are illuminating (and I have worked here to amplify them), they nevertheless fail to answer satisfactorily the fundamental question of why Joseph alone and not some other saint should have seemed to respond adequately to contemporary circumstances. While any attempt at historical explanation is necessarily partial, I have nevertheless sought to address this problem by taking a larger view, showing that the invention of Saint Joseph is related to a nexus of fundamental and long

seventeenth century, its most influential manifestation came in the form of the visions of the Visitandine nun Margaret Mary Alacoque.

[62] Herlihy argues that Joseph was intended to offer a model to fathers in an age when the family was threatened by war, famine, and plague ('The Making', p. 128; *Medieval Households*, pp. 128–9; 'The Family', p. 14). Chorpenning takes up the same idea, arguing also that 'these external assaults precipitated an internal crisis of affection within the late medieval family' (*Sermon Texts*, p. 27). However, the marriage patterns that Chorpenning identifies as symptomatic of this 'crisis of affection' (late marriage of sons, early marriage of daughters) are seen by Herlihy as characterising family life from the twelfth century onwards, as an agnatic (patrilineal) kinship system came to be superimposed on a pre-existing bilineal one (see works cited). Chorpenning also signals Gerson's association of Joseph with the effort to reunite the Church under a single pontiff (op. cit., p. 29). Glorieux discusses the origins of Gerson's devotion in the context of the troubles of 1413 and his committing of himself and France to Joseph's protection (see note 32 above).

term political, social, and psychological developments. While, like his spouse, Joseph admittedly remains a singular figure, he nevertheless stands, in many ways, as a prototype of the modern man.

2

Feminising the Warrior at Francis I's Fontainebleau

Kathleen Wilson-Chevalier

In early sixteenth-century France, the warrior ideal of masculinity ruled the (noble) roost. A code of military honour prevailed on the battlefield, in private quarrels, and in sexual affairs.[1] Logically then, for the urban-born Humanist scholar Guillaume Budé, Louis XII's realm was a culturally backwards state in which armour and weapons set the tone.[2] It is this chivalric world view that inflects the 'male page' of two conceptually pendant manuscript illuminations that Jean Bourdichon created for Anne of Brittany around 1510.[3] Shown but quickly passing through an impermanent room, King Louis XII has stripped off his suit of armour to compose a missive to his wife. Outside, still astride their mounts, a number of his military acolytes await the instant when he will regain his saddle, clearly his natural place. In these representations made for Queen Anne, interior castellar space is projected as feminine space, and book-based culture is depicted as unequivocally belonging to the female sphere — for while both royal protagonists are shown writing, a book figures solely on Anne's sheet. Bourdichon's image thus provides a neat visual frame for

---

[1]   On the French warrior in general, see *L'Homme de guerre au XVIᵉ siècle*, Actes du Colloque de l'Association RHR, Cannes, 1989, eds. G.-A. Pérouse, A. Thierry, and A. Tournon (Saint-Étienne: Université de Saint-Étienne, 1992). For aggressive sexual prowess seen through the eyes of Marguerite de Navarre ('…vostre plaisir gist à deshonorer les femmes, et vostre honneur à tuer les hommes de guerre'), see Christine Martineau's essay: 'L'Homme de guerre au XVIᵉ siècle dans *L'Heptaméron'*, pp. 312–24. The conceptual framework of my essay owes a debt to Eugene Giddons, 'Honourable Men: Militancy and Masculinity in *Julius Caesar'*, in *Renaissance Forum* (vol. V, no. 2, Winter 2001, 1–33).

[2]   See Gilbert Gadoffre, *La Révolution culturelle dans la France des humanistes: Guillaume Budé et François Iᵉʳ* (Geneva: Droz, 1997), 'Introduction', pp.13–41, for Budé's analysis of the then oft-denounced 'ignorance française'.

[3]   From the *Épîtres des poètes royaux*, St Petersburg, National Library of Russia, Fr. F.v. XIV, 8, f. 1ᵛ and f. 51ᵛ. See François Avril and Nicole Reynaud, *Les Manuscrits à peintures en France 1440–1520* (Paris: Flammarion-Bibliothèque Nationale, 1993), no. 168, 303–5.

FEMINISING THE WARRIOR AT FONTAINEBLEAU

the 'obsessional fear of devirilization through culture' that structured the imagination of the French warrior caste.[4] Two decades later, when Louis's successor Francis I began to commission his grand decorative undertakings at Fontainebleau, his political agenda would lead him to confront this fear head on.

The golden age of Fontainebleau corresponds to the post-captivity, second half of Francis's reign, when the King's determination to impose a royal monopoly of power meant taking control of the power to fight, and when, intrinsically linked to this design, a spectacular 'cultural revolution' was underway. Rosso Fiorentino and Francesco Primaticcio were the Italians charged with radically reshaping the King's artistic programme, from shortly after the damning of the memory of Constable Charles de Bourbon (1527) to — in Primaticcio's case — the period during and after the disgrace of his successor, Constable Anne de Montmorency (1541). And by reshaping the King's artistic programme, these painters wilfully contributed to the fundamental reshaping of his tool of governance, his court. The king was labouring to transmute the traditional *noblesse* (potentially turbulent lords) into educated courtiers (faithful allies), as the royal secretary Jacques Colin's 1538 translation of Castiglione's *The Book of the Courtier* attests, and as two of Rosso's stuccoes created just slightly before imply. This pair of male figures that flanks the fifth bay on the north side of the Galerie François Ier can be read as emblematic of the King's intent.[5] The cream of his own generation of aristocrats is exemplified by the aging barbarian warrior to the left: a wise and potent, yet

4 Gadoffre, op. cit., p. 23.
5 For a thorough study of the literary sources of the iconography of the fifth bay in its entirety, see most recently Philip Ford, '*Pietas* à Fontainebleau: Valère Maxime, Oliviero d'Arzignano, et la Galerie François Ier', in *Le Dialogue des arts* (no. 18), *Littérature et peinture du Moyen Âge au XVIIIe siècle*, eds. Jean-Pierre Landry and Pierre Servet (Lyon: C.E.D.I.C., 2001), I, 85–102. For global interpretations of the Gallery, see Dora and Erwin Panofsky, 'The Iconography of the Galerie François Ier at Fontainebleau', *Gazette des Beaux-Arts*, LII (1958); S. Béguin, O. Binenbaum, A. Chastel, W. McAllister Johnson, S. Pressouyre, H. Zerner, in *La Galerie François Ier au château de Fontainebleau*, Revue de l'Art, numéro spécial 16–17 (Paris: Flammarion, 1972); Eugene A. Carroll, *Rosso Fiorentino: Drawings, Prints, and Decorative Arts* [exhibition catalogue] (National Gallery of Art, Washington, 1987–1988), 222–97; Pierre and Françoise Joukovsky, *A travers la Galerie François Ier* (Paris: Honoré Champion, 1992). Rebecca Zorach has made a series of important remarks on the functioning of the 'overarching system' of the gallery in '"The Flower that Falls Before the Fruit": The Galerie François Ier at Fontainebleau and *Atys excastratus*', *Bibliothèque d'Humanisme et Renaissance*, LXII (2000–1), 63–87.

24

sorely outmoded Gaul.[6] By the 1530s, a few clairvoyant nobles — including Galiot de Genouillac, Louis Du Bellay, Jean de Baïf, Louis de Ronsard — had begun to invest heavily in the education of their sons. Such men had realised that their dynastic line would be able to counter the threat posed by all-too-well-educated men of the gown, by men of the calibre of Florimond Robertet, only if their progeny received an upbringing drastically different from their own; their descendants, they sensed, would need to wield not only the sword but also the plume. When Rosso envisioned opposite his barbarian Gaul a young 'Roman' who implicitly defers to the older generation to his right, the artist was invoking the valiant, learned young gentleman whose new intellectual capital had henceforth prepared him for the most prestigious positions in the realm.[7] Such was the profile of Guillaume and Jean Du Bellay, two young lords who had been intellectually armed at the Coqueret and Navarre colleges in Paris to serve magnificently both their dynasty and their king. Forward-looking youths of the noble elite, they were actively engaged in dissipating 'the fogs of boastful ignorance' (an expression used by Erasmus in a letter to Jacques Toussain in 1531) that had clouded the horizons of their father's peers.[8] By the time Brantôme wrote his *Vie des grands capitaines*, Guillaume Du Bellay was but one of the author's examples of a new race of gentlemen: eloquent warriors whose power and intellect had been harnessed to the public (monarchical) good.[9]

* * *

---

[6] The Gaul's two-pronged beard, a standard sign for Old Testament figures, affords a supplementary allusion to old and new. The young female terms to either side and the abundant fruit over his head express his potency.

[7] The young Roman's left elbow aggressively repels a naked (and discontent?) barbarian term who looks back nostalgically towards the first half of the gallery, while a pendant term gazes ahead, instead, towards the wiser and nobly clothed, if still barbarian, Gaul.

[8] For the quotation, see Gadoffre, op. cit., 45–6. All the preceding examples are taken from Gadoffre's chapters IV and V, which provide a detailed analysis of 'le moment où la noblesse d'épée, beaucoup moins sotte qu'on a voulu le croire, commence à comprendre avec quelles armes soutenir la concurrence de la classe administrative' (p. 121).

[9] 'M. de Langeais, certes, a esté un grand, sage et tres politicq capitaine; aussi avoit-il les deux, et l'espée et la plume, qui ayde fort à parfaire un grand capitaine.' Brantôme could affirm that 'les lettres et les armes maryees ensemble font un beau lict de noces' (as quoted by Gadoffre, op. cit., 128 and 159).

The Porte Dorée served as the main passageway into the palace of Fontainebleau during the age of Francis I, and the King and his team of advisors no doubt reflected at length on the content of the frescoes conceived to greet his noble subjects as they rode their horses through its portico. If Ovid's *Fasti* has long been identified as the source of the erudite tale which Primaticcio illustrated there no later than the early 1540s,[10] it has not yet been recognised that these (and other *bellifontain*) representations were envisioned to destabilise the King's arrogant, hyper-virile elite. Neo-Platonic thought had already begun to reign sovereign at Fontainebleau, and its interpretive thread was heat — both a structural component of the male body, and the motor of the universe in Marsilio Ficino's cosmic view.[11] This conceptual system underlies the two-piece Hercules cycle, tailored for the lords of the realm at the moment they were leaving behind the open spaces in which they fought their battles and hunted their game, to enter a sophisticated, highly encoded royal space in which courtly ladies were perforce more at ease. Both before and after the execution of these frescoes, male writers such as Philippe de Commynes and Michel de Montaigne gave voice to the deep-seated fear of the French warrior that culture would render him soft and effeminate;[12] and it is precisely this anxiety that drives Primaticcio's rendition of Omphale and her assistants dressing the demi-god in female garb. The artist has strategically positioned Hercules' small genitals on the straight line that marks the vertical axis of his preparatory drawing; and to our left, aged terms lower or hide their heads as a mature Hercules frowns at being unmanned.

---

[10] See Raymond Lebègue, 'Un thème ovidien traité par le Primatice et Ronsard', *Gazette des Beaux-Arts*, LV (1960), 301–6; K. Wilson-Chevalier, 'Women on Top at Fontainebleau', *Oxford Art Journal*, XVI-I (1993), 34–48; Suzanne Boorsch, in *The French Renaissance in Prints from the Bibliothèque Nationale de France* (Los Angeles: Grunwald Center for the Graphic Arts, UCLA, 1994), no. 45, 248–9 (who notes the importance of light and shade); Philip Ford, 'Hercule et le theme solaire à Fontainebleau: la Porte dorée et *Le Satyre* de Ronsard', in *Cité des hommes, cité de Dieu: Travaux sur la littérature de la Renaissance en l'honneur de Daniel Ménager* (Geneva: Droz, 2003), 245–58 (who cites Dorothee Herrig's — convincing — suggestion that these frescoes were executed in the early 1540s (*Fontainebleau: Geschichte und Ikonologie der Schlosslage Franz I.* (Munich: Tuduv, 1992), p. 165)). My iconographic interpretation of what Philip Ford refers to as 'deux scènes burlesques, voire même scabreuses', draws yet also differs from all of the above.

[11] Gadoffre notes that in the teachings of Robert Gaguin at the Sorbonne in the 1490s, Ficinian neo-Platonic thought had already crossed into France (op. cit., p. 57).

[12] See Gadoffre, op. cit., p. 23, who quotes Montaigne's assertion (Book II, chapter X) that 'l'estude des sciences amollit et effemine les courages, plus qu'il ne les fermit et aguerrit'.

Riveted on the cross-dressing scene are the (unequal) gazes of an agitated servant who prepares the banqueting table and a nonplussed, fully nude observer — the image of the ideal youthful spectator whose masculine identity is being redefined? To grasp fully the King's intent, the beholder must discover the key concealed in the (seemingly licentious) fresco on the opposite wall — for these pendant frescoes were designed to place the male beholder before a choice.

The second and concluding episode of Ovid's narration should be read as a novel modulation of the 'Hercules at the Crossroads' theme, in which light functions as a critical sign. In Leon Davent's magnificent print (Fig. 1), the mythological hero has just ejected a sexually aroused Pan from the bed he shares with Omphale; and the heat of anger has risen to his now cuckolded head. The body of Hercules, half cast in shadow, its right side alone reflecting the blinding light of the torch, reads as a binary paradigm: light/dark, right/left serve as markers of virtue and vice. Which form of heat will prevail? 'L'amour fole'[13] — the lowly carnal heat of a bestial Pan-of-many-horns? Or a higher type of heat, the multi-faceted celestial love that makes a harmonious world turn? The illumination provided by the flame of a distressed young torchbearer, his back turned to the cool nefarious moon, is angled out from Love's head, and two female terms absorb its glow. To Omphale's left, the queen's less-than-heroic aging companion retreats into the space defined by seductive female anatomy, perhaps to signify his marginalisation as she thrusts her arm forth to grab Love's bow. The gesture of the youth who plunges forward is synchronised with hers, instead; for she — Hercules' lion skin atop her head — is the agent charged with leading her consort along the virtuous path. But why then, in both of these frescoes, is a 'heroic' woman 'on top'? The crucial core of Francis's new definition of aristocratic manhood was discipline; and in a ploy to downplay military achievement and devalue the disruptive masculinity of potentially rival lords, women, conflated with culture, were being placed at the centre of the civilising function assigned to the King's court.

When a few years later Jacques Colin published another translation (in 1547, the year of Francis's death), his choice had fallen upon a differ-

---

[13] The term is used by Ronsard in a work addressed to Marc-Antoine Muret in 1553, in which he evokes Hercules and Iole (quoted by Ford, 'Hercule et le soleil...', p. 248, n. 11). In his later poem *Le Satyre*, Hercules — as in Primaticcio's fresco, 'se colere, / S'enfle de fiel'; and further along in the poem, Hercules is compared to a beast: 'Le feu venu, Hercule se colere [...] ainsy qu'un grand taureau' (ibid., 246 and 251). Ford aligns the numerous terms Ronsard invokes to suggest Pan's heat: '*s'allumer, luire, chandelle, ardre, flammes, allumé, enflammer*' (p. 250).

ent Ovidian tale which centred around the problem of ire. Extracted from the thirteenth book of *The Metamorphoses*, the text highlighted the struggle of Ajax and Ulysses over Achilles' shield, in which the shrewdness and the eloquence of Ulysses prevail over the this-time-fatal anger of Ajax.[14] Rosso's stucco pair suggests that this concern in the 1540s with redefining manly comportment underlies the programme of the Galerie François Ier as well. In the preceding decade, the goal had already been to prepare a re-gendered modern warrior for the treacherous road that might lead him from barbarian insufficiency to existential — and courtly — success.

* * *

To penetrate the meaning of this mind-bogglingly complex gallery, an iconographical tour was an absolute must; and His Majesty the Most Christian King himself, to whose glory this outstanding shrine was erected, was delighted to assume the role in which he was portrayed in the last main fresco — that of Enlightened Guide. So when he had deemed his guests worthy, he and his party set off from the royal chamber to work their way through the intellectual labyrinth at hand. On the narrow wall immediately to their left they discovered Rosso's *Bacchus, Venus, and Cupid* (Fig. 2),[15] a composition charged with introducing the theme of base instincts that governed the first, dismal half of the decorative cycle; that half which was placed under the influence of the lower elements of water (on the north wall) and earth (on the south wall); that half which was chronologically situated before the advent of the wise prince.[16]

---

[14] Jacques Colin, *Le proces d'Aiax, et d'Ulisses pour les armes d'Achille, contenu au treziesme livre de la Metamorphose d'Ovide, translatée en langue françoise* (Lyon: Pierre de Tours, 1547).

[15] See Sylvie Béguin, 'New Evidence for Rosso in France', *Burlington Magazine*, CXXXI (Dec. 1989), 828–38.

[16] See my complementary essay 'La Représentation de la lectrice bellifontaine et le système de civilité à la cour de François Ier', in *Lectrices d'Ancien Régime*, ed. Isabelle Brouard-Arends (Presses Universitaires de Rennes, 2003), 493–522. A passage in Claude Chappuis's *Discours de la Court* (Paris: André Roffet, 1543) offers an interesting addition to the neo-Platonic analysis of the iconography of the first bay on the north side of the Gallery proposed therein (496–7), which I see as dominated by cold water, in the absence of male heat and cosmic Love — and to the interpretation of the gallery which follows herein. Chappuis presents Fontainebleau as a 'fontaine de civilité' (being abandoned by men in this fresco, I believe): 'Si feiz ie tant qu'au donion me gectay / Et au meilleu ie vys une fontaine / ... / C'est celle la ou pour aprendre a vivre / Parmy le monde, en grand civilité, / Puyser se peult parfaicte honnesteté, /

Rosso's depiction of terrestrial love was coloured by his own homosexual preferences, no doubt;[17] and Cupid titillated the visiting elite by welcoming them with his buttocks. Artist was not King, however, and Rosso's personal sexual leanings did not direct the show. About to unfold was an unequivocally heterosexual programme that addressed issues of noble masculine identity within the divinely monarchical, the monarchically divine, cosmic scheme of things.

In the very first eye-level scene on the south wall (most legible in the corresponding tapestry, Fig. 3),[18] a putto fondles the genitals of a little companion — bluntly trusting virility to the fore. In the adjacent fresco of *The Battle of the Centaurs and the Lapiths*, this virility then literally explodes.[19] However valiant the efforts of historians to identify bearers of civilisation amidst the battling throng (Theseus and/or Hercules), no single man is demonstrably better than the beasts he fights. Lowly animal and human buttocks command the scene, while the potentially more noble Lapith heads have been reduced to impotence on the ground. In the corresponding passage of Ovid's *Metamorphoses*, the institutions of marriage and religion are cast asunder; and there can be no glory for the warrior in a universe so devoid of respect for the gods. Rosso's earth-dominated combat offers no glimpse of the sky; and in the stucco cartouche of the frame below, his figures turn their backs on the buildings of civilisation to ensconce themselves in nature, where they descend to the level of angry and lustful beasts.[20] Even the Salamander on the central axis above, head

---

Grace agreable, ung maintien asseuré, / Ung attraict doulx, discret & mesuré / Et qui en boit il vomist bien soubdain / Rusticité, & devient tout mondain — / Et ne fault point a aultre escolle aller / Affin d'apprendre a bien dire & parler.'

[17] I read Rebecca Zorach's comment that '[s]ensual male nudes are central to Rosso's œuvre' as an allusion to this penchant (op. cit., p. 63).

[18] On the six tapestries woven in the 1540s after each of the south wall frescoes, with the exception of the very last, see Sylvia Pressouyre in *Revue du Louvre*, op. cit., 106–11; Gerlinde Gruber, 'Les Tentures à sujets mythologiques de la grande galerie de Fontainebleau', *Revue de l'Art*, 108 (1995), 23–31; and Andrea Stockhammer, in *Tapestry in the Renaissance. Art and Magnificence*, ed. Thomas P. Campbell (New York: The Metropolitan Museum of Art, 2002), 465–76.

[19] See *Revue du Louvre*, op. cit., 49–52, 126–7, and Joukovsky, op. cit., 20–4. Carroll, op. cit., 232–5, reproduces an engraving that singles out the genital-fondling putti of this bay: in one instance a putto seems to pull another towards him 'as though to kiss him'; in the scene corresponding to my Fig. 3, a putto 'tickles the reclining putto's scrotum'. Carroll reads these scenes as suggesting 'lust, but of a playful and perverse kind', and attributes to their 'perversity' their nineteenth-century replacement by garlands (p. 235).

[20] See Carroll, op. cit., 232–4, for the corresponding anonymous etching.

lowered, seems full of rage. The sole glimmer of hope for protection from the mindless, unleashed heat of men is displaced to the sides, to the shields held by Old Testament priests, guarded by ascending angel-like lads. In conjunction with the contorted heralds above, these roundels display the royal initial and emblem, intimating some vague possibility of escape from this earthly chaos, somewhere, somehow, through King Francis I.

On the north wall, the explicit theme of problematic virility returns to colour the central fresco of the second bay (Fig. 4) in an unanticipated way.[21] *The Education of Achilles* includes a minor episode, seemingly marginalised at the back left, that has come to be known as 'the verification of the sex'. In this new instance of genital touching, positioned beneath a playful group of stucco putti fondling a companion anew, a couple of fine young boys confirm that the child on display belongs, indeed, to 'the stronger sex'. The point may well be, however, that this child's specific male trajectory has not yet been inscribed in the books. Directly to the right of this scene is a group of older men who pay no heed, for their attention has been mustered by the fencing lesson that engages the grey-haired Chiron and the budding warrior Achilles. Was Rosso picturing the ideal education of a prince, as historians have systematically surmised, and as Francis's monogram on a pedestal seems to imply? If the answer were affirmative, why then, on the vertical axis, and in the foreground of his scene, did he give pride of place to the buttocks of the most learned, yet nonetheless bestial, centaur, his tail provocatively raised?[22] Achilles' physique is surely being fine-tuned for glorious combat as master and pupil also swim, brandish a lance, or hunt. The future hero learns to play music at the top of a series of stairs, at the highest point of the composition, too. Chiron holds not his traditional lyre, though, but rather the lowliest of all musical instruments, the flute; and in a universe otherwise bereft of women, Achilles turns towards a breast-bared beauty as he strums a string instrument — amorously no doubt. Excellent corporeal training, and the element of water, cool the potentially bestial ardour of this noble youth. He manoeuvres, nevertheless, in the base realm of terrestrial love. However effective the lessons the 'male governor' Chiron has instilled in his young 'page', Achilles has faulted, for he has failed to enter into the

---

[21]   *Revue du Louvre*, op. cit., 53–6, 126–7; Joukovsky, op. cit., pp. 101–2.
[22]   See *Revue du Louvre*, op. cit., p. 55, fig. 74, for a reproduction of the nineteenth-century repainting of the buttocks and tail, clearly aimed at making them less 'offensive'.

superior civilisation of the book.[23] As a grown warrior, 'fierce Achilles', 'wild with rage', whose 'anger blazed up, just like that of a bull in the open arena' to slay Cygnus, was destined to succumb to the wrath of Neptune. Apollo then had him mowed down by Paris, 'a coward who had stolen away from Greece another man's wife'.[24] Water, at the beginning of the gallery, is not the sacred Christian element that saves.

The moral of the story is perhaps revealed in the delicate stucco notations of the frame below. Had Ulysses not yanked Achilles out of his hiding place amongst the daughters of Lycomedes; had Achilles not hung up his girlish slippers so quickly, but rather laboured further at the 'feminine' spinning wheel and spun more weighty (intellectual) yarn; then he and his warrior peers might not risk being compared to the goat that has usurped the baby's bed; for, as Guillaume Budé contended, when the human mind is instilled with bad habits from the cradle, 'the perpetual contagion of ignorance' will forever reduce man to an animal state.[25] Young

---

[23] This reading is consonant with Erasmus's hesitation to recommend to the young prince Plutarch's *Lives*: 'Un garçon batailleur et impétueux de nature pourrait être incité à la tyrannie en lisant sans précautions les histoires d'Achille, d'Alexandre le Grand, de Xerxès ou de Jules César' (quoted by Gadoffre; op. cit., p. 61).

[24] All citations are from Ovid, *Metamorphoses*, Book XII (Mary M. Innes' Penguin translation). Tellingly, the tale of Achilles' death frames Ovid's narration of the combat of the Lapiths and the Centaurs. Also of interest for the reading of the stuccoes which follows: during a respite in the fighting, on a feast day when Achilles 'was propitiating Pallas with the sacrifice of a cow', he turned to Nestor, 'the wisdom of our times, ripe in years and rich in eloquence', to understand why Caeneus, a countrywoman of his, changed to the opposite sex. Having been raped by Neptune, who promised her whatever she wished, she asked: 'Grant that I not be a woman, and you will have given me all.' Caeneus was then one of the Lapiths who participated in the battle against the centaurs. The centaur Latreus first assaulted Caeneus verbally, saying: 'Consider what you were born or, if you prefer, what you suffered, and go, take up your distaff and baskets of wool, twist the threads with your thumb, and leave war to men!' In the ensuing battle, although all the centaurs fell on Caeneus ('We, a whole people, are worsted by a single man, and scarcely a man at that! Yet truly he is a man, and we, by our weak efforts, are mere women, such as he used to be'), s/he ultimately escaped into the air: 'Hail to you, Caeneus, glory of the Lapith race, once a most mighty hero, and now a bird unique.' Had Achilles resembled the male/female Caeneus he inquired about, he might have escaped being ingloriously slain by a weakling and thus risen unfettered, he too, into the noble element of air.

[25] He states in his *De studio litterarum* that '[...] l'esprit humain, pénétré, dès le berceau et l'apprentissage de la vie, d'habitudes erronées et vicieuses, ne s'aperçoit même pas que, sous la perpétuelle contagion de l'ignorance, partout répandue, il est retombé au rang de leurs autres animaux' (cited by Gadoffre, op. cit., p. 276). Italians today still use the expression 'ignorante come una capra'.

boys slump to either side of a little scene of combat under the weight of
the central frame, while the outermost frescoes exhibit bulky, fettered,
plebeian brutes who almost overpower the central scene of this bay.[26] Although these Michelangelesque musclemen appear against the higher
element of air, and although one is adorned with a victory crown, neither
is able to break himself free from a club-like, sterile, unproductive tree.
Such, symbolically, is the condition of the able-bodied, but unlettered,
lord.

If the memory of the great warrior Achilles lives on to this very day,
his trajectory proved that his inferior mortal heat was no match for the superior cosmic heat of the god of the sun. In the fresco known as *The Loss
of Perpetual Youth*, located on the wall opposite *The Education of Achilles*, the same Apollo makes an explicit appearance, whereby he extends
his displeasure to humanity as a whole.[27] Hidden within this composition,
on the ill-explained left side of Rosso's image, which is best understood
by scrutinising the tapestry woven after the fresco (Fig. 5), is an Androgyne (as Frédérique Villemur first recognised) — a crucial neo-
Platonic key. In fact, the French fascination with this figure emerged just
as the decoration of the gallery was getting under way. In 1534, Rabelais's famed Gargantua began his literary career sporting an enigmatic
Androgyne badge on his fashionable princely hat. Meanwhile, Marguerite
de Navarre's 'pensionnaire' Antoine Héroët was fusing ideas from Plato's
Symposium on the one hand, and Marsilio Ficino's *Commentarium in
convivium Platonis* on the other, to compose 'L'Androgyne de Platon'
which he presented in manuscript form, in 1536, to the King. When he described a four-armed, four-legged, two-headed figure that '[...] se verroit
plus tost painct qu'escripte', was it not Rosso's representation of a
male/female Androgyne splitting into two parts that Héroët had in mind?[28]

---

[26]   Earlier in the same passage, Budé asserts that 'ceux qui avaient passé leurs années d'enfance et de jeunesse dans la promiscuité de la foule et loin de l'étude des lettres, ou bien ressemblaient à des bêtes, ou restaient si grossiers qu'ils en étaient
presque incapables de parler... l'usage de la langue se détériore progressivement, et de
patricien, pour ainsi dire, devient insensiblement plébéien...'.

[27]   For this scene, see *Revue du Louvre*, op. cit., pp. 57–60, 128–9; Joukovsky, op.
cit., 34–8.

[28]   Frédérique Villemur, 'Eros et Androgyne: la femme comme un autre "soy-
mesme"', in *Royaume de fémynie. Pouvoirs, contraintes, espaces de liberté des
femmes de la Renaissance à la Fronde*, eds. E. Viennot and K. Wilson-Chevalier
(Paris: Champion, 1999), 237–60. See also Marian Rothstein, 'Mutations of the Androgyne: Its Functions in Early Modern French Literature', in *The Sixteenth Century*

The consequences of the separation of the Androgyne, a classical stand-in for the sin of Adam and Eve, were seen as dire for mankind. For Ficino, in particular, it signified an arrogant rejection of God's grace, responsible for the loss of the specific form of light which allowed man to perceive the divine. In Rosso's fresco, Apollo drives his chariot away from the viewer above a mass of clouds that obscures the sky. To Apollo's left Mercury, the god of language, eloquence, and persuasion, and as such the link between earth and the heavens, seems to be burning his caduceus in front of supplicants, a sign of his refusal to transmit their prayer to the gods on high.[29] The female half of the Androgyne points in vain towards an isolated Muse, shown expiring alongside the abandoned tools of her trades:[30] magnificent books, which ought to allow humans to master the art of rhetoric and thus communicate with their kind; and musical instruments, which ought to sound the harmony of the cosmos, made possible, when all goes well, by the warmth of Apollo's sun. Yet the heavy clouds, reminiscent of Erasmus's 'fogs of boastful ignorance', block the sun's rays as the Androgyne's indifferent male side walks away. In synchrony with the right-hand side of this fresco, the (actual) 'Loss of Perpetual Youth', the nearby tondo reformulates the notion that mankind is henceforth condemned to grow old and debilitated; and even though mortals are actively preparing to pray to the earth goddess Cybele in the left-hand tondo, there is still no sign of communication between the celestial and the terrestrial domains.

Journal, XXXIV–2 (Summer 2003), 409–37. Rothstein quotes the passage I cite (p. 414) without linking it to Rosso's image.

It was thanks to female patronage that Héroët emerged at the French court (Raphaël Valéry, 'Qui était Antoine Héroët ? Biographic provisoire en attendant un colloque', *Bulletin d'art et d'histoire de la Vallée du Loing* [2002, no. 5], 147–58). After entering the service of (the future) Margueriite de Navarre in 1524, he became 'pensionnaire extraordinaire' of Marguerite and her mother Louise de Savoie in 1529. That the theme of the Androgyne was of particular interest to Marguerite is confirmed by the French translation of Ficino's *Commentary* which she commissioned in 1546.

[29]   According to Guillaume Budé, for whom Mercury is a fundamental reference: 'sans ce médiateur et cet interprète, la terre n'aurait eu nul commerce avec le ciel, les mortels nul gage de leur parenté avec les puissance d'en haut [...]; entre les hommes eux-mêmes ne se serait pas établi le droit des gens, d'où sont sortis, comme d'une source d'humanité, les pactes, traités, alliances, [...] — ciment des cités — d'où sont nées à leur tour les lois et les institutions politiques...' (from *De contemptu rerum fortuitarum*, as translated by Marie-Madeleine de La Garanderie, in *Christianisme et letters profanes* (Paris: Honoré Champion, 1995), 282–3).

[30]   Is Discord emerging from her flank as the Androgyne splits?

On both the north and the south sides of the next (the third) bay, angry gods provoke trials and tribulations to punish sorely overheated men for their venereal, hence generation-related, sins. In *The Revenge of Nauplius*, to the north, the enraged goddess of civilisation, Pallas, seconded by Neptune, has drawn Ajax's fleet onto the rocks in the blackest of ill-fated moon-lit nights.[31] The empty niches of the surrounding stucco frame read as emblems of Ajax's lack of respect for the two ancient deities, for the warrior had dared to rape the Palladian priestess Cassandra in one of her temples, just as he had dared to slay a member of Neptune's dynastic line. Since the element of water commands the first three gallery bays on the north wall, Neptune — father of Nauplius, in turn father of Palamedes, whom Ajax killed — fittingly effects Pallas's revenge.[32] No half-beasts intervene to justify the violence of Rosso's shipwreck scene, yet male heat is no less savagely unleashed than during the Lapith/Centaur struggle. Once again there is no glory for the warrior here. Men betray men, and then batter away at fellow human beings to save their own skins, in a most un-Christian way.[33]

Although the pendant fresco on the south wall has generally been interpreted as *The Death of Adonis*, Rebecca Zorach has argued that (at the very least) it is concomitantly a depiction of *The Punishment of Attis* (Fig. 6).[34] If, as I contend, noble masculine identity is at stake in the *bellifontain* artistic scheme, the presence of such a 'dangerously sexualised' tale makes consummate iconographical sense. While irreverent rape lies at the heart of Ajax's misdeeds on the opposite wall, the 'Adonis/Attis' bay presents a whole gamut of other forms of transgressive sex. In the lower left corner of the frame, a 'Cupid' holding a mask before 'Venus' serves to denounce as deceitful 'fol amour' the three other corner images of homosexual pairing and the coupling of human and beast. Even more ex-

---

[31] See *Revue de l'Art*, op. cit ., 61–2, 129–30 ; Carroll, op. cit., 238–41; Joukovsky, op. cit., 70, 73–5 (who noted, 73, the importance of the 'double punishment of the impious' Ajax).

[32] The theme of dynastic issue seems to reappear in the stucco and fresco putti of the frame. Genealogy, again, and revenge, are alluded to in the small oval fresco set below the main scene, in which Neptune is represented, the prow of a ship in his hand, along with Nauplius's mother Amymone. The central importance of lineage for the *noblesse* helps to explain the unbounded passion that irrupts in this scene. Yet in the global economy of the gallery, anger as a response to anger has undeniably negative overtones — no matter its structural roots.

[33] See note 41 for the use of the metaphor of a storm to signify the state of France during the King's captivity at Eleanor of Austria's entry into Lyon in 1533.

[34] Op. cit. The interpretation that follows is consonant with Zorach's reading.

plicitly, the large rectangular stucco to the right stages acts of sodomy and bestiality, performed outside a civilised palace to the sound of the sexually charged bag-pipe, and in the vicinity of an ominous skull (seen clearly in an anonymous drawing in the Louvre, Cabinet des dessins), Zorach has unravelled the thread that links the various scenes: the tale of the incestuous relation between the protagonist of the central fresco, Attis, and his mother Cybele, has a parallel in the little stucco below the main fresco, since its rigged chariot race is an episode from the incestuous love of Oenomaus and Hippodamia; the tiny painted upper roundels show Attis making a vow of fidelity to his mother/lover, which he will mindlessly break, as well as a bull, to be sacrificed in the goddess's honour. In fact, Cybele on her chariot drawn by lions dominates the rectangular stucco to the left, announcing to the approaching visitor that the great ancient earth goddess directs the entire bay.

Numerous attempts have been made to conflate this death of a pagan hero (whether Adonis or Attis or both) with the death of Christ. A humanist Christian programme drives the French King's masterpiece, and the first half of the gallery does afford a number of recognisable typological models for the scenes of the second half. Yet however much this intellectual worldview may be characterised by a desire for reconciliation, pagan is not equal to Christian, just as the Old Testament is not equal to the New. The little winged putti supporting the frame of *The Punishment of Attis* continue to cower under its weight; and the standing stucco children to the left provide a new instance of genital fondling, with a most uncommon twist. As the little boy touches himself, a rare little girl putto strains her neck to watch — unless, as Zorach surmises, the second putto is in fact a castrate, like Attis himself. Yet whatever 'her' real gender identity, the infant couple is most probably meant to draw attention to the dramatic core of the central scene where, in punishment for his betrayal, Attis dies of self-mutilation.

Members of the French King's Renaissance court would surely have associated Attis's genital tribulation with the fact that Attis died bereft of an heir; and suffering in the region of the crotch must have evoked syphilis, which too was perceived as a product of a (Christian) god's wrath. Yes, the theme of sacrifice is emphasised when one of the standing putti in the frame points up towards the sacrifice of a bull. And yes, in the central composition, a winged infant carries Attis's garments up towards the sky, reminding the viewer that the scene is about resurrection, too. The sacrifice of Attis/Adonis is nonetheless presented as less than the sacrifice of Christ. While the earth goddess governs appropriately this third and last bay of a trilogy dedicated to the element over which she presides, the season of Attis's castration is winter, and not one of these 'exorbitant sexualities' is procreative. The meagre earthly fruit in the arms of the last stucco putto of this portion of the gallery reminds us that generation is problematic under such heavy, sin-filled skies. As Venus descends earthwards in her chariot, clouds once again mask the rays of the cosmic motor, the sun. The heat of base terrestrial love offers no access to 'the wisdom that is the knowledge of the true, the honest, the useful' of which Budé spoke so highly to the King,[35] no hope of true salvation. However, for the King's select audience, the 'traversée du désert' had come to an end. A watershed awaited them in the central bays of the gallery, where Jupiter introduced his sacred heat. The passage to the higher elements of fire and air/ether was about to begin.[36]

* * *

Jupiter first 'entered' the King's gallery somewhat surreptitiously, hidden away in a cabinet that formerly opened off the north side of the gallery; and there, symbolically positioned above a potentially burning hot fireplace, he appeared in all his divine glory to Semele.[37] Nonetheless, Davent's etching after Primaticcio's non-extant composition (Fig. 7) shows that the supreme god wields his thunderbolt in such a way that the male principle, because isolated, still bears a negative edge. A Wind blows in vain, for the contorted Semele lies inanimate on the regal bed. To the right, Love masks his eyes in despair as he leads away a heavily laden water nymph, whose very body exudes the element which formerly con-

---

[35]   Such is one of Guillaume Budé's definitions of wisdom in his discussion with Francis I (*Philologie. De Philologia*, ed. & trans. M.-M. de La Garanderie (Paris: Les Belles Lettres, 2001), 18).

[36]   This reading corroborates Sylvie Béguin's observation that the first important visitor who inaugurated the Gallery was Charles V, and that: 'Entreprise après la libération de François Iᵉʳ, dès 1528, la Galerie apparaît comme la revanche sur l'adversité' (S. Béguin, 'François Iᵉʳ, Jupiter et quelques belles bellifontaines', in *Royaume de fémynie*, op. cit., 197). The problem at hand, after defeat and captivity, was to 'muer un destin contraire en gloire' (Gadoffre, op. cit., 218).

[37]   On the iconography of this cabinet, see the contributions of Sylvie Béguin: 'Two Notes on Decorations in the Galerie François I at Fontainebleau: A Religious Theme in the Cabinet of Semele', *Journal of the Warburg and Courtauld Institutes*, LVII (1994), 271; *Royaume de femynie*, op. cit., 193–4; and, most recently, 'Un *modello* pour la Galerie François Iᵉʳ?', in *Les Cahiers d'Histoire de l'Art* (2003–1), 19–24.

stituted the damp female essence of Semele.[38] Although the sexual union of Jupiter and Semele was procreative, its issue was only Bacchus, the god associated on the east wall with lower terrestrial love; a god born in parthenogenesis of Jupiter's own thigh; a god whose promise of resurrection, like Cybele's, was inferior to that of Christ.

Primaticcio's bold mythological scene of copulation reeks of tragic desolation, and despite Jupiter's flash of lightning, dark clouds obscure much of the sky. Produced at a court where powerful women were reciting on front stage, it was to be understood as a scene of rape, a metaphor for a poor choice. To be sure, the sacred heat of Jupiter was intentionally confounded with the sacred heat of the king of France. Yet the King's — and I daresay his sister's — ultimate message to the male elite of France was not lodged in this heat that destroys; the royal aim was to subordinate the King's noble subjects through education and discipline, not to scare them away. A subsidiary stucco (known solely through a seventeenth-century copy, Fig. 8), no doubt conceived by Rosso and plausibly identified as *Constantine Burning the Heretical Books*, provides a precious contemporaneous gloss on the burning of Semele. Rosso's historicised roundel was one piece of a puzzle fabricated during a period of increasingly exasperated religious oppositions, and it has been recognised as an allusion to the on-going Sorbonne-instigated burning of Lutheran books.[39] However, Constantine the Prince was shown intervening to stop priests from kindling their bonfire with books — for such omnipotent but fatal heat leaves no room for the tolerant exchange of ideas on which a harmonious society thrives. The royal goal being the latter, the King's gendered political discourse was given a radically different inflection in another scene of divine union that Primaticcio frescoed on the opposite, the south, wall.

Jupiter's more felicitous sexual performance with Danae marks the conceptual climax of the Gallery, its true turning point. In this, the supreme god's second metamorphosis, his fire no longer annihilates but

---

[38] The nymph (whose water cascades near Jupiter's thigh, depicted as if an extension of Semele's body) may also refer to the waters of the Styx, where Juno dispatches Semele out of revenge in Book III of Ovid's *Metamorphoses*.

[39] See note 37. Clément Marot also used water and fire as metaphors for religious conflict in a 1533 rondeau which R. Cooper ('Humanism and Politics in Lyon in 1533', in *Intellectual Life in Renaissance Lyon*, eds. Philip Ford and Gillian Jondorf (Cambridge: Cambridge French Colloquia, 1993), 19–20) reads as a 'reply to Sorbonne intégrisme': 'En l'eau, en l'eau, ces folz seditieux... / Ilz ayment tant les vins delicieux / Qu'on peult nommer cabaretz leurs escholles / Mais refroidir fauldroit leurs chauldes colles, / Par rebours de ce qu'ilz ayment mieulx, / En l'eau.'

mutates instead into a fertile golden rain (Fig. 9). Wedged in between the King's 'F' below and his salamander above, at the precise mathematical centre of the royal passageway, the concord of the opposites is assured: fire flanks water (a feat made perfectly explicit only in the sixteenth-century tapestry reproduced here); male flanks female (with all due respect); and Apollo flanks Diana on the upper rim of the main scene, for the moon occupies a salient place in the cosmic cycle alongside the sun. Terrestrial Love buries his head in defeat as his celestial brother, wings raised for action, prevents an ugly aging woman positioned on the nefarious side of the gallery from disrupting his winning game. Fruitful abundance invades the upper half of the bay,[40] and birds soar triumphantly into the heavens at the very moment that the ineffectual old system, driven by hapless masculinity, is harnessed to engender a promising new race. Apollo's rays single out the young and beautiful Danae — the female agent of change who reclines over a symbolic wing which Sylvie Béguin has judiciously linked to both Louise de Savoie, begetter of the fine new prince Perseus/Francis I, and Queen Leonora of Austria/France, whose marriage to Francis served as a potent emblem of peace.[41] Under the leadership of the new prince, and thanks to his self-sacrificing marriage to the sister of his most relentless enemy Charles V, cosmic harmony could henceforth foster prosperity, tolerance, and intellectual exchange. For the first time in the Gallery, little boys converse lovingly in pairs, song books in hand, or play instruments, both low and high, as they exhibit to the beholder both front and rear.[42] The heretofore tortuous path would henceforth be put straight by a charitable Christian world view, for the associa-

---

[40] In the tapestry, a suggestively phallic fruit extends over the frame, it too on the negative side, near a column with *isolated* flames.

[41] S. Béguin, *Royaume de fémynie*, op. cit., 194–201. The pun on Leonora's name which appeared in the Queen's entry into Lyon of 1533 — *A lié en or* — confirms Béguin's hypothesis. Moreover, Queen Leonora was compared to Juno, whose wedding torch 'quenches the flames coming from a fountain — "Amour qui fond haine"'; animals symbolising the royal couple included the salamander and the ostrich (Austria), 'one cold, one hot'; and the marriage was presented as bringing an end to the age of Iron, and calm after the storm — neatly parallel to the Gallery iconography — with the return of the King and the *enfants* from captivity and the restoring of a pilot to the ship of state (R. Cooper, op. cit., 26–7).

[42] In conjunction with Leonora's entry into Lyon in 1533, the Queen was identified with the Ark of the Covenant as a sign of the new alliance which had made possible the King and the royal children's return from captivity. Pairs of putti at each end of the chariot that bore the Ark actually stood for the hostage children of France (Cooper, op. cit., 29–30). This historical sub-text may well be hidden in the cheerful putti of the Danae bay.

tion of water and sacred fire was surely meant to evoke baptism, too. Under such auspicious skies, our aging barbarian — who figures in the very next bay on the north side of the gallery — could but cede his place to a more civilised courtier youth, better outfitted to serve his kingdom and his king (Fig. 10).[43]

These dissimilar male companions buttress the standard centre-of-the-bay salamander, and in this particular incarnation s/he stands erect in the midst of flames.[44] Aligned with burning towns, both in the subsidiary painting at the bottom of the frame and in the main fresco where a blaze consumes Catania/Troy, the salamander promulgates the good news that the superior element of fire will preside over the last three northern bays. The Renaissance was a troubled and pessimistic age, and even the finest of realms was perforce fraught with trials and tribulations. Yet thanks to the guidance of a wise Christian prince, culture could help keep the never-disappearing barbarian threat at bay; the renewed moral stance of the noble caste could provide a stronger link in a more sturdy monarchical chain. Little matter that a city is burning to the ground; in the face of disaster, positive neo-Platonic heat has fostered the unity of a heroic few. Circumspect adults, whom Philip Ford relates to the King and his sister, have turned their backs on material goods to save the eldest of their line;[45] and even more importantly in the eyes of worthy lords, they have bequeathed their laudable respect for dynasty to the infants who open the way. At the core of this ancient lesson of familial piety lies the comprehensive understanding that Budé refers to as 'une certaine disposition juste et parfaite de l'esprit et de l'intellect', which the merely physical instruction that Chiron dispensed to Achilles could not provide.[46] Further-

---

[43]   The content of the bay will make it clear that this young man has the profile of Marguerite de Navarre's 'seigneur de bonne maison, qui estoit aux escolles, desirant parvenir au sçavoir par qui la vertu et l'honneur se doibvent acquerir entre les vertueux hommes' (quoted by Gadoffre, op. cit., 162, from the thirteenth story of L'Heptaméron).

[44]   Because 'la salamandre' spits fire and water, it reads as the perfect emblem of a henceforth male, but also — because all powerful — androgynous king.

[45]   For the literary sources of both sides of this bay, see Philip Ford, Pietas, art. cit., who sews large and small scenes together with threads from Oliviero d'Arzignano and Valerius Maximus. He identifies the twins of Catania, Emantia and Crito, with Francis I and Marguerite de Navarre, which helps explain both the sexually ambiguous treatment of the adult who leads the way, and the precedence given to the old woman she bears. There could well be an allusion to the leading roles the King's mother and sister played saving the realm after the disaster of Pavia.

[46]   See Gadoffre's sub-chapter: 'L'Histoire comme pédagogie royale' (op. cit., 253–7); for Budé, History is 'une grand maistresse qui équipole toute seule à plusieurs

more, like the quality teaching of the masterful Louise de Savoie, in homage of whom this fresco was most likely conceived, this sober — and witty — lesson was directed not only at little boys, but at little girls too.

On the opposite wall, under the influence of the highest element, air, youths strain selflessly to serve their mother, and in return for their devotion they receive the unanticipated gift of death (Fig. 11). In ancient and 'modern' times, the pestiferous air of a plague could very well kill animals and men.[47] Yet when Cydippe's exemplary sons die, Cybele's chariot soars towards the heavens this time: in a model Christian realm, resurrection rewards the virtuous terrestrial conduct of the truly noble few. *Cleobis and Biton* almost certainly alludes to the two sons of Francis I who, as hostages, paid dearly for the release of their father the King. How then should we interpret the 'F' that adorns Cydippe's cart? Is Cydippe — an aged female figure whose arms open in the form of a cross — a stand-in for both the captive Francis and his war-weary, ransom-burdened realm of France? If so, here as on the north wall, gender slippage has seeped into the most poignant of royal messages, ones pregnant with uplifting historicised meaning.[48]

The degree to which shifting identities structure the King's iconography is heretofore remarkable, but the very best is yet to come. To top off the then highly popular (and instructive) stories excavated from the ancient Roman past, Renaissance addenda to Ovid's *Metamorphoses* were written for both sides of the next bay. Even in the supposedly licentious, semi-public secular arena of Fontainebleau, the passionate male fire of the pagan gods begged being reined in; so when Jupiter and Saturn perpetrate

---

grans precepteurs ensemble'. Jacopo Sadoleto's book on the *Education of Children*, which he dedicated to Guillaume Du Bellay in 1533, bears witness to broad interest in this theme in the royal circle (*De liberis recte instituendis liber*; Cooper, art. cit., 12–13).

[47] The plague hit France hard between 1531 and 1533, and R. Cooper (art. cit., 1–3) provides historical evidence of the gloomy outlook that characterised the years when the Gallery programme was initially being conceived. He also supplies the specific reference used in the Lyon entry of 1533 to link Valerius Maximus' reference to young men sacrificing themselves for their country and the Dauphin (p. 28).

[48] The spirit of this bay reflects Marguerite de Navarre's fascination with a perfect mystical union, based on a 'don total qui supprime les existences particulières', a 'sacrifice' 'en martyre / Et en malheur' (K. Wilson-Chevalier, 'La Représentation de la lectrice bellifontaine et le système de civilité à la cour de François Ier', in *Lectrices d'Ancien Régime*, ed. Isabelle Brouard-Arend, op. cit., 500–1) — all of which I take as a sign of Margaret's greater involvement in the programme of the Gallery as a whole. See also *Cléobis et Biton: un mythe oublié*, exhibition catalogue, Musée des Beaux-Arts de Carcassonne, 1995.

erotically charged divine rapes in the shapes of a bull and a horse, they are relegated to the margins of the north bay. In the fresco between them triumphs living animal proof of the Most Christian King's superiority over the turbulent immortal pagan lot. The god-like King Francis is metamorphosed into a tame civilising elephant, 'F'- and salamander-laden, and charged with assuring the social stability for which, in unison, three generations of his dynasty had toiled. A Jupiter in imperial guise (an allusion to Charles V?) recognises defeat by depositing his thunderbolt at his Master's feet. The Good Prince's rise to glory proceeds unimpeded from this point on.

After musing over a modern metamorphosis with what may well have international implications, the royal party turned to the opposite wall to behold the fresco known as *The Unity of the State* (illustrated by the corresponding tapestry, Fig. 12). At first sight, issues of political unity seem to prevail as representatives of the Orders of the realm come together around the King. The crux of the matter lies beneath the surface, though, invisible to the human eye. Mercury, mediator of discord because god of eloquence, has henceforth restored his power to mankind, thus enabling cosmic heat to circulate freely, through untainted air, to promote communication and foster rational problem-solving around an eminently approachable king.[49] Closest to Francis, on his left side, stand representatives of the Third Estate. A barbarian in the second row listens attentively to a magnificently dressed peer — a man of letters of the likes of Budé? Thanks to the mastery of language and culture, this learned soul has stripped off his uncouth breeches and has captured the ear of his prince, who in gratitude has elevated him above his estate.[50] The orator's extraordinary gift — which has materialised as the pomegranate of unity, but also resurrection — can position the human race amongst the immortal gods.[51] Francis responds magnanimously by pointing to his Court: the faithful servants, priests, and warriors alike, who flank him on his more favourable, palatial right; will they too benefit from 'prudence lettrée chose precieuse et don de Dieu inventé pour suppleer les faultes de nature hu-

---

[49]   On this theme, see *Mercure à la Renaissance*, ed. Marie-Madeleine de La Garanderie (Paris: Champion, 1988).
[50]   The Third Estate breeches seem to function as a sign for Étienne Dolet's horror of 'la tourbe rustique et quasi barbare des médicastres et juristes qui ne pensent qu'au profit' (Gadoffre, op. cit., p. 27).
[51]   '...les gens de lettres et mesmement ceulx qui ont grace d'elegance en histoire sont ceulx qui font la mémoire des princes immortelle, et à bien parler, qui ont pouvoir de les rédiger au cathalogue des dieux (*L 'Institution du Prince*, f. 38^r; cited by Gadoffre, op. cit., p. 254).

41

maine'?[52] On the left margin a finely dressed, but unlettered, barbarian noble can only turn away. In the tapestry only, his face mirrors that of another barbarian — a peasant, or a 'sorbonnatre' priest? – while his gaze seems riveted on the men who struggle in the large oval to his right. Their fate is his. Like them, he will forever remain fettered and earthbound. Never will he accede to the Word of Mercury, which binds heaven to earth.

The enigmatic little fresco below the main scene encapsulates the neo-Platonic movement that, from left to right, traverses this entire bay. Men imprisoned in closed spaces give way to a messenger whose action is a function of the prince he serves. Saddled horses allude to the frenetic diplomatic activity made possible by Mercury the divine messenger's return. The nature of the progression of the large-scale figures in the side ovals and central composition is exactly the same. The men in the oval to the left struggle to become one, yet remain grounded in the terrestrial realm despite their positioning against an open blue sky. In the central scene, a magnificent architectural setting proclaims that raw nature has ceded to civilisation under the aegis of the king and his court. Even the marginal figures to the right form pairs; and while bare-breasted beauties enter a palace directly above the humanist busy engaging the king, the proximity of such a learned court seems to have propelled even a lowly sinful monkey to new heights. The ascension reaches its climax in the oval to the right: as Mercury's acolyte Charon transports a soul to God, his and his passenger's profiles fuse. The Androgyne crosses the Christian waters of baptism, achieving the difficult union of body and soul. Its heads in the clouds, it has managed to break free.

In the last bay to the north, the fire of pagan sacrifice (on the sides) yields to the sacred fire of Christianity (in the centre), with its true promise of procreation and salvation in the confines of the king's civilised realm. Below, the Muses dance a round, for 'circular knowledge', 'the harmony of the sciences', has enabled mankind to reach Wisdom and communicate with the divine.[53] Finally, in the very last fully extant bay, stucco barbarian followers of Bacchus and their no-future progeny share the margins with hopelessly carnal humans and exotic painted animals

---

[52] From *L'Institution du Prince* (cited by Gadoffre, op. cit., 255).

[53] In his *Institution du Prince*, Budé refers to a 'savoir en cercle': 'faisans ung cercle des ars liberaulx et sciences politiques, ayans connexité et coherence de doctrine qui ne se doibt ne peut bonnement separer par estude, pour ce que toutes ces sciences s'entretiennet comme font les parties d'ung cercle qui n'a commencement ne fin' (Gadoffre, op. cit., 256; see also 296–8).

while the Enlightened Guide steals the show, abandoning a hoard of ges-
ticulating monstrous personifications of the vices on their ignorant (cold)
fogs. The just and learned leader — empowered by the cultural revolution
underway, and sure of his role as the wisest defender of the true faith —
strides self-confidently into the superior element of ether, where he knows
that he, more than even the immortal Jupiter, belongs. In the little stucco
below (known through an etching by the Master I.♀.V), a celestial Venus,
aided by favourable winds and her celestial son whose huge wings are
opening for flight, was preparing to rejoin the king. A mere instant later,
she would have handed over her theoretically female realm of water to a
little troop of too muscular, clearly unlearned, men.

Having reached this hard-to-scale iconographical peak, poorly
schooled noble visitors, silenced by the eloquence of their flesh-and-blood
sovereign, were surely forced to concede defeat. Nevertheless, a brilliant
cultural display and a profound political transformation are two very different things.

* * *

At the south centre of the Galerie François Ier, the king presented his male
heat, equated with that of the sun, as positively counterbalanced by the
cold nature of the female moon. Yet following a major administrative crisis that led in 1541 to Constable Montmorency's fall, the sun at times ex-
erted its heat to the detriment of the moon — for in 1536 the cold satellite
had become the emblem of the new dauphin Henri, a close friend of
Montmorency.[54] The lessons proffered to the courtier were instinctively
rejected by this high-ranking member of the King's barbarian generation,
this all-too-powerful feudal lord. As a result, Francis felt obliged to reiterate the monarchical fact of life that the king's 'bon plaisir' alone bestowed
grace and disgrace. A drawing Primaticcio made for the vault of the
King's Galerie d'Ulysse illustrates the new royal message with brio (Fig.
13). As the glorious sun, confounded with the frontally displayed male
genitals of Apollo and his horses, rises to transmit its heat to the cosmos,
Diana and her horses descend with the moon into obscurity, their base rear
ends turned towards the viewer as a polemical sign of the subordinate

---

[54]   On this theme, and the drawing that follows, see my article 'Les Déboires de
Diane au château de Fontainebleau', in *Le Mythe de Diane en France au XVIe siècle*,
Actes du colloque de l'ENS Boulevard Jourdan, Paris, eds. Jean-Raymond Fanlo and
Marie-Dominique Legrand, *Albineana* 14 (Niort : Cahiers d'Aubigné, 2002), 409–41.

status of the moon/dauphin. Additional female figures, metaphors of the king's monopoly of favour, rise and fall with the sun and the moon.

The idea of 'feminising the warrior' through culture was hatched during Francis's reign to serve as a tool to draw courtiers into the service of the king. When ineffectual, as in the case of Montmorency, the King was not loath to elevating a real woman to serve as living proof that he alone was in control. Such is the sense of the grandiose decorative cycle which the King had Primaticcio undertake in honour of the duchess of Étampes, his mistress and his (wilful) creature, in the former lodging of Montmorency; and such is (one of) the meaning(s) of another androgynous figure which Primaticcio concocted for the King (Fig. 14). Executed for the non-extant Diana fresco cycle that adorned the king's baths, this *Jupiter as Diana* went a full step further than the earlier, well-known *Androgynous Portrait of Francis I* (see Fig. 16, p. 145), in which the King's identification with both male and female gods positions Diana on his sinister side. In Primaticcio's androgynous figure, female (Diana) appears 'unnaturally' positioned above male (Jupiter), as a forceful statement that the king was powerful enough, literally, to turn the world upside down. Yet during this culturally extraordinary reign, even when, as was the case here, the aging father was furious with his rebellious son, his ultimate message was one of tolerance and concord. Jupiter assumes a position of subordination under Diana, the ambiguously gendered allusion to his son, as an emblem of the King's recognition that if his body was sacred, it was unfortunately mortal too.

At Fontainebleau, male can be portrayed as female, but the corollary that female can be portrayed as male is also true. Himself the son of a strong, politically engaged mother, Francis I never hesitated to lay real power in the hands of the ladies in whom he placed his trust. Despite, but no doubt also because of, the lack of heat that kept them off the battle-field, women were endowed with, and able to nourish, the two natural prerogatives of intelligence and language that Budé so highly esteemed. From the day he was born, the King had understood that women were capable of contributing to the decision-making process, and his mother entered his privy council as soon as he became king. I would argue that Marguerite de Navarre — his intrepid diplomat and open-minded 'minister of the cult', she who so thoroughly confounded his masculine and her feminine self — played one of the major roles in elaborating the gender-unstable cultural system scrutinised here. In turn, the duchesse d'Étampes came to reside on the *étage noble* at Fontainebleau, on the same level as both Queen Eleanor and His Majesty the King, and it was in her chamber that Primaticcio was charged with actualising the story of Alexander the

Great. Above her fireplace, the artist represented Alexander and his captains vacillating at the arrival of a hoard of Amazon queens, ingeniously equating the virility of the Amazons with overheating from the logs below. No message could be more destabilising for unruly captains of war than this representation which intimated that women could be valorous too. In fact, by empowering a real Omphale, a real Thalestris, the King was playing his trump card in a tough political game.

The symbolic system which underpins the unique artistic achievement of Francis I's reign flirts with, but cannot be reduced to, mere sexual licence (as historians have almost unanimously supposed).[55] The fascination with Ovid's *Metamorphoses* should be read as a symptom of highly unsteady times; and rarely have such elaborately gendered body politics been put so boldly in the service of political change. The final results were perhaps no less ambiguous than gender at Fontainebleau. In subsequent decades, the Wars of Religion would demonstrate that the destabilising of aristocratic masculinity was an overwhelmingly difficult task for even an increasingly assertive Most Christian King. Present-day critical thinking continues to elaborate on the humanist politics of education and tolerance embedded in the figurative system which the King set in place with the help of his male and female allies, nevertheless.

---

[55] In his 1554 *Mémoires*, however, Arnould Du Ferron had described the King's system with remarkable clairvoyance: 'Ainsi meslait-il tellement la sévérité de la Philosophie avec les jeux amoureux qu'il pouvoit sembler, que ceux-ci empruntassent de l'autorité de celle-là, et tirast réciproquement de la gaillairdise de ceux-ci' (as quoted by Gadoffre from a seventeenth-century translation from the Latin, op. cit., 198). Need I underline the extent to which Gadoffre's project and my own have proceeded on parallel tracks?

Fig. 1, Léon Davent after Francesco Primaticcio, *Hercules, Omphale and Pan* (engraving, Paris, Bibliothèque nationale de France)

Fig. 2, Rosso Fiorentino (?), *Bacchus, Venus and Cupid*
(oil on canvas, Collection Musée national d'histoire et d'art, Luxembourg)

Fig. 3, Tapestry after *The Battle of Centaurs and Lapiths* bay of the Galerie François Ier, 1540s (Vienna, Kunsthistorisches Museum)

Fig. 4, Rosso Fiorentino, *The Education of Achilles* bay, 1530s (Galerie François Ier, château de Fontainebleau)

Fig. 5, Tapestry after *The Loss of Perpetual Youth* bay of the Galerie François Ier, 1540s (Vienna, Kunsthistorisches Museum)

Fig. 6, Rosso Fiorentino, *The Punishment of Attis* bay, 1530s (Galerie François Iᵉʳ, château de Fontainebleau)

Fig. 7, Léon Davent after Francesco Primaticcio, *Jupiter and Semele*, etching (Vienna, Albertina)

Fig. 8, Anonymous seventeenth-century drawing of a tondo by Rosso for the Cabinet du roi, Fontainebleau, *Constantine burning the heretical books* (location unknown)

Fig. 9, Tapestry after the *Danae* bay of the Galerie François Ier, 1540s (Vienna, Kunsthistorisches Museum)

Fig. 10, Rosso Fiorentino, *The Fire of Catania/Troy* bay, 1530s (Galerie François Ier, château de Fontainebleau)

Fig. 11, Rosso Fiorentino, *The Cleobis and Biton bay*, 1530s (Galerie François Ier, château de Fontainebleau)

Fig. 12, Tapestry after *The Unity of the State* bay of the Galerie François Ier, 1540s (Vienna, Kunsthistorisches Museum)

Fig. 13, Francesco Primaticcio, *The Antipodes*, early 1540s
(Paris, Louvre, Département des Arts Graphiques, Inv. 8512)

Fig. 14, Francesco Primaticcio, *Jupiter as Diana*, early 1540s (Paris, École des Beaux-Arts, M1155)

3

Situating the Masculine: Gender, Identity, and the Cosmos, in Maurice Scève's *Délie*, Marsilio Ficino's *De amore*, and Leone Ebreo's *Dialoghi*

Kathryn Banks

Introduction: Histories of Ideas and Literary Texts

The sixteenth-century cosmos was a gendered one. In French scientific poetry for example, it was a common topos that the sun was the earth's husband; the light and heat of the male sun, poured beneficently into the lap of the female earth, caused her to give birth to beautiful flowers.[1] Or, alternatively, the male sun was the lover or husband of the female moon; the sun bestowed his light upon his wife the moon, just as a husband's greatness bestowed status upon his lowly wife.[2] Thus the relations between cosmic bodies resembled human gender relations.

---

[1]   See, for example, Du Bartas' hugely popular *Sepmaine* of 1578: 'Le ciel, bruslant d'amour, verse mainte rousee / Dans l'amarry fecond de sa chere espousee, / Qu'elle rend puis apres, syringuant ses humeurs / Par les pores secrets des arbres et des fleurs' (in *The Works of Guillaume de Salluste Sieur Du Bartas*, ed. Urban Tigner Holmes et al. (Geneva: Slatkine Reprints, 1977), 3 vols, II. 193–440, book II. 185–8); 'Le ciel, masle, s'accouple au plus sec element, / Et d'un germe fecond, Qui toute chose anime, / Engrosse a tous momens sa femme legitime' (II. 360–2). Similarly in the *Premier des Meteores*, Baïf writes: 'Tout s'échauffe d'amour: et la terre amoureuse / Pour plaire au beau Soleil prend sa robe odoureuse / De fleurons damassée' (in Jean-Antoine de Bäif, *Le Premier Livre des poèmes*, ed. Guy Demerson (Grenoble: Presses Universitaires de Grenoble, 1975), pp. 57–79 (60, ll. 169–71)). The marriage between earth and heavens is also a topos in Ebreo's *Dialoghi*.

[2]   'J'estime que ton corps est rond comme une bale, / Dont la superficie en tous lieux presque egale, / Comme un miroir poli, or dessus or dessouz, / Rejette la clarté du Soleil, ton espoux. / Car comme la grandeur du mari rend illustre / La femme de bas lieu, tout de mesme le lustre / Du chaleureux Titan esclaircit de ses rais / Ton front, qui de soy-mesme est sombrement espais' (Du Bartas, *La Sepmaine*, IV. 655–62). The representation of the sun and moon as husband and wife is frequent in both Classical and Renaissance literature, appearing, for example, in Rabelais's *Tiers Livre* (See J. C. Monferran, 'De quelques lunes du XVIe siècle: *L'Amour des amours* de

61

Conversely, sixteenth-century love lyric often compares human lovers to cosmic bodies. Such comparisons in lyric are particularly interesting if we bear in mind that cosmic bodies were often considered to be gendered in reality, and genuinely involved in love relationships. If cosmic bodies are in reality like human lovers, then comparisons of human lovers with cosmic bodies should not be dismissed as 'simply' figurative language; cosmic images should not be reduced to imagery. It is a commonplace of Scévian criticism to refer to the 'universe' of the *Délie*, yet the word 'universe' is used as a metaphor for the relation between the two lovers, for their mental 'world'.[3] Or, if modern critics do evoke the very real nature of the human–cosmos relation in the sixteenth century, they tend to assume that love lyric simply reiterated a received and unquestionable view of microcosm–macrocosm similarities, and thus grounded poetry's figurative images in a pre-existing ontological reality.[4]

Such analysis implicitly depends upon the dichotomisation of 'philosophical ideas' and 'literary texts' and, more specifically, upon the presupposition that 'philosophical ideas' logically precede and determine 'literary texts'. However, recent research in sixteenth-century studies has undermined this belief. In particular, Terence Cave has detected 'fragments d'un moi futur' in the writing of Rabelais, Béroalde de Verville, and Montaigne, thus troubling the dominant historical narrative of the

---

Jacques Peletier du Mans, *La Sepmaine* de Du Bartas', *Revue d'histoire littéraire de la France*, V (1995), 675–89).

[3] It is used this way by, for example, Marcel Tetel, *Lectures scéviennes: l'emblème et les mots* (Paris: Klincksieck, 1983); Nancy Frelick, *Délie as Other: Towards a Poetics of Desire in Scève's 'Délie'* (Lexington, KY: French Forum, 1994); and JoAnn DellaNeva, *Song and Countersong: Scève's 'Délie' and Petrarch's 'Rime'*, French Forum Monographs (Lexington, KY: French Forum, 1983).

[4] For Jean Rousset, the system of 'universal analogy' and microcosm–macrocosm correspondences was unquestioned in the sixteenth century, and constituted the 'fondement ontologique de la métaphore' (*L'Intérieur et Extérieur: Essai sur la poésie et sur le théâtre au XVIIe siècle* (Paris: Librairie José Corti, 1976)). For Fenoaltea, writing more specifically about the *Délie*, the cosmic system is similarly fixed and given. She sees it less as 'grounding' images of the human than as a background against which the non-fixity of human relations may be put into relief but, like Rousset, assumes that love lyric does not question the structure and functioning of the cosmos, or the place of the human within it (Doranne Fenoaltea. *'Si haulte Architecture': The Design of Scève's 'Délie'* (Lexington, KY: French Forum, 1982)). Christine Raffini makes a similar assumption (*The Second Sequence in Maurice Scève's 'Délie': A Study of Numerological Composition in the Renaissance* (Birmingham, AL: Summa, 1988)).

self.[5] Cave thus suggests that literary texts can give us an insight into six-teenth-century modes of thinking that is different from the one offered by the 'generalising' philosophical treatises which make up the traditional 'histoire ponctuelle des idées'.[6] In a similar vein, the present essay shows that Maurice Scève's *Délie* of 1544 does not simply reiterate concepts of the human and the cosmos from earlier philosophical texts but also *explores* ways of thinking about them.

However, my methodology differs from Cave's in that I begin by reading a literary text not together with the ideas of *future* thinkers but rather with those of *earlier* thinkers; I focus not upon 'fragments' of later thought but upon divergences from earlier or contemporary thought. I read the *Délie* together with Marsilio Ficino's commentary on Plato's *Symposium, De amore*, and Leone Ebreo's *Dialoghi*. At the end of this essay, I do briefly discuss similarities and differences between Scève's concep-tions of space and the subject and seventeenth-century conceptions. How-ever, as Cave suggests, we might be able to avoid a teleological, present-centred history of ideas if we cast from our minds future thinkers such as Pascal and Descartes;[7] I endeavour to do this as much as possible by con-sidering future thought only after my consideration of the *Délie*.

The *Délie* might make an interesting contrast to any contemporary treatise depicting an ordered cosmos which grounds and valorises man's

---

[5]   See the excellent *Préhistoires: Textes troublés au seuil de la modernité*, espe-cially chapter 4, 'Fragments d'un moi futur: de Pascal à Montaigne' and chapter 6 'Fragments d'un moi futur: le récit et son sujet' (Geneva: Droz, 1999). Jean Lecointe's impressive study similarly aims to 'décrire, en quelque sorte, une "préhistoire"' by ex-amining the self's gradual conquest of literary legitimacy even before the self was well established (*L'Idéal et la différence: la perception de la personnalité littéraire à la Renaissance*, Travaux d'Humanisme et Renaissance (Geneva: Droz, 1993), 275, pp. 12–14). Like Cave, Lecointe considers that 'ce n'est pas tant quelles réponses la Renaissance a pu apporter aux questions posées, que sous quelle forme, justement, elle est arrivée à partiellement se les poser' (p. 12); however, by contrast to Cave, Lecointe considers the 'prehistory' of a text (Montaigne's *Essais*) which is already considered an object for literary studies as well as for philosophy.
[6]   Cave, op. cit., pp. 11–13. In addition, the extremely interesting volume *Philoso-phical Fictions and the French Renaissance* troubles the dichotomisation of literature and philosophy in a different way, by highlighting the intertwining of philosophy and fiction in the Renaissance: ed. Neil Kenny (London: The Warburg Institute, 1991).
[7]   Cave, op. cit., p. 113. An excellent example of a teleological account of the conception of the self is Charles Taylor, *Sources of the Self: The Making of the Modern Identity* (Cambridge, MA: Harvard University Press, 1989).

identity.[8] However, a comparison with the *De amore* and the *Dialoghi* promises to be particularly fruitful: these texts influenced the literary production of Scève's contemporaries, and the *Délie* recalls their key concepts while also subverting them. There were nineteen editions of the *De amore* published between 1484 and 1590, and many French literary works bear witness to its influence, especially those of the 1530s and 1540s.[9] These works include those composed in Lyon by acquaintances of Scève, such as Symphorien Champier.[10] Finally, Symon Sylvius was apparently working on the first translation into French at the same time as Scève was preparing the *Délie* for publication.[11] Ebreo's *Dialoghi* were first published in Rome in 1535, and editions appeared in Venice in 1541 and 1545; they were translated into French by Pontus de Tyard, a friend and admirer of Scève's, and published in Lyon in 1551;[12] they also influenced literary texts of the period, particularly in Lyon.[13] Critics have observed that the *Délie* is greatly indebted to both Ficino and Ebreo.[14]

---

[8] Man's dignity was often grounded in his role and position in the cosmos. See Jill Kraye, 'Moral Philosophy', in *The Cambridge History of Renaissance Philosophy*, ed. Charles B. Schmitt, Quentin Skinner, Eckhard Kessler, and Jill Kraye (Cambridge: Cambridge University Press, 1988), 303–86 (306–16).

[9] See the introduction to Raymond Marcel's edition of the *De amore* (Paris: Les Belles Lettres, 1956).

[10] See Jean Festugière, *La Philosophie de l'amour de Marsile Ficin et son influence sur la littérature française au XVIᵉ siècle* (Coimbra: Imprensa da universidade, 1923).

[11] See Marcel (ed. cit.).

[12] Another translation of the *Dialoghi* was published in the same year by the seigneur du Parc, alias Denys Sauvage.

[13] V.-L. Saulnier claimed that Ebreo's *Dialoghi* represented the 'grand bréviaire du platonisme lyonnais': *Maurice Scève (ca. 1500–1560)* (Geneva and Paris: Slatkine, 1981), first published 1948–9, pp. 209, 249. Jacqueline Risset suggests that the 'École lyonnaise' were particularly indebted to Ebreo (*L'Anagramme du Désir. sur la 'Délie' de Maurice Scève* (Paris: Fourbis, 1995), p. 73).

[14] For Festugière (op. cit.), Scève 'est de ceux en effet chez qui se retrouve, de la façon la plus complète et la plus fidèle, la philosophie du *Commentaire*' (p. 96). Dorothy Gabe Coleman also shows that neo-Platonism had an important influence upon the *Délie* but argues that Scève does not follow this model exactly: love in the *Délie* is not spiritual and chaste as it is in neo-Platonism; in this respect Scève preferred the model of Roman love poetry and Classical mythology (*Maurice Scève, Poet of Love: Tradition and Originality* (Cambridge: Cambridge University Press, 1975), pp. 128–134; 178; 195). See also T. Anthony Perry, *Erotic Spirituality: The Integrative Tradition from Leone Ebreo to John Donne* (Tuscaloosa, AL: The University of Alabama Press, 1980); Saulnier, op. cit.; Jean-Claude Margolin, 'Du *De amore* de Ficin à la *Délie* de Scève: lumière, regard, amour et beauté', in *Marsilio Ficino e il*

SITUATING THE MASCULINE

More specifically, though, why does a comparison of this particular poetic text and these particular prose treatises promise to be so productive? In the literary texts Cave analyses, changes of themes, illogical arguments, and the strange use of grammar reveal problematic areas on the edge of thought.[15] Certainly the subversion of logical structures, syntax, and grammar in the *Délie* could be examined in this context.[16] However, I

---

ritorno di Platone: studi e documenti, ed. G. C. Garfagnini, 2 vols (Florence: Olschki, 1986), II. 587–614; Thomas Hunkeler, *Le Vif du sens: corps et poésie selon Maurice Scève* (Geneva: Droz, 2003), pp. 137–93; James Helgeson, *Harmonie divine et subjectivité poétique chez Maurice Scève* (Geneva: Droz, 2001); Deborah Lesko Baker, *Narcissus and the Lover: Mythic Recovery and Reinvention in Scève's Délie*, Stanford French and Italian Studies (Saratoga, CA: Anma Libri, 1986); Risset, op. cit.; H. Weber, 'Macrocosme et microcosme dans la *Délie* de Maurice Scève', in *Poétique et narration: mélanges offerts à Guy Demerson*, ed. F. Marotin and J.-P. Saint-Gérand (Paris: Champion, 1993), pp. 157–66, and *La Création poétique en France au XVIᵉ siècle de Maurice Scève à Agrippa d'Aubigné*, 2 vols (Paris: Nizet, 1956), II. 161–7; Tetel, op. cit.; Fenoaltea, op. cit., pp. 87–92; Madeleine Soudée, 'Maurice Scève: mystique et penseur', *Romance Notes*, XXXV (1994), 129–143; Albert Baur, *Maurice Scève et la Renaissance lyonnaise* (Paris: Honoré Champion, 1906), chapter 5, 'Relations avec Marguerite de Navarre: le platonisme'; Pierre Boutang, *Commentaire sur quarante-neuf dizains de la Délie* (Paris: Gallimard, 1953), pp. 20–1. Other thinkers whom critics have discussed in relation to the *Délie* include Sperone Speroni (himself very much influenced by Ebreo; see Risset, op. cit., pp. 110–13; Fenoaltea, pp. 90–1), Nicholas of Cusa (see Hans Staub, *Le Curieux Désir. Scève et Peletier du Mans, poètes de la connaissance* (Geneva: Droz, 1967)); Fenoaltea, op. cit., pp. 84–92), and Charles de Bovelles (see Risset, op. cit., pp. 91–100; Fenoaltea, op. cit., pp. 84–92). My essay 'The Human and the Cosmos: Difference, Cognition and Causality in the *Délie* of Maurice Scève' approaches the relationship between Scève and Charles de Bovelles with a similar methodology as that used in this essay; in other words, the philosophical treatise and the poetry are treated not as source and result but rather as very different ways of grappling with conceptions of difference, cognition, and causality.

[15] Cave, op. cit., p. 15.
[16] For analyses of the *Délie* relating to these stylistic features, see Jerry Nash, 'Logic and Lyric: Poetic Closure in Scève's *Délie*', *French Studies*, 38 (1984), 385–96; Michael J. Giordano, 'Reading *Délie*: Dialectic and Sequence', *Symposium (Syracuse)*, 34 (1980), 155–67; R. Hallett, 'Three Analytical Dizains in Scève's *Délie*', *Romance Notes*, 18 (1977), 237–42; Doranne Fenoaltea, 'The Polyphonic Quality of Scève's *Délie*', *Symposium (Syracuse)*, 29 (1975), 330–44; Thomas M. Greene, 'Styles of experience in Scève's *Délie*', *Yale French Studies*, 47 (1972), 57-75; and Fenoaltea, op. cit. My own essay 'Order and Disorder: The Space of Discourse in Rudolph Agricola's *De inventione dialectica* and in Maurice Scève's *Délie*' takes a similar methodological approach to that of this essay, in reading dialectic and poetry as very different attempts to order language in spatial terms.

65

shall focus in particular in this essay on Scève's use of neo-Platonist images and, more specifically, on the image of the dazzling sun. This image is frequent in the *Délie*, and its meaning in Ficino's text is subtly transformed with far-reaching implications for gender, identity, and cosmic order. While some of my analysis could be extended to other love lyric of the period, this image is particularly insistent in the *Délie*.[17] Cave also suggests that the literary object is different from the philosophical treatise because it is concerned with the particular rather than with the general. This points to one reason for reading the *Délie* together with neo-Platonist prose treatises: the poetic text focuses upon the love of a *ie* for a *tu* or an *elle* rather than upon an analysis of love in the abstract.[18] Indeed, the use of cosmic images — together with the depiction of a love relationship with an 'elle' — means that the *Délie* approaches differently issues which are more directly examined in the prose treatises of Ficino and Ebreo; it is for this reason that an analysis of the *Délie* promises to enrich our understanding of sixteenth-century thinking about gender, cosmic order, and masculine identity.[19]

Resemblance, Gender, and Narcissism

Ficino mentions in passing that 'since it is proper to the male to give and to the female to receive, for that reason we call the sun male, since it re-

---

[17] The dazzling sun is often Délie's eyes, and Lance K. Donaldson-Evans observes that 'of all the poets of the French Renaissance, none makes more extensive use of the aggressive eye topos and its associated imagery than Scève' ('Love's Fatal Glance: Eye Imagery and Maurice Scève's *Délie*', *Neophilologus*, 62 (1978), 202–11, p. 206). Examples and analysis can be found in Lance K. Donaldson-Evans, *Love's Fatal Glance: A Study of Eye Imagery in the Poets of the Ecole Lyonnaise* (University, MS: Romance Monographs, Inc, 1980), chapter III; see especially 'The Eye as Source of Fire' (pp. 127–30), 'The Eye as Lightning' (pp. 130–35), and 'The Eye as Source of Blinding Light' (pp. 135–44). Dizains which represent dazzling cosmic bodies (usually the sun) and dazzling 'sun-like' eyes include D24, D51, D80, D92, D105, D106, D115, D128, D186, D212, D269, D386 and D443.
[18] I examine this specificity of the love lyric in my essay on the *Délie* and the texts of Charles de Bovelles (see n.14): human beings are present in the former as a *ie*, a *tu* and an *elle* but in the latter as the singular abstract *Homo*, and this difference helps me to analyse different ways of thinking about difference and the subject in these texts.
[19] In this essay I use the terms 'male' and 'female' as well as 'masculine' and 'feminine' because these correspond to terms used by Ficino and Ebreo. For Ficino and Ebreo 'maleness' is defined by the role the (cosmic) body plays in relation to others, and in relation to what it desires. Therefore Ficino and Ebreo's terminology does not match the twentieth-century distinction between 'maleness' as defined by the body itself and 'masculinity' as defined by the role one plays.

ceives light from none and gives to all'; on the other hand, 'the earth, since it receives from all and gives to none, we call female'.[20] The masculine is defined as active and light-giving by contrast to the feminine, which is passive and receives light.

Light emanates through the Ficinian cosmos. The sun is both a symbol of God and a paler image of Him created by the emanation of His divine light. The light of the 'divine sun' spreads outwards through the intelligences or angels, the soul, and physical bodies, becoming 'paler' at each level of this hierarchy. This explains human love. The lover desires the divine light which is in the beloved:

> For it [the lover's passion] does not desire this or that body, but desires the splendour of the celestial divine shining through bodies, and is amazed and awed by it.[21]

The souls of both lovers contain a light derived from the divine but the beloved has imprinted this image upon his body more successfully than the lover, and so the lover recognises the divine light in the beloved as 'almost exactly like the image which the soul of the lover has long possessed within itself'.[22] The lover desires something which he also pos-

---

[20] 'Quia uero maris dare, femine suscipere proprium est, iccirco solem qui lumen a nullo accipiens exhibet omnibus, marem uocamus... Terram, cum accipiat quidem ab omnibus, tribuat nulli, feminam nuncupamus', IV. v, ed. Pierre Laurens (Paris: Les Belles Lettres, 2002), p. 79. All quotations are from Laurens's edition. English translations are my own but I have consulted those of Sears Reynolds Jayne, *Marsilio Ficino, Commentary on Plato's Symposium on Love* (Dallas, TX: Spring Publications, 1985).

[21] 'Non enim corpus hoc aut illud desiderat, sed superni luminis splendorem per corpora refulgentem ammiratur, affectat, et stupet' (II. vi, p. 37).

[22] 'Therefore those who, as we have said, are born under the same star are so constituted that the image of the more beautiful of them, penetrating through the eyes into the soul of the other, matches and corresponds completely with a certain identical image which was formed in the astral body of that soul as well as in its inner nature from its creation. *The soul thus stricken recognises the image before it as something which is its own. It is in fact almost exactly like the image which this soul has long possessed within itself,* and which it tried to imprint on its own body, but was not able to do' ('Proinde qui, ut diximus, eodem sub astro sunt orti, ita se habent, ut pulchrioris eorum simulacrum, per oculos in alterius animum permanans, consimili cuidam simulacro tam in corpore ethereo quam in animi penetralibus ab ipsa generatione formato quadret et undique consonet. *Ita pulsatus animus obuium illud simulacrum tamquam suum aliquid recognoscit. Quod quidem tale est pro uiribus quale et ipse iam olim intra se possidet,* et suo in corpore cum uellet effingere, minime potuit' (my italics; VI. vi, p. 141)).

sesses yet does not possess completely. Put simply, the lover desires a
beloved who is similar to himself but superior.

Love is caused by resemblance: 'Amorem procreat similitudo.'[23] The
closer the resemblance the better, so men are more easily seduced by men
than by women, although women with masculine characteristics will do:

> Certainly women can easily seduce men, especially those women who
> display masculine characteristics. Men seduce men all the more easily
> because they are more similar to them than women are....[24]

Love exists between men who resemble one another, rather than between
the masculine and feminine which, in their relation to activity and passivity of light-emission, are different from one another. According to Ficino's definitions of the male and female in his brief reference to the sun–
earth relationship, givers of light should be considered male and receivers
female but in the fundamental hierarchy of God, angel, soul, body, which
structures the Ficinian cosmos, all terms are considered to be endowed
with light in progressively weaker form, rather than some terms being
defined as recipients of light and others as donors of light. The emphasis
is on resemblance, and difference occurs only in terms of superiority or
inferiority rather than in terms of a male–female opposition. Masculine
desire is focused on 'brighter' superiors, on ideal images of the masculine,
rather than on the feminine.

The lover strives to become more like his beloved and thus more like
the truly superior 'celestial light' of the divine sun; his desire for the beloved is essentially a desire to be the beloved. Human love, then, could be
said to be narcissistic: images of masculinity — as that which bestows
light — are situated throughout the cosmos, and the masculine subject
identifies with images of masculinity more perfect than his own in order
to himself approach those ideal images. Fernand Hallyn has argued that
the concept of the microcosm is inherently narcissistic;[25] since Ficino's
De amore bases the human–cosmos similarity in celestial light, which is
aligned with the masculine and the divine, the narcissism of the
microcosm–macrocosm relationship seems to be specifically masculine.
The resemblances which structure the sixteenth-century cosmos are re-

---

[23] II. viii, p. 158.
[24] 'Femine profecto viros facile capiunt; facilius autem ille que masculam quandam
indolem pre se ferunt. Et tanto facilius masculi quanto similiores sunt viris quam
femine ...' (VII. ix, p. 253).
[25] Fernand Hallyn, 'Le Microcosme ou l'incomplétude de la représentation',
Romanica Gandensia, XVII (1980), 183–92.

semblances between masculine terms, and are the basis for masculine identity-formation.[26]

By contrast, in Scève's *Délie*, as in other sixteenth-century French male-authored love lyric, the beloved is feminine. Yet, as in Ficino's *De amore*, the beloved is described as a source of light which illuminates the lover,[27] and as an 'Idole', a neo-Platonist term used to describe a simulacrum of divine light.[28] Thus one could argue that despite her gender the lady plays the same role as the male beloved does in Ficino. After all, in the previous quotation Ficino claims that, although men make better beloveds, masculine women will do. Moreover, in Ebreo's *Dialoghi*, love between men is not the norm. Dialogue 1, which discusses human love rather than cosmic love, does not specify the gender of the beloved, referring to 'la chose aymée' or 'iceluy',[29] and all of the dialogues are situated within the context of Philon's love for Sophie; furthermore, the dialogues discussing cosmic love focus on an alternation of the feminine and the masculine rather than on a masculine of decreasing potency as in Ficino. Despite this gender difference, Philon emphasises that lovers desire to be converted into the beloved, 'eslongnans d'eux tant qu'il est possible toute division et diversité':[30] gender difference does not prevent the beloved from being an ideal self-image for the lover.

Indeed critics have often interpreted the feminine beloved in love lyric — and not least in the *Délie* — precisely as a narcissistic image of the masculine subject.[31] Deborah Lesko Baker argues that the *Délie* has an

---

[26]   Arguably this is the case for many conceptions of the relationship between macrocosm and microcosm. For example, when the relationship is conceived as linking the parts of the human body with parts of the cosmos, the body is a male body. Indeed since the female body was commonly conceived as an imperfectly-formed male body (see Maclean, *The Renaissance Notion of Woman*, Cambridge Monographs on the History of Medicine (Cambridge: Cambridge University Press, 1980), chapter 3), it is not surprising that it was not chosen to depict the relationship between the human and the perfection of the heavens.

[27]   '...toy, de qui m'est tousjours derivée / Lumière' (D200).

[28]   D1. See also D3, 'Idolatrer en ta divine image'.

[29]   All quotations are from Pontus de Tyard's 1551 translation of the *Dialoghi*, ed. T. Anthony Perry (Chapel Hill: University of North Carolina Press, 1974).

[30]   Dialogue I, p. 69.

[31]   For discussions of narcissism in the *Délie*, see Lesko Baker, op. cit.; Helgeson, op. cit.; Tetel, op. cit.; Lawrence D. Kritzman, *The Rhetoric of Sexuality and the Literature of the French Renaissance*, Cambridge Studies in French (Cambridge: Cambridge University Press, 1991), chapter 9; Françoise Charpentier, 'En moi tu luis la nuit obscure', *Europe: Revue Littéraire Mensuelle*, 691–2 (1986), 83–94. Gisèle Mathieu-Castellani has analysed in detail the narcissism of a range of sixteenth-

SITUATING THE MASCULINE

'implicit, obsessive rapport with the Narcissus myth' (op. cit., p. 136), and 'makes a considerable step...towards the modern literary and psychic interpretations of Narcissus' (p. 38), in which the *ie* sees the world in terms of himself (chapter 3). Whereas, for Ficino, desire is *explicitly* dependent upon resemblance ('Amorem procreat similitudo'), the proclaimed femininity of the object in love lyric thinly disguises her similarity to the lover, and thus veils the importance of resemblance and identification in masculine desire. Love lyricists may imply that their desire is narcissistic but they also deny it.[32]

The Lady and the Sun: Reversing Cosmic Gender Hierarchies

As is frequently observed, motifs of light and of darkness recur insistently in Scève's *Délie*.[33] Although the lady's name recalls the moon goddess Diana, she is also — as in much sixteenth-century love lyric — depicted as the sun. Scève's use of this lady–sun topos is quite distinctive: whereas, a few years later, Joachim Du Bellay in his *Olive* (1549) and Jacques Peletier Du Mans in his *Amour des amours* (1555) evoke the sun more often in its role of engendering flowers, Scève insistently represents the lady–sun as an illuminating or dazzling source of light and only rarely as producing flowers.[34]

---

century love poets: 'Narcisse ou la mélancolie', *Littérature*, 37 (1980), 25–36; 'Narcisse au giron de Mélancolie', *Versants: Revue Suisse des Littératures Romanes*, 26 (1994), 95–110. However, Lesko Baker suggests that narcissism is more important in the *Délie* than in other sixteenth-century poetry: Ronsard evokes Narcissus frequently but distances himself from him more than Scève does (pp. 15–16) and, whereas Scève recovers the neglected role of self-recognition in the Ovidian myth, Ronsard neglects it in favour of the standard medieval and Renaissance view of Narcissus's plight as representing a fall into deception, pride, and vanity (p. 35; pp. 141–2), or uses the myth to represent erotic conquest of the other (p. 127).

[32] Dizain LX attempts to reject the comparison with Narcissus suggested by its accompanying emblem: the poetic persona has never offended 'Amour' and has always loved beyond himself ('aimant autrui, je me désaime'). He does, however, like Narcissus seem to melt like wax next to a fire and he loves in vain, as is underlined by the repetition of the emblem's 'devise' to conclude the dizain. Moreover, Délie is not mentioned by name and the verb 'aimer' is used twice intransitively and once with 'autrui'. On this dizain, see Lesko Baker, op. cit., pp. 2–5.

[33] See, for example, Hans Staub, 'Le Thème de la lumière chez Maurice Scève', *Cahiers de l'Association Internationale des Études Françaises*, 20 (1968), 125–36; Tetel, op. cit., chapter 3, 'Une lueur dans les ténèbres'; Hans Staub, op. cit.; H. Weber, op. cit., II, pp. 181–6; Thomas Greene, art. cit..

[34] In addition, the sun as producer of flowers does not appear in connection with the 'jealous sun' topos which I will go on to discuss in this section; by contrast, in

70

The *ie* compares and contrasts the effects of cosmic light on the viewer with the effects of the lady's light upon himself:

> Quand l'œil aux champs est d'esclairs esblouy,
> Luy semble nuict quelque part, qu'il regarde:
> Puis peu a peu de clarté resiouy,
> Des soubdains feuz du Ciel se contregarde.
> *Mais moy*, conduict dessoubs la sauuegarde
> De ceste *tienne*, & unique lumiere,
> Qui m'offusca ma lyesse premiere
> Par tes doulx rayz aiguement suyuiz,
> Ne me pers plus en veue coustumiere.
> Car seulement pour t'adorer ie vis [.]³⁵

Similarly, the *ie* says that looking at the sun makes it seem to him as if he looks at the lady:

> Sur nostre chef gettant Phebus ses rayz,
> Faisoit bouillir de son cler iour la None ;
> *Aduis me fut de veoir* en son taint frais
> Celle, de qui la rencontre m'estonne,
> De qui la voix si fort en l'ame tonne:
> Que ne puis d'elle vn seul doulx mot ouir:
> Et *de qui l'oeil vient ma veue esblouir*
> Tant qu'aultre n'est, fors elle, à mes yeux belle.
> *Me pourra donc tel Soleil resiouir,*
> *Quand tout Mydi m'est nuict, voire eternelle ?*³⁶

One could interpret these dizains as meaning that the lady is a sort of paler reflection of the sun, like the human beloved in Ficino's *De amore*. However, in the first quotation above, it is implied that the lady's light is *more* powerful than cosmic light. In the second quotation it is the sun which reminds the *ie* of the lady rather than the other way around, which re-

---

sonnet XVII of the *Olive*, the sun is 'honteux' in response to the lady–sun's performing the sun's creative role rather than its illuminating role. Thus the lady usurps the sun's illuminating role rather than its role in producing flowers.

³⁵   D24; my italics. I refer to I. D. McFarlane's edition of the 1544 text; (Cambridge: Cambridge University Press, 1966).

³⁶   D92; my italics. The sun also reminds the *ie* of the lady in D386: 'Quand Apollo apres l'Aulbe vermeille / Poulse le bout de ses rayons dorez, / Semble a mon œil, qui lors point ne sommeille, / Veoir les cheueulx de ce Monde adorez, / Qui par leurs noudz de mes mortz decorez / M'ont a ce ioug iusqu'a ma fin conduyct. / Et quand apres a plaine face il luyt, / Il m'est aduis que ie voy clerement / Les yeulx desquelz la clarté tant me nuyt, / Qu'elle esblouyt ma veue entierement.'

verses the order of comparison in Ficino's reference to a deified human character:

> It is said that the deified Augustus had eyes so bright and shining that when he stared at someone very hard, he forced him to lower his face, as if before the glow of the sun.[37]

In other dizains it is explicit that the lady is brighter than the sun. Her superior light and brightness undermine the sun's own light, causing it shamefully to hide its rays behind a cloud:

> Si Apollo restrainct ses raiz dorez,
> Se marrissant tout honteux soubz la nue,
> C'est par les tiens de ce Monde adorez,
> Desquels l'or pur sa clarté diminue.
>   Parquoy soubdain, qu'icy tu es venue,
> Estant sur toy, son contraire, enuieux,
> A congelé ce Brouas pluuieux,
> Pour contrelustre à ta diuine face.
> Mais ton tainct frais vainct la neige des cieulx,
> Comme le iour la clere nuict efface.[38]

Thus the cosmic gender hierarchy of the *De amore* is reversed, since the female beloved is 'brighter' than the sun, usually considered to be male.[39]

In other dizains, the beloved is not superior to the celestial sun but is confused or conflated with it, as in D106:

> I'attens ma paix du repos de la nuict,
> Nuict refrigere a toute aspre tristesse,
> Mais s'absconsant le Soleil, qui me nuyt,

---

[37] 'Fertur et diuus Augustus oculos adeo claros et nitidos habuisse ut, cum acrius quemquam intueretur, cogeret eum quasi ad Solis fulgorem uultum submictere' (VII. iv, p. 219).

[38] D124. See also ll. 1–2 of D51, quoted below.

[39] Similarly, when Délie is represented as a moon she occupies a masculine position in Ficinian terms. Although she is represented as the female moon goddess Diana she is also represented as the cosmic body, 'lune'. This cosmic body was traditionally defined by its mid-position between the heavens and the earth, between man and the gods (see Monferran, art. cit.). For Ficino and Ebreo, this meant that it was of mixed gender, since it received light from the sun but gave light to the earth. However, the lady–moon in the *Délie* always plays the latter role of giving light rather than receiving light, and thus performs a masculine function. In the case of the moon, though, the reversing of cosmic hierarchy is less striking than in the case of the sun, since the sun was at the top of the cosmic hierarchy and associated with the divine.

Noye avec soi ce peu de ma liesse.

The 'Soleil' apparently represents the lady, since it hurts the poet. Yet the 'Soleil' also represents the literal cosmic body, since its presence is contrasted to the night in which — like the Petrarchan lover — the poet hopes in vain to find peace. Rather than being compared to the sun or said to be a human equivalent of the sun, the lady is confused or conflated with it. Rather than being a reflected image of the celestial sun, she occupies the sun's position. She does not only replace the human male beloved of the *De amore*, but also plays the role of the celestial or divine sun. Whereas Ficino depicts a series of hierarchically-ordered celestial and human images of masculinity, in the *Délie* an image of femininity occupies the human, lunar, and solar cosmic positions.

One could interpret the lady's usurping of the sun's position as a sort of displaced hubris on the part of the *ie*.[40] It reverses the celestial–human hierarchy which was absolutely central not only to the neo-Platonist systems of Ficino and Ebreo but also more generally to the so-called 'medieval' hierarchical cosmos. Such an interpretation fits a reading of the lady as narcissistic ego ideal: the *ie* desires a human object powerful enough to usurp the top position in the cosmic hierarchy, because he himself would like to occupy this position, which, after all, is usually a masculine one. James Helgeson makes a similar argument in relation to images not of the sun but of cosmic harmony: the *ie* narcissistically constructs the *Délie* as the perfect incarnation of cosmic harmony which he himself would like to be. Thus, for Helgeson, the *ie* defines himself by means of the lady, violently delimiting her space in order that she might serve as an image representing his own ideal demarcated identity.

For Helgeson, this move heralds the arrival of the 'ego philosophique' or the 'sujet moderne', who strives to delimit his subjectivity within clearly-demarcated boundaries: the disintegration of neo-Platonism in the *Délie* is bound up with the advent of this modern subject (op. cit., p. 135). Teresa Brennan suggests that a similar process was going on in early modern fantasy more generally: in the early modern period, according to Brennan, the lady replaced God as the object of fantasy, thus heralding in the 'era of the ego', in which the masculine subject aggressively controls the feminine object so that she can serve as his self-image.[41]

---

[40]   Thus for Lesko Baker the fact that the lady is more powerful than the sun implies that the *ie* is more important in the poem than the cosmos, and that our interpretations should commence from a consideration of selfhood (op. cit., p. 60).

[41]   Teresa Brennan, *History after Lacan* (London and New York: Routledge, 1993), pp. 62–8.

Dazzling Suns: The Darkness and Formlessness of the ie

However, I will argue that the *Délie* is not *closer* than neo-platonism to the 'modern' concept of the subject as striving to conceive of itself as a contained whole, but *further away*. Thus the *Délie* points less to a 'préhistoire' of the modern subject than to other conceptions of the subject which sixteenth-century minds might have been moving towards, which might have been born later, and might perhaps still be latent, underlying our dominant conceptions of the self. Furthermore, while I would not deny that narcissism is present in the *Délie*, focusing upon it can be very misleading, since the crucial role played by the lady in relation to masculine identity is not a purely narcissistic one.

Rather than being similar but superior to the *ie*, the lady precisely prevents the *ie* from resembling her. In the *De amore*, the human soul, identified with the human subject, is a light source resembling the 'sun' which endows it with light.[42] This is sometimes the case in the *Délie*, yet the lady's light also subjects the *ie* to darkness. For example, in the following quotation of D51, the light from the lady–sun causes a light to emerge from the soul, yet her light becomes dazzling and thus the *ie* is cast into darkness:

> Si grand beaulté, mais bien si grand merueille,
> Qui a Phebus offusque sa clarté,
> Soit que ie sois present ou escarté,
> De sorte l'ame en sa lueur m'esueille
> Qu'il m'est aduis en dormant que ie veille,
> Et qu'en son iour vn espoir ie preuoy,
> Qui de bien brief, sans deslay, ou renuoy,
> M'esclercira mes pensées funebres.
>   Mais quand sa face en son Mydy ie voy,
> A tous clarté, & a moy rend tenebres

The scenario of the dazzling sun and the poet's darkness is frequently repeated in the *Délie*:

> Ces deux Soleils nuisamment penetrantz,
> Qui de mon viure ont eu si long Empire,
> Par l'œil au Cœur tacitement entrantz
> Croissent le mal, qui au guerir m'empire.

---

[42] This idea was not restricted to neo-Platonist treatises. For example, for Du Bartas the light of the human 'esprit' is derived from the light of God, and shines out through the 'lantern' of the body (Du Bartas uses 'esprit' and 'ame' interchangeably, as was fairly common; op. cit., VI. 709–722).

Car leur clarté esblouissamment pire
A son entrée en tenebres me met.[43]

The image of the dazzling sun is familiar from the *De amore* and the *Dialoghi*. In Ficino's *De amore*, God — the celestial sun — cannot be directly viewed because he would be too dazzling.[44] Similarly, for Ebreo the sun is a simulacrum of the divine intellect,[45] and sunlight represents a splendour or knowledge too bright for us to perceive.[46] However, for Ficino and Ebreo, the divine sun's dazzling poses no danger to the human subject since the subject encounters it only in its diluted form in the human beloved. By contrast the lady in the *Délie* is *both* the directly-encountered human lover and the dazzling divinised sun; therefore she subjects the *ie* to darkness rather than endowing him with light. The *ie* does not internalise derived light but only passively experiences it, as do the baser parts of the Ficinian cosmos situated below the level of the human. The lady does not bolster the *ie*'s identification with the valorised term of light but forces him towards its opposite, darkness.

The masculine is severed from its usual connection not only with light but also with form. In the sixteenth century, form is usually associated with the soul and light, and gendered male, by opposition to female

---

[43]   D269. See also D106 quoted above: 'le Soleil qui my nuyt.' Since Scève often plays on the double meaning of 'nuyt' ('harms' and 'night'), the use of 'nuyt' here also recalls the recurrent paradox in Scève that, for the *ie*, the sun may herald night rather than day.

[44]   'The eye perceives this light [the light of the sun] reflected in bodies, but it cannot endure the light itself at its source... Thus it is by the light of God that we know all things. But we cannot see this pure light, nor its source, during our lives' ('Hoc quidem lumen in corporibus reflexum oculus percipit, ipsam uero in fonte suo lucem minime substinet... Itaque per dei lumen omnia intelligimus. Ipsum uero purum lumen eiusque fontem hac in uita uidere non possumus' (VI. xiii, pp. 228–9)).

[45]   '...le Soleil, au monde corporel visible, est simulacre de l'intellect divin au monde intellectuel invisible' (pp. 163–4). See also pp. 62–3.

[46]   Ebreo refers to '...[les] choses spirituelles et eternelles, l'Essence desquelles, quant à la Nature, est plus grande et congnoissable que celle des choses corporelles et corruptibles, combien que, à cause qu'on ne les peult comprendre par les sens, nous en ayons moins de congnoissance. Aussi nostre Entendement est à l'esgard de la congnoissance dicelles comme l'œil d'une chauvesouriz à la clarté et choses visibles: car elle *ne peult voir la lumiere du Soleil, qui est la plus resplendissante de toutes, pource que son œil n'est bastant à recevoir telle splendeur*, mais bien void elle le lustre de la nuict lequel luy est proportionné' (pp. 61–2; my italics). In addition, the image of the dazzling sun was widely used to represent the divine and the celestial in the sixteenth century: for example, the philosophical poets Du Bartas and Jean-Édouard Du Monin both use it.

matter; and neo-Platonism is no exception.[47] However, the lady–sun makes the lover melt like snow in the sun,[48] and a whole range of other verbs refer to his disintegration or fragmentation.[49] Furthermore, often his soul is not ravished into the perfect harmonious spaces of the beloved or the heavens but into formless places such as the depths of an abyss,[50] or a Chaos,[51] or a sea.[52]

Whereas Helgeson and Brennan emphasise a violence which stems *from the masculine subject* and serves *to limit the space of the lady*, violence in the *Délie* stems *from the lady* and serves *to fragment the masculine subject*: he is violated by the dazzling force of the lady, and his love means that he is melted, burned, dispersed through space and so on. The lady apparently *prevents* — rather than *facilitates* — a narcissistic construction of the *ie* as whole and complete. Thus, whereas for Ficino the subject moves between his own space and that of a more perfect other, and strives to become the other so that he can become a 'complete' or 'whole man',[53] in the *Délie* the subject disintegrates and is dispersed through space in a much less ordered manner.

---

[47]   For example, Ebreo says that matter desires forms as a woman desires a man: 'la Premiere matiere desire et ayme toutes les formes des choses engendrées, comme la femme l'homme, et ne pouvant son amour estre contenté par le desir et l'appetit jouissant d'une forme...aucuns l'ont surnommée Putain' (pp. 87–8).

[48]   'comme neige au Soleil ie me fondz' (D118).

[49]   These verbs include *congeler, abîmer, fondre, réduire en cendre, réduire en poudre*.

[50]   D79, D118, D103, D164, D439. The image of the abyss does appear in Ficino but in the specific context of representing the soul's alienation in the body, which does not correspond to its use in Scève.

[51]   D103.

[52]   D164, D393, D243.

[53]   'True man and the Idea of man are one and the same. Therefore each of us separated from God on earth is not a true man since he is separated from the Form and Idea of himself. To this Idea divine love and piety will lead us. And although we are here divided and mutilated, joined then, by love, to our own Idea, *we shall become whole men*, so that we shall seem first to have worshipped God in things, in order later to worship things in God, and shall seem to worship things in God in order to recover ourselves above all, and seem, in loving God, to have loved ourselves' ('Verus autem homo et idea hominis idem. Ideo quisque nostrum in terris a deo separatus, non uerus est homo, cum a sui idea sit formaque disiunctus. Ad eam nos diuinus amor pietasque perducet. Cumque hic discerpti simus et mutilati, idee tunc nostre amando coniuncti, *integri homines euademus*, ut deum primo in rebus coluisse uideamur, quo res deinde in deo colamus, resque in deo ideo uenerari, ut nos ipsos in eo pre ceteris amplectamur, et amando deum, nos ipsos uideamur amasse' (VI. xix, p.239)).

SITUATING THE MASCULINE

Therefore the *Délie* represents a move away from the Ficinian conception of love as an exchange between the positions of human subject,
human object, and divine object; however, this departure from Ficino represents not a firmer delimitation of the space of the subject in preparation
for the 'sujet moderne' but rather a spatial 'dispersion' of the subject. Indeed, Ficino's conception of people (or souls) as spaces within which a
divine light may exist is arguably closer to Descartes's subject than is
Scève's 'dispersed' and 'darkened' subject; the 'light' in Ficino's subject
comes from the divine rather than belonging to him as it does in Descartes, yet they share a notion of selfhood as internal space which is much
less dominant in Scève's poetry.[54]

*Benevolent 'Masculine' Love: Anxieties about the Neo-Platonist Cosmos
and Neo-Platonist 'Man'*

In neo-Platonist terms, the lady's failure to bestow light upon the *ie* represents a refusal to love him, since neo-Platonism equates the emanation of
light through the cosmos with the emanation of love from celestial superiors towards celestial inferiors. Of course, the unloving lady is a topos of
many types of love poetry, including the courtly lyric which predated Ficinian neo-Platonism by several centuries at least.[55] However, she is a
particularly interesting figure when she resembles the neo-Platonist divine
sun, since the potential absence of the celestial superior's love is a central
problem in neo-Platonism, at least in Ebreo's *Dialoghi*.

---

[54]   Indeed a passage in Ficino's *Theologia Platonica* recalls Descartes's famous
cogito, except insofar as for Ficino the *cogito* is proof not so much of the thinking
subject as of *the truth*: 'siquando animus de re aliqua dubitat, tunc etiam de multis est
certus. Nam se tunc dubitare non dubitat. Ac si certum habet se esse dubitantem à veri-
tate certa id habet certum. Quippe qui se dubitantem intelligit: verum intelligit: & de
hac re quam intelligit, certus est: de vero igitur est certus' (Hildesheim: Georg Olms
Verlag, 1975), XI. vii, p. 187; 'if the mind doubts a thing, then it is certain of many
things. For it does not doubt that it doubts. And if it is certain that it is doubting then it
considers this certainty as a certain truth. For he who knows he is doubting: knows a
true thing: & of this thing which he knows, he is certain: he is therefore certain of a
true thing'. However, Timothy Reiss's view of Descartes would reduce this diver-
gence between Ficino and Descartes: Reiss argues that the sense of an *internal* self as
an *individual subjective* self is a concept that Descartes made possible — and that we
read back into Descartes — but which Descartes himself had not conceived of
(*Mirages of the Selfe: Patterns of Personhood in Ancient and Early Modern Europe*
(Stanford: Stanford University Press, 2003)).
[55]   Jacqueline Risset (op. cit.) argues that Scève, and Lyonnais writers in general,
were influenced by medieval models more than the *Pléiade* were.

77

Philon spends much time explaining that love is to be equated with desire, that one loves that which one lacks. This troubles Sophie: if one loves what one lacks, why should celestial superiors love inferiors? She is very insistent in this objection, and returns to it again in the following dialogue, demanding that Philon justify why God should love. Indeed Philon does justify much more convincingly the love of the lacking inferior than the love of the perfect superior, and Anthony Perry suggests this is 'perhaps the crucial problem of [Ebreo's] entire thought'.[56] The anxiety is partly suppressed because Philon seems to be the authoritative voice, yet Sophie's argument makes sense and her name does, after all, imply wisdom. Arguably the same problem underlies Ficino's system but since Ficino emphasises resemblance — rather than lack — as the cause of love, it is less striking.

In response to Philon's attempts to justify God's love, Sophie replies 'je croy bien cela, et toutefois ton dire ne satisfait pas à mon doute' (p. 187). Unsurprisingly for a sixteenth-century French subject, Sophie says she believes that God loves us; however, she would like this belief to be backed up logically, 'with reasons'.[57] A logical inconsistency in neo-Platonism is glossed over thanks to the impossibility of questioning a central tenet of Christianity — God's love. Therefore, it is perhaps unsurprising that when, in the *Délie*, the celestial superior is not the Christian God but a deified lady,[58] the lady fails to provide the purely benevolent love that neo-Platonism grounds in the Christian conception of God rather than justifying logically. The lady's replacement of benevolent love with aggressive 'dazzling' may represent the dark underside of neo-Platonism's emphasis on light emanating downwards: cosmic inferiors are dependent upon a gift of love or light which is purely benevolent, and, logically speaking, there seems to be no very good reason why this gift should be provided.[59]

Ebreo's cosmic hierarchy is structured around gender difference between the masculine and the feminine rather than around a 'dilution' of

[56] Introduction to his edition, p. 19.
[57] As Perry observes, Sophie's 'most persistent difficulty' is 'that of justifying philosophically or "with reasons" God's love for man' (ibid, p. 23).
[58] Weber points out that in the *Délie* the celestial is *never* associated with the Christian God as it is in Petrarch's poetry (art. cit., p. 166).
[59] One could argue that Tyard's 'Disgrace' manifests similar anxieties without expressing these through the figure of the lady–sun. Kathleen Hall suggests that this poem points to the suffering of a man for whom stock knowledge regarding the benevolence of the universe — and the very existence of God — has suddenly become unconvincing ('Pontus de Tyard and his "Disgrace"', *Esprit Créateur* (1965), 102–9).

masculinity as in Ficino, and so benevolent love is defined not only as divine love in contradistinction to human love but also as masculine love in contradistinction to feminine love. Love for a celestial superior defines the 'lover' as feminine, since 'she' receives light; by contrast, love for a cosmic inferior defines the 'lover' as masculine, since 'he' gives light. For example, the soul loves the divine intellect — its superior — as the female loves the male:

> L'entendement divin et pourveü de souveraine et parfaite beauté, de laquelle l'ame (qui n'est autre chose qu'une splendeur procedante d'iceluy) devient amoureuse, comme de son superieur et origine: ainsi que l'on void la femelle imparfaite s'enamourer du masle qui luy accomplit sa perfection (p. 174).

On the other hand the soul loves the corporeal world — its inferior — as the male loves the female, that is to 'render it perfect'.[60] Similarly, the moon's love for the sun 'duquel sa lumiere, sa vie et sa perfection dependent' is 'comme l'amour de la femelle au masle', but its love for the earth 'ressembl[e] celuy du masle à la femelle... comme si elle desiroit de donner perfection à la Terre'.[61] Finally, the corporeal world loves the spiritual world as the female loves the male, whereas the spiritual world loves the corporeal world as the male loves the female.[62]

For Philon, the benevolence of masculine love renders it far superior to the needy love of the feminine. Love has been defined as lack, that is in the same terms as what is later feminine love, yet paradoxically benevolent masculine love is considered 'plus vray et entier' (pp. 143–4). As the masculine does not love for his own gain, his love is more complete: 'trop plus parfaitement ayme le masle qui donne que la femelle qui reçoit.'

In the terms of the *Dialoghi*, the *ie* in the *Délie* is in the feminine position; his love is needy like feminine love, and he appeals to his celestial

---

[60] 'Outre cest amour fault encor en adjouster un autre[,] que l'ame porte au monde corporel son inférieur (comme l'on void le masle estre amoureux de la femelle) pour le rendre parfait et imprimer en luy la beauté qu'elle tire de l'entendement' (p. 174).

[61] 'en cecy est elle [la Lune] encor simulacre de l'ame. car l'amour qu'elle porte au Soleil, duquel sa lumiere, sa vie et sa perfection dependent, est comme l'amour de la femelle au masle: et la fait iceluy amour estre curieuse de l'union du Soleil. Encore est elle [la lune] inclinée à l'amour terrien (amour ressemblant celui du masle à la femelle) comme si elle desiroit de donner perfection à la Terre avec la lumiere et influence qu'elle reçoit du Soleil' (p. 175).

[62] 'En oultre l'amour du monde spirituel envers le monde corporel est semblable à celuy du masle à la femelle, et celuy du corporel au spirituel est semblable à celuy de la femelle au masle, comme par ce devant je t'ay amplement dit' (p. 144).

superior to satisfy his need, to fill his lack, and to share her perfection with him. In a sense the relationality of gender in neo-Platonism means that it has a dangerous potential for slippage or indeterminacy. A twenty-first-century mind would probably define sexuality in terms of the object desired, that object being literally other, and, by contrast, consider gender to be defined within the subject itself in some sense, whether by nature or by performance. On the other hand, for Ebreo, gender, on a cosmic level at least, is definitely defined by the object of desire. Thus there is a potential in Ebreo's system for gender to be unstable, since it is at the vagaries of the object desired.

If the male lover is in a feminine position, the female beloved, on the other hand, has not adopted all the characteristics of the masculine position in the cosmos: she has masculine superiority without masculine benevolence. The masculine ideal is not displaced onto a woman with masculine traits but is completely lost. The *ie* suffers because he experiences needy lacking 'female' love but there is no 'male' and divine benevolent love to satisfy his need, to allow him to identify with the superior masculine term. The *Délie* reveals an anxiety underlying the reliance upon the logically-superfluous benevolence of this superior masculine or divine term.

The lady's replacement of the masculine beloved does not prevent her from functioning as a narcissistically comforting ego ideal for the masculine subject but her replacement of the divine sun — or Christian divine — *together with* that of the masculine beloved, has a crucial effect. While one might claim that there is a sort of hubris involved in placing an apparently human entity at the top of the celestial hierarchy, in fact the replacement of God with another term entails a very great threat for the human subject. The conjunction of neo-Platonism and the poetic tradition of unloving ladies means that anxieties can be expressed about neo-Platonism's logical inconsistency concerning the love of divine masculine superiors. The masculine subject in neo-Platonism is dependent upon the love of a masculine superior which is logically superfluous; in the *Délie* this love is absent and so the masculine subject no longer resembles the divine, and has relinquished to the feminine his association with the positive poles of neo-Platonist oppositions, namely form and light.

Masculine Identity and Cosmic Disorder

The grounding of the fragmented *ie* in the logical flaws of neo-Platonism could support the argument that the poet seeks wholeness in vain. However, it could also provide a way out of the longstanding critical impasse

SITUATING THE MASCULINE

in Scévian studies between partisans of this argument and those who believe that fragmentation is ultimately overcome. The fragmented and
'darkened' *ie* might point towards other possible ideals of identity than as
coherent, whole, and 'illuminated'. Since the *Délie* manifests anxiety
about the neo-Platonist construction of masculinity, it seems reasonable to
assume that it might explore other possible constructions. The subject
pushes his identification with formlessness so far that — in a fairly extreme and insistent version of Petrarchan motifs — he burns, melts, and
becomes rivers which stream away. I would like to suggest that this might
imply a different way of valorising identity in relation to space, an alternative to considering the masculine self as a mirror image of valorised
cosmic terms (the sun) or of cosmic harmony.

The co-existence of an identification with lack and of more typically
narcissistic tendencies could be theorised in terms of Jacques Lacan's
model of dual identification in the *Quatre concepts fondamentaux de la
psychanalyse*.[63] In this model, the subject identifies both with a supreme
marker of (male) form and discrete identity — Descartes's God, a sort of
ideal subjectivity — but also with a marker of formlessness and self-
destruction, the formlessness of 'intersubjectivity' as the concept is inflected by psychoanalysis, that is, as uncertain differentiation between
subject positions rather than as an exchange between them like the exchange between subjects in neo-Platonism. According to this model, the
subject identifies with a marker of male form yet also implicitly acknowledges the impossibility of that position by identifying with the space of
formlessness, or of uncertain differentiation between human subjects. This
model could provide a fruitful avenue for psychoanalytic Scévian criticism which — unfortunately, it seems to me — has tended to concentrate
upon models of purely narcissistic identification, often supported by the
common imagery of mirrors in psychoanalysis and love lyric.[64]

---

[63] Jacques Lacan, *Le Séminaire, livre XI: les quatre concepts fondamentaux de la
psychanalyse* (Paris: Éditions du Seuil, 1973).
[64] Critics of the *Délie* using psychoanalytic concepts of narcissism and the ego
ideal include Helgeson, who aligns the *ie*'s violence towards the lady with that of the
self's aggression towards the other during the Lacanian mirror stage (op. cit., pp. 92–
3); Kritzman, op. cit., and Charpentier, op. cit.. Other psychoanalytic criticism of the
Délie includes Frelick, op. cit., and Gregory de Rocher, 'The Curing Text: Maurice
Scève's Délie as the *Délie*', *The Romantic Review*, 78 (1987), 10–24. De Rocher sees
Délie as representing not the narcissistic other but the Other. Lesko Baker uses Freud's
concept of trauma (op. cit.). For general discussions of the use of psychoanalytic criticism in sixteenth-century literary studies, see Gisèle Mathieu-Castellani, 'Des anciens
et des modernes, ou Freud au XVIe siècle', in *Lire avec Freud: pour Jean Bellemin-*

81

However, I prefer not to use the terms of this psychoanalytic model at this stage, since in relation to my particular line of enquiry they could be misleading. I am interested in the question of the extent to which conceptions of the subject in the *Délie* do or do not foreshadow the 'ego philosophique' of Descartes, and so will avoid using a model which conceives of one mode of identification in terms of Descartes. Similarly, since I consider the breakdown of cosmic order in favour of disordered space, I do not wish to refer to the abstract 'space' which in Lacan's model represents the relations between human subjects and objects.

The attempt paradoxically to ground identity in lack can be considered in relation to sixteenth-century notions of (masculine) human beings and the cosmos. The subject in the *Délie* proclaims that he is unique because the sun makes him suffer darkness whereas it illuminates everybody else: 'quand sa face en son Mydy ie voy, / A tous clarté, & a moy rend tenebres.'[65] Thus he grounds his uniqueness in his inability to be 'enlightened' by the celestial sun. Juliana Schiesari suggests that a form of self-valorisation in lack was available to the masculine subject in the Renaissance because of the concept of melancholia, which Ficino championed as the 'illness' of great men.[66] For Schiesari, though, melancholia and lack imply a narcissistic conception of masculine identity as oneness rather than an identity of fragmentation like that in the *Délie*. Moreover, this oneness may be expressed in terms of the cosmos: Schiesari observes that in the *De amore*, the centre and circumference of the cosmos are 'joined together in the concentrated understanding of the divinely gifted melancholic', so that the melancholic is associated with oneness and perfection (p. 129). However, the relation between melancholia and the cosmos could be conceived differently, as was indeed the case in France for the Pléiade: Noel Brann[67] has shown that the Pléiade poets — although enamoured of Ficino's idea of divine frenzy — rejected his valorisation of melancholia because, defined by Aristotle as an imbalance of the four humours, it implied disharmony and therefore was not suitable to help the

Noël, ed. Pierre Bayard (Paris: Presses Universitaires de France, 1998); Stephen Greenblatt, 'Psychoanalysis and Renaissance Culture', in *Learning to Curse: Essays in Early Modern Culture* (New York: Routledge, 1990).
[65] D51, quoted in full above.
[66] Juliana Schiesari, *The Gendering of Melancholia: Feminism, Psychoanalysis, and the Symbolics of Loss in Renaissance Literature* (Ithaca and London: Cornell University Press, 1992).
[67] Noel L. Brann, 'Melancholy and the Divine Frenzies in the French Pléiade: Their Conflicting Roles in the Art of *Beaux Exercices Spirituels*', *Journal of Medieval and Renaissance Studies* (1979), 81–100.

divinely-inspired soul in its ascent towards the heavens and harmony. Scève's fragmented subject plunging into an abyss of darkness recalls this conception of melancholia; yet, by contrast with the theoretical writings of the Pléiade, the *ie*'s proclamation of the uniqueness of his suffering implies that the subject on a trajectory towards the abyss may be a valorised subject. Although Scève departs from Ficinian conceptions of the subject, this may be related to ways of thinking about Ficino's concept of melancholia which Ficino himself did not conceive.

Scève does not say that he valorises melancholy positively, nor that a movement into the lower realms of the cosmos is a legitimate move for a masculine poetic subject. However, Risset observes that Scève did not write a poetics or theorise poetry in the way that many of his contemporaries in the Pléiade did and, furthermore, that this might result from the fact that his poetic practice was in advance of concepts which had been directly expressed.[68] The insistent depiction of the *ie* in darkness and in the abyss seem to ground poetic identity not in an upward movement towards the heavens and the celestial sun which the masculine subject resembles, but rather in a downward movement into less harmonious parts of the cosmos. This conception of the identity of the *ie* in the *Délie* recalls Lesko Baker's suggestion that the *ie* might transcend Narcissus's position by the gradual constitution of a 'pain persona', a 'lyric self whose posture is defined by its assimilation of anguish' (op. cit., p. 98). I hope I have shown that, in the first half of the sixteenth century, such a conception of the subject might be related to a reworking of neo-Platonist conceptions of the relationship between man and the cosmos. Thus the coexistence of a narcissistic urge towards wholeness and light together with a proclamation of fragmentation and darkness, may relate to efforts to conceive of the masculine subject differently, in a world where men can no longer be sure of the existence of a benevolent cosmic order.

Concepts of Subject and Space in the Délie, *and in the Writings of Descartes and Pascal*

The 'darkened' and fragmented self thus appears as one possible mode of identity construction present in the sixteenth century. It was not the con-

---

[68] Op. cit., p. 124. For Risset, the absence of theory results from the fact that Scève's poetry extends to language the underlying implications of philosophical thought in his period; this 'extension' means that any theory of language would have been 'behind' his practice. One could argue that this would also have been the case for any theorisation touching upon the poetic persona, since the concepts of the *ie* implied by his poetry diverge from those which had been explicitly expressed elsewhere.

ception which was ultimately taken up and reinforced by the theoretical writings of Descartes, Pascal, and others. One might argue from these two observations that the fragmented self was firmly suppressed by the Cartesian conception; such an argument would support Lacan's aforementioned claim that the subject identifies with Descartes's God and ideal subjectivity but also — in a less obvious way — with formlessness.

One could also argue that, although Descartes's conception overrides the one manifested in the *Délie*, the two respond to a similar set of problems. The *Délie*'s conception of a fragmented subject was one response to anxieties about the conception of man based on an ordered cosmos. In this essay, I have argued that the reversal of the cosmic gender hierarchy seen in the lady–sun topos represents not man's narcissism but rather anxiety about precisely his narcissistic grounding in an ordered and benevolent cosmos; thus the insistence upon the darkness and formlessness of the *ie* implies a valorising of the subject in a lack of order instead of in order. This way of thinking does not see man as *different* from the cosmos or from physical space. Descartes, on the other hand, responds to the loss of man's privileged position in an ordered cosmos by arguing that, in a world of 'indefinite' space, the only 'fixed point' is provided by the thinking subject;[69] and that, furthermore, if man is perfect, this is linked to his morality and not to a central position in the cosmos.[70] Man should not valorise himself with respect to space but with respect to his own thought, which is something entirely separate from space.

In addition, the *uniqueness* of the *ie* in the *Délie* recalls concepts of the subject in Descartes's writings and certainly Pascal's:[71] the subject's experience is not that of every man. However, the uniqueness of the *ie* in the *Délie* often is *not* conceived as *interiority*. It has been observed that interiority and subjective individuality are conjoined only by a particular cultural construction of the subject.[72] This observation usually serves to point out that interiority can exist without subjective individuality, as is usually considered to be the case for a period leading up to that of the 'Cartesian self' or the modern self.[73] However, logically, the observation also implies that the reverse could be true, that subjective individuality could be conceived without a conception of the subject as internal space. The *Délie* gestures towards just such a notion of the subject.

---

[69] See in particular part II, article 13 of the *Principia Philosophiae*.
[70] See in particular Descartes's 1647 correspondence.
[71] See n. 54 for objections to this interpretation of Descartes.
[72] See, for example, Lecointe, op. cit., p. 11.
[73] See Reiss, op. cit.

4

Rhetoric and Virility in Ronsard's *Folastries*

Cathy Yandell

In April of 1553, *Le Livret de folastries* was published anonymously by the same printer who had produced Ronsard's *Amours* the preceding year. These poems appeared four months after the resolution of Ronsard's famous quarrel with Saint-Gelais, itself a microcosm of the larger conflict between the lofty, classically inspired poets of Du Bellay's *Deffence* and Ronsard's *Odes,* on the one hand, and the Italianate court poets producing lighter fare, on the other.[1] Yet the larger stylistic conflict was far from resolved. Ronsard again sought public approval for his poetic experiments two years later in the first sonnet of the *Continuation des Amours*, 'Thiard, chacun disoit a mon commencement', in which the poet lamented the multi-headed monster, the fickle public, who found fault with both his high and his low styles.[2]

This literary conflict is significant in the context of the *Folastries* because it announces the hybridity that dominates the collection, a hybridity that is not only stylistic, but also sexual and generic. From the outset, the anonymous publication of the *Folastries* reveals the blurred relationship between the poet and his work. Acknowledging the complexity of the concept of 'masculinity', particularly within the context of sixteenth-century culture, one can nonetheless profitably pose the question: to what extent can the poetic identity that Ronsard establishes within the collection be said to be male or masculine? In these potentially most 'masculinist' of poems, both *gaillards* and *gaulois*, does what might be called 'masculine' rhetoric prevail? I will argue here that it does not, and that the

---

[1] See Melin de Sainct-Gelays, *Œuvres*, ed. Prosper Blanchemain (Paris: Paul Daffis, Bibliothèque Elzévirienne, 1873), I. 23–5. Du Bellay specifically recommended as a form the hendecasyllabic, following Catullus, Pontanus, and Johannes Secundus, in *Deffence et Illustration de la langue francoyse* (Geneva: Droz, 2001), p. 137.
[2] Pierre de Ronsard, *Œuvres complètes*, Bibliothèque de la Pléiade, ed. Jean Céard, Daniel Ménager, and Michel Simonin (Paris: Gallimard, 1993–4), I. 172. The Pléiade edition will hereafter be designated by 'P'.

virility embodied in the poems is frequently mollified or challenged. Ronsard both posits and subverts masculine ideals in the *Folastries*. The present essay will not be the first to suggest sexual ambivalence in Ronsard's work. In 'Ronsard the Poet, Ronsard the Hermaphrodite', Ann Moss fruitfully studies the ambiguous sexuality in several of Ronsard's mythological poems of the 1560s. Lawrence Kritzman explores Ronsard's 'phallocentric masquerade' in the *Amours* of 1552, and Kirk Read calls attention to Ronsard's lactating mentor in 'A Jan Dorat'. Daniel Ménager treats the stylistic effects of Ronsard's use of the female voice, and I examine more specifically Ronsard's assumption of a lesbian voice in his elegy of 1567. In another study, I address Ronsard's substituting male for female referents, as when the poet himself becomes a flower in 'Dedans des Prez je vis une Dryade'.[3] But the 'folastries', arguably the poems most fraught with sexual ambivalence, have heretofore been neglected in criticism focusing on the problems of gender.

From the outset, the *Folastries* situate themselves within an isotopy (to use Greimas's term) or a semantic field of sexuality.[4] Both the title and the epigraph of the collection signal a blurring of genders or sexual behaviours. 'Folastrerie', which replaced 'folastrie' during the course of the sixteenth century, is defined by Cotgrave as 'fond [meaning 'foolish' in the sixteenth century] trickes, lascivious prankes, wanton fashions, effeminate actions'. Since the collection was printed by Veuve Maurice de La Porte in five hundred copies, the anonymous collection was intended to be a commercial success, perhaps because of its licentious nature.[5]

---

[3]   Ann Moss, 'Ronsard the Poet, Ronsard the Hermaphrodite', *Ronsard, figure de la variété*, ed. Colette H. Winn (Geneva: Droz, 2002), pp. 115–23; Lawrence D. Kritzman, *The Rhetoric of Sexuality and the Literature of the French Renaissance* (Cambridge: Cambridge University Press, 1991), pp. 113–29; Kirk Read, *High Anxiety: Masculinity in Crisis in Early Modern France*, ed. Kathleen Perry Long, (Kirksville: Truman State University Press, 2002), pp. 71–87; Daniel Ménager, 'L'Amour au féminin', *Sur des vers de Ronsard, 1585–1985* (Paris: Aux amateurs de livres, 1990), pp. 105–16; Cathy Yandell, '*L'Amour au féminin*? Ronsard and Pontus de Tyard Speaking as Women', *Ronsard, figure de la variété*, op. cit, pp. 65–83; *Carpe Corpus: Time and Gender in Early Modern France* (Newark: University of Delaware Press; London: Associated University Presses, 2000), pp. 72–5.

[4]   'Isotopy' is defined by A. J. Greimas as 'a complex of manifold semantic categories making possible the uniform reading' of a text. Greimas, *Du sens* (Paris: Seuil, 1979), p. 88; cited by Umberto Eco, *Interpretation and Overinterpretation,* ed. Stefan Collini (Cambridge: Cambridge University Press, 1992), p. 62.

[5]   Randle Cotgrave, *A Dictionarie of the French and English Tongues* (London, 1611; rpt Columbia: University of South Carolina Press, 1968). See also Michel Simonin, *Ronsard* (Paris: Fayard, 1990), pp. 144–5.

However, its author assures readers on the title page in a distich from Catullus 16 that the salacious verses should not be read as reflecting the author's own character:

> Nam castum esse decet pium poëtam
> Ipsum, versiculos nihil necesse est.[6]
> (For the sacred poet ought to be chaste himself, though his poems need not be so.)

That an unidentified poet should seek to protect his reputation is curious if not paradoxical. Against what is the nameless poet seeking protection? Many literary historians agree that erotic literature was for the most part well accepted in the French Renaissance and that modern pornographic literature — both marginal and transgressive — is inconceivable before the Reformation and especially before Classicism. Indeed, Jean-Marie Goulemot has argued hyperbolically that 'foul language, scatological descriptions, and scenes of joyous fornication abound everywhere in the literature of the [pre-modern] time: from Rabelais to Sorel's *Francion.* They constitute an essential part of the literary production of the period'.[7] Yet if there were no norms to transgress, why did Ronsard publish anonymously? Could it be that his anonymity served as a subterfuge to test the critical waters for his lower, bolder style? If so, Ronsard's wager produced mixed results: the *Folastries* were well received by at least some of his contemporaries. Pierre des Mireurs, immediately guessing the author's identity, wrote laconically: 'Descendat quantum volet e sublimi sacrae poesis fastigio, semper Terpander erit' ('As much as he descends from the heights of sacred poetry, he will still be Terpander').[8] Olivier de Magny, in his own imitation of the *Folastries* published in 1554, praises the grace

---

[6]   Pierre de Ronsard, *Œuvres complètes* (Paris: Société des Textes Français Modernes, 1914–75), V. 1. According to some classical scholars, Catullus was the first to claim that a poet's character cannot be inferred from his work. See *The Poems of Catullus*, ed. Guy Lee (Oxford: Clarendon, 1990), p. 154. Charles Fontaine had already used this same distich to exonerate his youthful follies in his *Fontaine d'amour* of 1546. See Ronsard, ed. Laumonier, V. vii. Unless otherwise indicated, all subsequent references to Ronsard will be from the fifth volume of the Laumonier edition.
[7]   Jean-Marie Goulemot, *Forbidden Texts,* trans. James Simpson (Philadelphia: University of Pennsylvania Press, 1994), p. 11. See also David Dorais, 'Les Païens de la Pléiade: L'Érotisme dans les *Folastries* de Ronsard et dans les *Gayetez* d'Olivier de Magny', *Renaissance and Reformation/Renaissance et Réforme* 23: 3 (1999), p. 66.
[8]   Pierre de Nolhac, 'Documents nouveaux sur la Pléiade: Ronsard, Du Bellay', *Revue d'Histoire littéraire* (1899), p. 358.

and perfection of 'ce livret de doctes folies'.[9] Charles Fontaine, a disciple
of the Marotic school, also predictably assesses the collection in laudatory
terms.[10] The ultimate measure of success for Ronsard's anonymous
experiment can be ascertained by the poet's choice to republish almost all
of the *folastries* under his own name in later collections.

The fact remains, however, that at the time of their publication, the
Folastries were inextricably embroiled in literary quarrels. Five days after
the *privilège du roi* had been issued, Henry's entourage complained of the
poems, citing their libidinous turpitude and their affront to good morals.[11]
To complicate matters further, Ronsard's epigraph is extracted from
Catullus's response to another literary quarrel, this one about the sexual
practices of its author:

> Pedicabo ego vos et irrumabo,
> Aureli pathice et cinaede Furi,
> qui me ex versiculis meis putastis,
> quod sunt molliculi, parum pudicum.

> (1. I'll bugger you and stuff you, you catamite Aurelius and you pervert
> Furius, who have supposed me to be immodest, on account of my verses,
> because these are rather naughty.)
>> (Trans. Francis W. Cornish, 1913)

> (2. I'll fuck the pair of you as you prefer it, oral Aurelius, anal Furius, who
> read my verses but misread their author: you think that *I'm* effeminate,
> since *they* are!)
>> (Trans. Charles Martin, 1992)[12]

The origins of this passage would have been well known to Ronsard's humanist readers. Because Catullus had written a so-called Sapphic ode, that
is a *basium* poem in which the poet begs his lover for kisses, he is accused

---

9   O. de Magny, *Les Gayetez,* ed. Allistair McKay (Geneva: Droz, 1968), p. 55.
10   'Ne creins, ne creins, Ronsard, ce dous stile poursuivre, / Stile qui te fera, non
moins que l'autre, vivre: / Autre, obscur et scabreux, s'il ne fait à blamer, / Si se fait-il
pourtant trop plus creindre qu'aymer.' Charles Fontaine, *Odes, enigmes, et épigrammes* (Lyon: J. Citoys, 1557), p. 67. See also Marcel Raymond, *L'Influence de
Ronsard sur la poésie française, 1550–1585* (1927; Geneva: Slatkine Reprints, 1993),
I. 32–3.
11   Simonin, op. cit., pp. 145–6.
12   *Catullus, Tibullus, Pervigilium Veneris,* trans. Francis Warre Cornish, Loeb
Classical Library (Cambridge, MA: Harvard University Press; London: William
Heinemann, 1937), pp. 22–3; Charles Martin, *Catullus* (New Haven: Yale University
Press, 1992), p. 78. Subsequent references will be to the Loeb edition.

by Aurelius and Furius of being a sodomite. While this charge may initially appear illogical since Catullus's lover is female, the operative element is not the lover's gender, but rather his role. Both their accusations and Catullus's threat in these hendecasyllabic verses involve sexual passivity. It is interesting to note that the term 'molliculi' is translated in 1913 as 'naughty' and in 1992 as 'effeminate'. A number of classical scholars now agree that the term 'mollis' denotes in Roman times not homosexuality or womanlike behaviour per se, but passivity or penetrability in sexual relations with either gender.[13] Nonetheless, in other poems, notably those addressed to Juventius, Catullus's speaker describes in detail his homosexual desire. Ironically, then, Ronsard has chosen an extremely sexually charged passage to defend himself against charges of extremely sexualised poetry.

In addition to the sexual ambiguity present in Ronsard's model, his poet also uses imagery befitting a female in a preface to 'Janot Parisien', identified by Laumonier as Jean de Baïf. Ronsard describes himself (pp. 4–5) as ravished by the muses to conceive his verses:

> Livre que les sœurs Thespiennes,
> Dessus les rives Pympléennes,
> Ravi, me firent concevoir,
> Quand jeune garson j'allay voir
> Le brisement de leur cadance
> Et Apollon le guidedance.

While Catullus has been acknowledged as Ronsard's model for this preface, the Roman poet refers neither to ravishing nor to conceiving. Indeed, Catullus evokes the image of polishing his book with pumice stone, and, save a mention of his 'patrona virgo' (p. 3), sexual allusions are com-

---

[13]   'Mollis' comes from the verb *mollesco*, to become soft or gentle. Compare Iarbas's declaration in *Aeneid* IV. 215 that Aeneas is a 'Paris', again not necessarily homosexual but passive. On the anachronistic concepts of 'heterosexual' and 'homosexual' as applied to Roman society, see Craig Williams's *Roman Homosexuality: Ideologies of Masculinity in Classical Antiquity* (Oxford: Oxford University Press, 1999) and James L. Butrica's review of *The Priapus Poems*, ed. Richard W. Hooper (Urbana and Chicago: University of Illinois Press, 1999) in the *Bryn Mawr Classical Review* 23: 2 (2000), http:// ccat.sas.upenn.edu/bmcr/2000/2000-02-23.html. Jonathan Walters notes 'the Roman sexual protocol that defined men [of high rank] as impenetrable penetrators', a status that symbolically protected the male body from invasion by a more powerful external force. See 'Invading the Roman Body: Manliness and Impenetrability in Roman Thought', *Roman Sexuality*, ed. Judith P. Hallett and Marilyn B. Skinner (Princeton: Princeton University Press, 1997), pp. 29–43.

pletely absent from his preface. Ronsard thus departs from his model not only by sexualising the metaphor for his book, but also by assuming in the process a feminised body capable of conception.

Ronsard enacts a further sexualising of the preface — albeit playfully — by addressing to 'Janot' the expression 'tu m'aymes mieux, / Ny que ton Cœur, ny que tes yeux' (p. 4). Readers of Catullus would recognise this expression as describing Lesbia's attachment to her pet sparrow, with whom (as we all know) Lesbia often played 'whilst she [held it] in her lap' (Catullus 2, p. 3). Once again the sexual implications in the text arise dialogically in relation to Catullus, the invisible but omnipresent model.

The poet of the *Folastries* thus establishes a problematic relationship with his publication in a number of ways — by his absent name, by his radically new style, and by his poet's sexuality, which through imitation is in constant dialogue with that of his model. Given that this collection situates itself under the aegis of sexuality, readers might well expect to find Ronsard, 'poète de la conquête amoureuse',[14] the most 'virile' or manly in his most lascivious collection of poems. Upon closer examination, however, it becomes clear that Ronsard's poet is strangely lacking in virility — 'virile', that is, in its sixteenth-century reading, namely 'manlie' (as in *vir*), 'bold, courageous, valiant, strong, substantiall'.[15]

To what extent does the lyric narrator, Ronsard's 'je', fulfil masculine ideals as delineated in these sixteenth-century definitions? In both cultural and literary terms, the proving grounds for such a question remain constant: the bed (or verdant pasture) and the battlefield, that is, sexual conquest and military valour.[16]

To be sure, erotic episodes abound in the *Folastries*, as in the pastoral 'Jaquet et Robine'. Of the eight poems bearing the title of *Folastries*, only this one recounts an unproblematic coupling. The staging of the amorous exploits of Jacquet and Robine includes the rhetoric of exchange and reciprocity from the rustic poem's opening:

> Jaquet ayme autant sa Robine
> Qu'une pucelle sa poupine,
> Robine ayme autant son Jaquet

---

[14]   André Gendre, *Ronsard, poète de la conquête amoureuse* (Neuchâtel: Éditions de La Baconnière, 1970).

[15]   Cotgrave, op. cit.

[16]   Compare François Billon's claim that Louise Labé was skilled in 'tout honneste exercice viril, et par especial aux Armes', *Le Fort inexpugnable de l'honneur du Sexe Femenin* (Paris: Ian d'Allyer, 1555), p. 15.

RHETORIC AND VIRILITY IN RONSARD'S *FOLASTRIES*

Qu'un amoureux fait son bouquet.
O amourettes doucelettes,
O doucelettes amourettes,
O couple d'amis bien heureux,
Ensemble aimez et amoureux.

(pp. 29–30)

These verses establish both linguistic symmetry and a blurring of genders. First, the names Jaquet and Robine recall the prototypical characters of French pastoral, Robin and Marion, except that the masculine 'Robin' figures here in its feminine form, Robine, and the diminutive that traditionally designates the young woman, Marie-on, now applies to the young man, Jacques-et. Symmetry is created not only by the lines 'Jaquet ayme autant /.../ Robine ayme autant', but also by the *rejet* following the enjambment of each verse which logically should follow the other verse in question. In this arrangement, Jaquet loves as a girl (*une pucelle*) and Robine loves as a boy (*un amoureux*). As if further to reflect a perfect semantic symmetry, the anaphoric verses 5 and 6 are identical save the chiastic reversal of 'amourettes' and 'doucelettes'. While Catullus frequently uses the rhetorical figure chiasmus, the diagonal arrangement of terms as in the Greek letter X, never is it used to establish an equalising effect as it is throughout Ronsard's fourth *Folastrie*. Finally, the abundance of terms denoting togetherness and equality throughout the poem is striking, as evidenced in lines 7 and 8 above: *couple / amis / ensemble / aimez / amoureux*.

The erotic vision sketched in this pastoral proves to be unrealistic, symmetrically depicted in almost caricatural terms: just as Jaquet spies his mistress's 'grosse motte...et son petit cas barbelu', so Robine eyes his 'tribart qui luy pendoit entre les jambes' (pp. 32 3). Their desires are united in the text with the repetition of the word 'rouge', once for Jaquet and once for Robine: his member is 'Plus rouge que les rouges flames / Qu'elle atisoit songneusement' (p. 33). When this mutual magnetism reaches its pinnacle ten lines later, the female Robine initiates the consumation: 'Si tu n'aymes mieux ta galette / Que ta mignarde Robinette, / Je te pry, Jaquet, jauche moy...' (p. 33). The shepherd and shepherdess's erotic antics are such that, upon observing them, even the goats mimetically begin to copulate. In rhetorical terms, also, copula are so readily understood as to be unnecessary: 'O couple d'amans bien heureux, / Ensemble aymez, et amoureux' (p. 34).

Both Catullus's and Ronsard's pastoral poems conclude with an elegiac description of reciprocal love, yet in quite different ways. While Ronsard's Jaquet and Robine are united in parallel rhetorical terms,

Catullus's lovers Septimius and Acme (Catullus 45, 53), though blessed by Venus, are shown to have distinctly male and female ways of loving. Catullus's male Septimius prefers Acme to the military conquests of Syria and Britain, whereas Acme's desire is to take her fill of love and pleasure only in Septimius: 'unam Septimius misellus Acmen / mavolt quam Syrias Britanniasque: uno in Septimio fidelis Acme / facit delicias libidinesque' (Catullus 45, p. 54).

Not coincidentally, Ronsard's pastoral poem portraying a symmetrical coupling is also the only *Folastrie* in which no poetic *je* is present. Like Montaigne, who in painting himself 'tout nud' reveals only those weaknesses he imagines that the reader will find endearing (such as being too quick in sex and having a poor memory), so Ronsard's poet in the *Folastries* assumes the voice of the former or thwarted lover, the loser, the has-been. Failure, sometimes stigmatised as effeminate, takes on a humorous dimension in the *Folastries*.[17] This comic stance invites the reader both to side with the underdog and to bemoan the bumbling poet's fate.

A dog of a different sort plays the protagonist in *Folastrie* 5 and successfully obstructs Ronsard's poet's amorous success. Poets from the Greek Anthology as well as Catullus and Ovid had written praises of various animals, especially dogs.[18] Here Ronsard takes the opposite position, chastising the dog for betraying him and his mistress in the midst of their secret lovemaking. The poem begins with the traditional image of the faithful dog, companion to historic heroes:

> Au viel temps que l'enfant de Rhée
> N'avoit la terre dedorée,
> Les Heroes ne dedaignoient
> Les chiens qui les accompagnoient,
> Fidelles gardes de leur trace...

(p. 35)

The Golden Age sets the stage for Ronsard's tale, before the dethroning of Chronos by Zeus and before the poet's own fall from amorous grace. But the masculine image of heroes and their valiant dogs is undercut by a humorous interruption:

---

[17] On the notion of failure as effeminate and 'psychic virility' in Catullus, see Marilyn B. Skinner, '*Ego Mulier*: The Construction of Male Sexuality in Catullus', *Roman Sexuality*, op. cit., p. 146.

[18] Catullus 2. 3. In the Greek Anthology, birds sing love songs or interrupt erotic dreams: *The Greek Anthology,* ed. Peter Jay (Oxford: Oxford University Press, 1973), IX. 286 (p. 202), and IX. 87 (p. 203). See also Marot, *Œuvres poétiques*, ed. Gérard Defaux (Paris: Bordas, 1993), II. 210.

> Mais toy, chien de mechante race,
>
> . . . .
>
> Desloyal et traistre mastin,
> Japant à la porte fermée
> De la chambre, où ma mieux aymée
> Me dorlotoyt entre ses bras,
> Counillant de jour dans les dras...

(p. 36)

In this passage, the poet is depicted as doubly passive, identified in both cases by the objective pronoun: the dog discovers him as he is being fondled by his 'mieux aymée'. The verbs *combler*, *japer*, *dorloter*, and *couniller* are carried out not by the poet but by the dog and the mistress. When the speaker finally takes action in the poem, 'Tout seul je faisoy la chosette / Avecque elle dans sa couchette' (p. 36), the mannerist diminutives serve to diminish any masculine power that the speaker might otherwise have claimed. The only other instances of the poet's assuming the subjective pronoun in the poem are followed by the pluperfect subjunctive, describing the poetry he would have written in honour of the dog, had circumstances been different: 'Je t'eusse fait chien immortel, / Et t'eusse mis parmy les signes, / Entre les astres plus insignes' (p. 37). Thus in all these examples, the poetic 'je' is in some sense emasculated, physically by the interruption of the sex act within the poem, and grammatically by its position as object, or as subject to a purely putative action.

A final foiling of Ronsard's erotic designs illustrates the extent to which Ronsard's poet depicts himself as equally priapic but more sexually thwarted than any of his models, Catullus, Martial, and Johannes Secundus. The image is identical in all of the poets, namely an erect penis futilely protruding into a tunic, but in Catullus, the first-person narrator is awaiting his lover's arrival and urging her to hurry. Martial employs the image to chide his prudish reader, and Johannes Secundus, after evoking the same image, returns to a vision of union through a kiss.[19] In contrast,

---

[19]   Catullus 32; Martial, *Epigrams*, XI. 16: 'If you are too grave, Reader, you can go from here where you will... How often will your stiffness push out your robe, although you be sterner than Curius and Fabricius!', trans. [Mitchell Starrett Buck] ([New York?]: Privately Printed for Subscribers Only, [1921]), p. 305. Compare Johannes Secundus, *Basium* XIV, *Le Livre des baisers*, ed. Thierry Sandre (Paris: Renaudot et Cie, 1989), p. 70:

> Tanti istas ego ut osculationes
> Imbelles faciam, superba, vestras,
> Ut, nervo toties rigens supino,
> Pertundam tunicas meas tuasque,

RHETORIC AND VIRILITY IN RONSARD'S *FOLASTRIES*

Ronsard's poet in *Folastrie* 3 remains perpetually frustrated with no hope of relief. Since his lubricious lover has changed her ways, now refusing her services, the poet's sufferings are visibly manifest:

> Ainsi depuis une semeine,
> La longue roydeur de ma veine,
> Pourneant rouge et bien enpoint,
> Bat ma chemise et mon proupoint.
> Qu' cent diables soit la prestresse
> Qui a bigotté ma maistresse.

(p. 28)

In this poem, the shrivelled and repentant Catin serves as the antagonistic impediment to the poet's fulfilment. The poet's former lover has been converted by Catin, who in her youth serviced priests and monks, rich and poor alike, 'Pourveu qu'il servist bien en chambre / Et qu'il eust plus d'un pié de membre'. Now, because of the old woman's influence, the poet's mistress rejects his every move:

> Si qu'or, quand baiser je la veux,
> Elle me tire les cheveux:
> Si je veux tater sa cuissette,
> Ou fesser sa fesse grossete
> Ou si je mez la main dedans
> Ses tetins, elle à coups de dens
> Me dechire tout le visage,
> Comme un singe émeu contre un page.

(p. 27)

Et, desiderio furens inani,
Tabescam miser, aestuante vena?

Quo fugis? Remane; nec hos ocellos,
Nec nega mihi flammeum labellum.
Te jam, te volo basiare, mollis,
Molli mollior anseris medula.

(Do you think I'm so taken by these debilitating kisses, haughty one, that are yours, if, every time I stiffen like a pulled bow, I have to protrude through my clothing and yours, and afterwards, furious from my own unsuccessful desire, I am consumed, my pulse beating feverishly? Where are you going? Don't go. Stay. Don't refuse me those eyes, nor your lips that enflame me. Yes, I want to kiss you, my sweet, you who are softer than a gosling's down [my translation]).

94

Once again, despite the poet's former success, now he remains either the object of his mistress's ire ('elle me tire les cheveux'...'me dechire tout le visage'), or the ineffectual, desiring subject ('quand baiser je la veux', 'si je veux tater'). The speaker's only action is preceded by the hypothetical 'si' and thwarted in the poem by the mistress — here depicted as a masculine ape — with her violent response.

So much for manly pursuits in the bedroom. Ronsard's poet also fails on the battlefield by subverting the masculine ideal of military prowess, particularly in *Folastrie* 2. In this heptasyllabic poem (again stylistically modelled on Catullus's hendecasyllables), the poet's comfortable access to his lover has been foiled by her brothers' return home from war. The poet's plan consists in sending them off again to fight as soon as possible, appealing to their patriotism: '...allez Soldars, / Allez bienheureux gendarmes, / Allez, et vestez les armes, / Secourez la fleur de lis' (p. 18). The poet first develops an incitement of the brothers to glory, followed by an attempt to induce guilt should they choose not to serve their country:

> A ce bel œuvre, guerriers,
> Ne serez vous des premiers?
> Ah, que vous aurez de honte
> Si un autre vous raconte
> Combien le Roy print de fors,
> Combien de gens seront mors...
>
> (p. 20)

The mock heroic praise of military might humorously undercuts the power of this most masculine of institutions. Ronsard had established himself in the *Odes* of 1550 as a great promoter of Henri II's battles and victories. Here, however, the poet's triumph will consist in having his mistress to himself if her brothers return to war — but his success will be achieved by cunning rather than by conquest:

> Soldars, ne cagnardez point
> Suivez le train de voz Peres,
> Et raportez à voz Meres
> Double honneur, et double bien:
> Sans vous je garderay bien
> Vos sœurs: allez donc gendarmes...
>
> (p. 21)

The principal refrain of the poem, 'Le bon Bacchus portelance / Soit tousjours votre defence', underscores the sword's double edge as it figures metaphorically in both the world of war and the world of pleasure. Inter-

95

estingly, in the midst of images of masculine warriors, Bacchus or Diony-
sus appears as a sexually ambivalent contrast. Often termed 'the effeminate god', under his soft, rounded appearance Bacchus is said to hide
nerves of steel and Herculean strength, thus uniting woman's beauty and
man's force.

The last two poems in the *Folastries*, two parallel sonnets blazoning
male and female genitalia, provide a final example of Ronsard's blurring
of genders throughout the collection. What is striking is not the difference
between the sonnets, which would be expected given the clearly masculine point of view of the poet's voice, but rather the similarities between
the two. First, both adopt a strongly religious and chivalric vocabulary.
The verses 'Sans toi le Monde un Chaos se feroit' (l. 9) and '...combien à
ton honneur / Doit on de vœux, combien de sacrifices' (ll. 13–14) of the
first poem announce the laudatory lines 'Je te salue, ô vermeillette fante'
of the second (P. I, p. 571). The prayer addressed to the genitals is of
course reminiscent of the quintessential 'Je te salue Marie pleine de grâce'
and especially the eleventh-century *Salve Regina*: 'Je te salue O Reine,
Mère de miséricorde.' The repetition of 'ô' in Ronsard's blazon ('ô vermeillette fante... ô bienheuré pertuis... ô petit trou') further recalls the
Salve Regina, 'O clémente, ô si bonne, ô douce, Vierge Marie'. Just as
readers are called upon to offer sacrifices to the male organ in the first
sonnet, so are all 'vers galans' invited to worship the female organ on
bended knee in the second.

Rhetorical consonances between the two poems abound as well.
Both Marotic sonnets are constructed as apostrophes to the genitals, calling them into being and thereby creating the speaker's subjectivity.[20] Further, both sonnets include active verbs describing the genitals' achieve-
ments: *poindre, choquer, rendre,* and *domter*. Paradoxically, while the
term 'combat' figures in the sonnet to male genitalia, the only conquering
that occurs in the two poems is accomplished by the female genitalia,
'Qui à ton gré domtes les plus rebelles'. A *contrepet* in line 13 of the first
sonnet, proposed by the most recent editors of Ronsard, 'Par qui l'on vit' /
'Par lui con vit', produces an internal rime in lines 13 and 14 ('con' /
'doit-on'), and again creates a parallel: just as the male genitals figure in
the sonnet for the female, so the female genitals are suggested in the sonnet for the male.

The use of images in the sonnets further obscures a clearly gendered
reading. The initial image of the first sonnet, the lance, draws from chival-

---

[20]   See Jonathan Culler, 'Apostrophe', *Diacritics* 7: 4 (1977), pp. 59–69 and 'Reading Lyric', *Yale French Studies* 98 (1985), pp. 98–106.

ric imagery, and the terms 'combat', 'choquer', and 'poindre' in the quatrains continue the bellicose rhetoric. Yet in the final tercet of the sonnet, when the reader might well anticipate victory in the battles mentioned in lines 4 and 11, the rhetoric of manlihood is instead strangely sublimated or moralised. The 'lance au bout d'or' becomes the 'instrument de bon heur / Par qui lon vit',[21] and the sonnet ends with the male member not in conquest but in a position of reception, receiving sacrifices. Similarly, while the female genitalia are depicted in the first tercet as taming even the most rebellious, at the end of the poem, they too become a passive object of worship.

While Baldassari Olimpo degli Alessandri has been suggested as the inspiration both for these sonnets and for the collected blasons of the 1540s, no poem to a male body part can be found in Olimpo, nor is there any attempt in the *Blasons anatomiques* to construct parallel poems to male and female genitals.[22] Ronsard's original juxtaposing of these rhetorically parallel poems seemingly underscores the poet's desire to provide equal exposure, as it were, with the effect of complicating the preponderantly male discourse.

One might argue that in all lyric poetry, the indeterminate 'I' is in perpetual contingency, and thus that the male voice is never entirely stable. Yet while the semi-lyric genre of *ineptiae* or *nugae* inherited from Catullus is said to have a more supple rhythm in distinction to the ode, allowing the poet freer expression, it does not necessarily lend itself to a less masculine rhetoric. Olivier de Magny, for example, whose *Gayetez* published in 1554 were directly inspired by both Catullus and the *Folastries*, asserts a 'substantiall' masculine voice by employing terms of conquest and force, as in the lyric addressed to Denis Durant:

> Toutes les fois que j'aperçoi
> Ma nymfelette aupres de toi,
> Qui te tend à demy farouche
> Sa petite vermeille bouche,

---

[21]   This turn is reminiscent of Clément Marot's famous blazon in which the 'Beau tetin', an erotic enticer, is transformed into the bearer of an infant's milk. See Marot, *Œuvres complètes*, ed. cit., II. 241–2.

[22]   Baldassare de Olimpo degli Alessandri (Olympo de Sassoferrato), *Pegasea* (Venice: Bernardino di Bindoni, 1539). In the French collection of anatomical blazons, the 'Blason du con' and the 'Blason du con de la pucelle', have no male counterparts. *S'ensuivent les blasons anatomiques du corps femenin*. ([Paris]: Charles Langelier, 1543), f. D2^r-D3^r. The digital facsimile can be consulted online at http://iris.lib.virginia.edu/speccol/gordon/ gordonimages/_B53/.

RHETORIC AND VIRILITY IN RONSARD'S *FOLASTRIES*

> Lors que captive soubz ta main
> Je te vois, fierement humain,
> Forcer sa levre cramoisie
> A te donner de l'ambrosie...[23]

This use of terms denoting power echoes other passages in which Magny employs more imperatives than does Ronsard, indicating a tension between man and woman, as well as a desire for domination of the addressee.[24] In contrast to Magny, then, Ronsard invents in his collection a rhetoric that is patently lacking in masculine *virtus*.

Unlike Magny, Ronsard's poet undoes expectations for virile or 'manlie' behaviour in both amorous and military exploits in the *Folastries*. Ultimately, what would become of Ronsard's highly sexed and ambivalently gendered *style bas*?[25] The prefatory poem to the *Nouvelle Continuation des Amours* in 1556 responds in part to this question.[26] The preface is dedicated to the Parisian humanist Jean de Morel, who had apparently criticised the *Folastries* three years earlier. Through the use of mythological characters and hypotyposis, or vivid description, Ronsard initially sets a lofty tone for his new work. The poet might seem at first glance to be assuring his colleague that he has repented from the follies of the *Folastries*, as he offers verses more acceptable to Morel's easily offended sensibility:

> Et plus dignes de toy qui n'as l'oreille attainte
> Sinon de chastes vers d'une Muse tressainte,
> Qui parle sagement, et qui point ne rougit

---

[23] Olivier de Magny, *Les Gayetez*, ed. Allistair McKay (Geneva: Droz, 1968), p. 25.

[24] See David Dorais, op. cit., pp. 67–8.

[25] Concerning the stylistic function of eroticism in the *Folastries*, David Dorais argues that the erotic qualities serve to illustrate a different concept of love from that of the 1552 *Amours* and announce the carnal desire, rather than the Petrarchan adoration, that will dominate the *Continuation des Amours* (p. 66). Claude Faisant suggests that since the poet's ardour in the *Folastries* is neither sincere nor serious, the obscenity of the poems can be seen as an accessory to the burlesque, creating dissonance to produce a parodic effect; 'L'Érotisme dans les *Folastries* de Ronsard', *Europe* 247–62 (November–December 1986), p. 61. Michel Jeanneret concludes that Ronsard's opting for the *style bas* has the effect of including voices other than his own in the text; '*Les Amours de Marie*: inscription de la deuxième personne et stratégies dialogiques', *Sur des vers de Ronsard* (1585–1985), op. cit., pp. 61–70. See also François Rigolot, *Poésie et Renaissance* (Paris: Seuil, 2002), p. 198.

[26] I am grateful to Marc-André Wiesmann for having called my attention to this poem in relation to the *Folastries*.

RHETORIC AND VIRILITY IN RONSARD'S *FOLASTRIES*

De honte, ny l'auteur ny celuy qui la lit.
(P. II, p. 823)

Yet these assurances form only part of the equation, and the rest of the poem systematically dismantles their claim. A note in the *princeps* edition exhorts the reader to consult Apollonius's fourth *Argonautica* for a better understanding of the elegy.[27] Like Apollonius, Ronsard recounts the gift of a clump of earth from the sea god Triton to Euphemus. Euphemus then dreams that the clump of earth is transformed into a young woman with whom he physically unites. When Euphemus awakens, Jason interprets the symbolic meaning of the dream: if Euphemus casts the clump of earth into the sea, it will become an island on which his descendants will flourish. Ronsard's recounting of the tale once again draws upon implicit sexual imagery:

> Or la nuict il songea qu'une douce rousée
> De laict avoit par tout cest motte arrousée,
> Qu'il tenoit cherement embrassé en son sein,
> Et qu'elle se changeoit en fille sous sa main,
> Et que luy tout ardant de la grand beauté d'elle
> Accolloit par amour ceste jeune pucelle,
> Qui sembloit dans le lict piteusement crier
> Comme une de quinze ans que lon va marier.
> (Ronsard, P. II. 821)

> ...Euphemus bethought him of a dream of the night, reverencing the glorious son of Maia. For it seemed to him that the god-given clod of earth held in his palm close to his breast was being suckled by white streams of milk, and that from it, little though it was, grew a woman like a virgin; and he, overcome by strong desire, lay with her in love's embrace; and united with her he pitied her, as though she were a maiden whom he was feeding with his own milk.
> (Apollonius, ll. 1731–1740)[28]

Whereas in Apollonius, the earth-woman drinks milk from the maternal Euphemus's breast, in Ronsard the more masculine 'milk' sprays the earth, the 'motte', which is not coincidentally the same term Ronsard had used to describe female genitals in the *Folastries*. Further, the sixteenth-

---

[27] P. II. 1531–2, n. 1. The note also refers readers to Pindar's fourth Pythian Ode. Pindar's ode recounts some of the story of Euphemus and the clump of earth, but with no mention of his dream.
[28] Apollonius, *Argonautica*, The Online Medieval and Classical Library, http://omacl.org/Argonautica/book4.html.

99

century poet insists more on Euphemus's sexual power over the young virgin, who cries out in the marriage bed. These examples demonstrate Ronsard's rendering of Euphemus as more stereotypically masculine than that of Apollonius.

Yet once again the masculinity that Ronsard erects in the poem is followed by precious images undermining that stance. The poet asserts that his verses, unassuming and tiny like a stream, form a favourable contrast to oceanic and torrential works.

> Un petit ruisselet a tousjours l'onde nette:
> Aussi le papillon et la gentile avette
> Y vont puiser de l'eau, et non en ces torrens
> Qui tonnent d'un grand bruit par les roches courans.
> Petits Sonets bien-faits, belles Chansons petites,
> Petits Discours gentils, sont les fleurs des Charites...
>
> (P. II. 822)

The word 'petit' appears four times within the six verses, and 'gentil' twice. The dainty diminutive 'ruisselet', along with references to flowers and butterflies, hardly describes a land of masculine conquest. But here the paradox emerges: in this poetic scene, smaller and sweeter are better. Comparing his work to Euphemus's bit of earth, which when thrown into the sea becomes a beautiful island, Ronsard notes that his 'petit labeur' is not as small as one might think, and indeed perhaps it is worth more than grandiose offerings:

> Peut estre qu'il vaut mieux que la grosse apparence
> De ces tomes enflez, de gloire convoiteux,
> Qui sont fardez de mots sourcilleux et vanteux,
> Empoullez et masquez, où rien ne se descœuvre
> Que l'arrogant jargon d'un ambicieux œuvre.
>
> (P. II. 822)

Further asserting his ability to write as he chooses, Ronsard's poet renounces responsibility for the reception of his work by calling upon Morel, and by extension all his readers, to choose among verses, both 'graves' and 'fols', as a bee among flowers.[29]

---

[29] Ainsin en feuilletant ce mine petit ouvrage
Tu sçauras bien tirer (comme prudent et sage)
Les vers qui seront fols, amoureux, esvantez,
D'avec ceux qui seront plus gravement chantez. (P. II. 823)

Resisting a clearly masculine discourse and univocal poetic style, Ronsard reveals in the *Folastries* both his dialogic relationship to gender and his ultimate adherence to the principle of *varietas*. The subsequent *Discours à Jean Morel,* ostensibly a palliative to appease Ronsard's detractors, serves instead as a manifesto of the poet's commitment to literary experimentation. Just as the sex act between the nubile maiden and Euphemus in the *Discours* serves as a metaphor for poetic production, so the sexualised language of the *Folastries* announces Ronsard's hybrid style. In both cases, the place of gender in the poems remains unstable, as virile rhetoric is at once established and challenged. In the final argument of the *Discours à Jean Morel,* the poet asserts that like Nature itself, his poetry will be both high and low, 'ore mal, ore bien...une herbe venimeuse / Tout aupres d'une bonne' (P. II. 823). Perfection, the poet concludes, belongs only to God...and poetry, he implies, to humanity.

5

Re-Reading Platonic Sexuality Sceptically in Montaigne's 'Apologie de Raimond Sebond'

Todd W. Reeser

In his book *How to Do the History of Homosexuality*, David Halperin challenges the recurring convention in pre-modern gay studies that, before modernism, sexual deviance was conceived of in terms of acts and not in terms of identities.[1] Gay identity, he argues, did not simply spring up in the late nineteenth century, in opposition to what were previously sodomitical acts. Because early modern studies of same-sex sexuality have often been based on what Halperin sees as a misreading of volume one of Foucault's *Histoire de la sexualité*, we should 'forget Foucault'. Instead, a more complicated model of (homo)sexuality should be employed: 'We need to find ways of asking how different historical cultures fashioned different sorts of links between sexual acts, on the one hand, and sexual tastes, styles, dispositions, characters, gender presentations, and forms of subjectivity, on the other' (pp. 43–4). Renaissance forms of same-sex subjectivity — or what Halperin calls 'partial identities' — should thus be considered in their relation to sexual acts.

The difficulties of understanding this act/identity relation — or lack thereof — are many in the French Renaissance. There are no 'complete' homosexual texts, no French Marlowe-like figure, and documentation of sexual acts is rare.[2] Still, I would like to attempt to study this act/identity

---

[1]   See his 'Forgetting Foucault', chapter one in David M. Halperin, *How to Do the History of Homosexuality* (Chicago: The University of Chicago Press, 2002). The earlier published version of the chapter is 'Forgetting Foucault: Acts, Identities, and the History of Sexuality', *Representations*, 63 (Summer 1998), 93–120.

[2]   Jonathan Goldberg formulates a similar idea when he writes that 'any inquiry [into sodomy (such as that of Bray)] will never deliver the sodomite per se, but only...sodometries, relational structures precariously available to prevailing discourses'. See *Sodometries: Renaissance Texts, Modern Sexualities* (Stanford: Stanford University Press, 1992), p. 20. For Bredbeck, Renaissance sodomy's 'lack of sexual specificity allowed the term to be used in unspecified ways, ways that signify broad fields of sexual aberration all additionally stigmatised by the prurience of male-male

relation in a context perhaps slightly different from what Halperin may have intended. My form of 'proto-identity' will be the Renaissance configuration of Platonic male–male sexuality, a key manifestation of what could anachronistically and problematically be called 'homosexuality' within humanist culture.[3] The type of 'sexual act' I will focus on here will be the 'act of reading', or more precisely, humanist acts of re-reading Platonic sexuality. 'Platonic sexuality' will serve as a kind of discursive umbrella that links together various types of same-sex sexuality in the Platonic corpus (e.g. the male/male androgyne of Aristophanes' tale in the *Symposium*, or the sexuality of Agathon or of Socrates himself), a semantic approach also used by certain humanists in attempts to stabilise diverse forms of Platonic sexuality and talk about them coherently.[4] These re-reading acts are repeated throughout Humanism, and by virtue of their repetition, are partially responsible for the Renaissance construction of this brand of identity often considered disruptive to heteronormativity, a pervasive form of identity deeply grounded in the regulatory institution of marriage. One way to think about this act/identity relation is to consider how the repetition of acts creates identity, an approach to subjectivity most famously discussed in the work of Judith Butler.[5] In this case, the reading act creates an image of a homosexual identity in the ancient world for Humanism, but it also has implications for Renaissance homosexuality and heteronormativity.

Whereas studies of Renaissance homosexuality often focus on discursive constructions of homoeroticism, homosexuality, or sodomy,

attraction'. See Gregory W. Bredbeck, *Sodomy and Interpretation: Marlowe to Milton* (Ithaca: Cornell University Press, 1991), p. 11.
[3]   Following one approach in early modern sexuality studies, I employ the anachronistic term 'homosexuality' as an umbrella, precisely because it is such a complicated phenomenon in the period (and in Montaigne) and can include a number of pre-modern representations (e.g. homoerotic desire, sodomy, friendship, effeminacy, same-sex marriage). On this issue, see chapter four ('How to Do the History of Male Homosexuality') in Halperin. I will evoke various elements of 'homosexuality' throughout my discussion.
[4]   Ficino, for example, uses the expression 'Platonic Love' (*amore Platonico*) in one of his letters. See Marsilio Ficino, *Opera omnia*, vol. I (Turin: Bottega, 1962), p. 716.
[5]   See, for example, Louise Fradenburg and Carla Freccero, 'Caxton, Foucault, and the Pleasures of History', in *Premodern Sexualities*, edited by Louise Fradenburg and Carla Freccero (New York: Routledge, 1996), p. xx. Judith Butler's works implying such an approach would include *Gender Trouble: Feminism and the Subversion of Identity* (New York: Routledge, 1990) and *Bodies That Matter: On the Discursive Limits of 'Sex'* (New York: Routledge, 1993).

and their role in literature and culture, I will focus on the interpretive process, in which the reader is confronted with ancient homosexuality and responds in some conscious or unconscious way. Like early modern homosexuality, this reading act is a complicated and diffuse phenomenon, and does not necessarily imply a simple 'reading out' of Platonic sexuality, rather a dialogic relation between reader and text in which the reader can be affected by the text of which he or she is supposed to have an intimate knowledge. Elsewhere, I have examined the effect of the potential homoerotics of Ficinian neo-Platonism on Marguerite de Navarre as she represents the process of the establishment of heterosexuality in the *Heptaméron*.[6] Here, I will focus on a text that treats the issue more explicitly, one of Montaigne's *Essais* not known for its discussion of sexuality — the 'Apologie de Raimond Sebond' (II. 12). In my reading, the essay critiques those who, by avoiding sceptical methodology, attempt to read same-sex sexuality out of Plato, as it suggests unexpected ways in which the reading act and sexual identity function together.

Reading Plato Anachronistically

The issue of reading Platonic sexuality arises in the 'Apologie' within the context of the issue of the subjective nature of reading. After discussing the subjectivity of law, Montaigne is reminded that, like law, textual hermeneutics is subjective: 'il n'est aucun sens ni visage, ou droict, ou amer, ou doux, ou courbe, que l'esprit humain ne trouve aux escrits qu'il entreprend de fouiller' (p. 569).[7] Regarding this excessive hermeneutic openness as unfortunate, Montaigne continues his lament that ancient and biblical texts are re-read from the point of view of the reader. The first problem is essentially what is read *into* such a text: 'Est-il possible qu'Homere aye voulu dire tout ce qu'on luy faict dire', he wonders (p. 570). The reading in of what is contrary to authorial intention is problematic, but so is the reading out of what an author means, a reading act that Montaigne discusses with reference to Plato:

(c) Voyez demener et agiter Platon. Chacun, s'honorant de l'appliquer à soi, le couche du costé qu'il le veut. On le promeine et l'insere à toutes les nouvelles opinions que le monde reçoit; et le differente lon à soy-mesmes selon le different cours des choses. On faict desadvoüer à son sens les

[6] See Todd W. Reeser, 'Fracturing the Male Androgyne in the *Heptaméron*', *Romance Quarterly*, 51 (Winter 2004), 15–28.
[7] All citations from Montaigne are taken from the *Œuvres complètes*, edited by Maurice Rat (Paris: Gallimard, 1962). Further parenthetical references to Montaigne will be to this edition.

mœurs licites en son siecle, d'autant qu'elles sont illicites au nostre. Tout
cela vifvement et puissamment, autant qu'est puissant et vif l'esprit de
l'interprete.

(p. 571)

Clearly, Montaigne is referring to the various and numerous translations,
commentaries, and interpretations relating to the Platonic corpus and to
neo-Platonism.[8] To efface homosexuality in these texts is to separate Plato
from himself ('le differente lon à soy-mesmes') as well as from his cultural context ('On faict desadvoüer à son sens les mœurs licites en son
siecle, d'autant qu'elles sont illicites au nostre'). This form of same-sex
sexuality includes what could be assumed to be the institution of pederasty and pederastic acts ('les mœurs licites'), presumably as described in
greater detail in the famous passage on 'licence grecque' in 'De l'amitié'
(pp. 185–6). It is difficult, however, to determine to what extent these
'mœurs' are linked with the sexual act as opposed to some kind of identity. By virtue of mentioning that such 'mœurs' are 'illicites' in his own
period, Montaigne makes reference to legal and cultural interdictions on
homosexuality, implying their real or discursive presence, in his own
'siecle'. But since pederasty, at least in its classic formulation, does not
exist in the Renaissance, the sexual customs in question would be much
more undefined than the way they were assumed to be in the Greek institution. A further reason this contemporary brand of homosexuality is difficult to define is Montaigne's implication that it may transcend simple
'mœurs': if the reader 'separates' Plato from himself, homosexuality
would appear to be more embedded in the self than 'mœurs' would imply,
and to be an integral part of what 'Plato' is (be it the man himself or, by
metonymy, Socrates, the Academy, or the Platonic textual corpus). Affirming the instability of Renaissance homosexuality, this passage would
not seem to be conducive to articulating a relation between act and sexual
identity.

If the distinction between act and identity is unclear, this suggestive
passage maintains what appears to be a clear distinction between the in-

---

[8]   Villey concludes that Montaigne's knowledge of Plato, acquired mostly after
1585, is based largely on his reading of Ficino in Latin. He assumes that Montaigne
did not know the various contemporary French translations of Plato and that he did not
have much knowledge of the 1578 Henri Estienne Latin edition of the Platonic corpus.
See Pierre Villey, *Les Sources et l'évolution des Essais*, volume I (Paris, 1908),
pp. 192–4. Ficino would thus most probably be one of the 'interpretes' to whom Montaigne is referring here. Still, it is clear that Montaigne is not referring to any specific
'interprete', but responding to a trend in Renaissance Humanism.

tended meaning of the author and the meaning the reader establishes. It is
in the author/reader relation, instead of in ancient sexuality per se, that I
will look for an act/identity relation. The importance accorded here to
how one reads is suggested by the use of the verb 'coucher', which in one
sense denotes a writing down as a committing to memory. In Nicot's
Thrésor de la langue française (1606), the French phrase 'Coucher par
escrit la parole d'aucun' translates as 'Memoriae prodere sermonem ali-
cuius', and 'Coucher ou rediger par escrit' as 'Mandare scriptis, Com-
mendare monumentis, Peragere res gestas', and Nicot mentions the phrase
'Coucher par escrit et garder par le benefice de l'escriture la memoire des
choses'.[9] In this sense, 'coucher' means to take a 'vertical' text and to
make it one's own by rendering it metaphorically 'horizontal'. Here, hori-
zontalising the text renders it a biased one, no longer 'standing' on its own
and unable to 'walk' ('on le promeine') and 'talk' (the secondary sense of
'demener' is to talk, discuss, or debate[10]) for itself. So readers who interpret Plato 'selon le different cours des choses' of their own period inscribe
a new interpretation as a *monumentum*, spreading their readings to a larger
public as a reconstructed *lieu de mémoire* that transforms how Platonic
sexuality is conceived. Both act and identity are transformed as the ancient 'mœurs' become contemporary ones, and as 'Plato' takes on a new
identity. Montaigne's use of Plato as example of reading out corresponds
quite well to his earlier complaint of the twisting of 'la parole la plus
nette, pure et parfaite qui puisse être' that produces so much 'fausseté'
and 'mensonge' (p. 569). When interpreters of an ancient writer interpret
his 'stile nubileux et doubteux en si frequent et ancien usage' (p. 570) in
various ways, they locate a 'quantité de formes...qui lui feront honneur'
(p. 570). These readers, instead, do 'honneur' to themselves ('s'honorant
de l'appliquer à soi') as they separate Plato from himself, much as the offended gods split the original male/male androgyne in the *Symposium*.
Authorial meaning has been transformed by the vague 'on' in question,
but even more so by the cultural context of the interpreter ('les nouvelles
opinions que le monde reçoit'), which creates this reading 'on' even as it
linguistically erases the specificity of its identity. In addition, the very fact
of focusing on the same-sex aspect of ancient male sexuality is itself cul-

---

[9]   Jean Nicot, *Thresor de la langue francoyse tant ancienne que moderne* (Paris:
David Douceur, 1606). I have consulted the ARTFL on-line dictionary at:
http://www.lib.uchicago.edu/efts/ARTFL/projects/dicos/TLF-NICOT/.   See   also
Edmond Huguet, *Dictionnaire de la langue française du seizième siècle*, volume II
(Paris: Champion, 1925–1973), pp. 576–9.
[10]   See Huguet, volume II, p. 782.

turally anachronistic. It is well known that object choice in the ancient Greek world was not as central to sexuality as other aspects relating to sexuality — particularly degree of sexuality (excess, moderation) and whether the active or passive role was taken. So, to disavow 'les mœurs licites' is culturally anachronistic on two levels: first, it disavows an important element of ancient culture, and second, it disavows the reason for the disavowal in the first place. In any case, the reading act and Platonic sexuality are assumed to be discrete entities, a situation that permits the reading act to construct what I might call a 'heteronormative hermeneutic identity' and that allows 'one' to 'honour' the self by fabricating an identity in opposition with a transformed Platonic sexuality ('s'honorant de l'appliquer à soi'). The act of reading *out*, then, becomes an act of reading something else *in*.

Still, the distinction between text and reader could be more complicated than it first appears. One tenet of reading is that the text can invite the reader to perform a given reading, in this case what I might anachronistically call a homophobic one. In this context, Montaigne proposes the possibility of this approach as part of reading practices: 'Sur ce mesme fondement qu'avoit Heraclitus et cette sienne sentence, que toutes choses avoient en elles les visages qu'on y trouvoit' (p. 571). Plato's 'visage' could be assumed to invite a heteronormative re-reading of itself. The Platonic use of sexuality as metaphor and as beyond corporal sexuality, for instance, could invite the reader to read out male/male sexuality as it could be transformed into heterosexuality or into no clearly identifiable sexuality at all, as was often done in re-inscriptions of Ganymede and of neo-Platonism, and as the myth of the male/male androgyne was rewritten.[11] Platonic sexuality would be a kind of sexual Silenus box, where the ugly outward casing should be opened up to reveal the internal beauty beyond physical sexuality and the body. More directly, Plato himself provides fodder for this kind of reading; in the *Laws*, Plato refers to homo-

---

[11]   For the role of Ganymede in Renaissance culture, see James M. Saslow, *Ganymede in the Renaissance: Homosexuality in Art and Society* (New Haven: Yale University Press, 1986), pp. 4–7, 33–9; Leonard Barkan, *Transuming Passions: Ganymede and the Erotics of Humanism* (Stanford: Stanford University Press, 1991). On the heterosexualised male/male androgyne, see Marian Rothstein, 'Mutations of the Androgyne: Its Functions in Early Modern French Literature', *The Sixteenth Century Journal*, 34 (Summer 2003), pp. 427–30. Louis Le Roy's 1582 French translation/commentary of the *Symposium* effaces homosexuality. See Rothstein, pp. 427–8; Reeser, p. 25.

sexual sex as what was later interpreted to mean 'contrary to nature'.[12] By inviting a reading contrary to certain aspects of Platonic sexuality, the Platonic text does not convey a stable meaning to its Renaissance readers, and the 'interprete' could be assumed to be in harmony with a certain aspect of the original text. In this vein, Montaigne also cites 'les Cyrenayens', who 'tenoyent que rien n'estoit perceptible par le dehors', and believed that the only way to perceive is by something that 'nous touchoit par l'interne attouchement, comme la douleur et la volupté' (p. 571). Presumably, because Platonic sexuality does not 'touch' the interpreter, as it were, it cannot be 'perceived' and thus can only be effaced, and the interpreter would be justified in finding a heteronormative identity within the text.

When the larger context of the 'Apologie' is taken into account, however, Montaigne's discussion of these re-readings appears critical of the 'interpretes'. The verb 'coucher' refers back to Montaigne's earlier response to Sebond's detractors — the only other time he uses it in this sense in the essay — and links these readings of Plato with the central issue of the interpretation of Sebond's text, in turn linked with larger questions of reading. Those who 'disent que [Sebond's] arguments sont foibles et ineptes à verifier ce qu'il veut' are 'dangereux' (p. 425), according to Montaigne, who then offers his larger ideas on interpretation as proof of this aspect of his apology: 'On *couche* volontiers le sens des escris d'autrui à la faveur des opinions qu'on a prejugées en soi; et un atheïste se flate à ramener tous autheurs à l'atheïsme, infectant de son propre venin la matiere innocente' (p. 425, my emphasis). Though reading out Platonic sexuality and reading in atheism may be opposed in terms of ideological motivation, they are similar in their resistance to interpretive openness. On one level, it is normal to 'coucher' a text, to add one's unfortunate prejudices ('son propre venin') to 'la matiere innocente' of the original text. Re-reading the ancients from one's own perspective is a simple result of an inability or 'impuissance' to see outside one's own senses. But the references to the readers' 'puissance' in the last sentence of the Plato passage ('Tout cela vifvement et puissamment, autant qu'est puissant et vif l'esprit de l'interprete') imply their blindness to more proper ways of reading that accept mankind's inherent 'impuissance'. In the larger framework of the essay, of course, Montaigne is very concerned with the 'impuissance' of human beings' ability to know and to interpret with cer-

---

[12]   See K. J. Dover, *Greek Homosexuality*, second edition (Cambridge, MA: Harvard University Press, 1989), pp. 165–8. Ironically, Aristotle's views on this matter are less condemning. See Dover, pp. 168–70.

tainty: 'Voyons donq si l'homme a en sa puissance d'autres raisons plus fortes que celles de Sebond, voire s'il est en luy d'arriver à aucune certitude par argument et par discours' (p. 426). As human beings, we cannot see or conceive even what is represented by the word 'puissance' (p. 479). It is not so much problematic, then, that the reader applies a culturally anachronistic reading self to an ancient text: rather, the problem is presenting such a reading as 'certitude' and not acknowledging interpretive 'impuissance'.

Not surprisingly, Montaigne views religion as particularly guilty of creating 'puissant' and anachronistic readings. Because Montaigne's larger goal in this section of the 'Apologie' is to show how all arguments are weak and inept, many of Montaigne's examples dealing with re-reading the ancients are about Catholicism. In this case, however, authorial intention hardly figures in, as cultural ideology performs the reading. The reader who re-reads does so almost in spite of the self, 'needing' oracles and being unable to leave behind the 'opinion' that Homer confirms the bias of the 'interprete'.[13] The central interpretive issue is the non-dialogic approach of such readers, who do not interact with the text. In terms of the famous metaphor in 'De l'expérience', such a reader does not play 'à la paume' with the text and does not accept that '[l]a parole est moitié à celuy qui parle; moitié à celuy qui l'escoute' (p. 1066).[14] The issue, then, is not the rejection of ancient sexuality per se, but its rejection as refusal to allow the text half of the 'parole'.

Montaigne's suggestive use of 'couche' ('Chacun...le couche') also points to a horizontal/vertical problem with religious undertones. Our status as human, in the religious scepticism of the essay, implies that we are 'couchez' in front of God: 'C'est à Dieu seul de se cognoistre et d'interpreter ses ouvrages. Et le faict en nostre langue, improprement, pour s'avaller et descendre à nous, qui sommes à terre, couchez' (p. 479). God's verticality (as suggested by 's'avaller' and 'descendre') is contrasted with human beings' more modest horizontality, implying that

---

[13]   Before his discussion of reading Platonic sexuality, Montaigne states: 'Quiconque a eu besoin d'oracles et de predictions, en y a trouvé pour son faict. Un personnage sçavant, et de mes amis, c'est merveille quels rencontres et combien admirables il en faict naître en faveur de nostre religion; et ne se peut ayséement departir de cette opinion, que ce ne soit le dessein d'Homere' (pp. 570–1).

[14]   On this metaphor and its relation to reading in Montaigne, see Cathleen M. Bauschatz, 'Montaigne's Conception of Reading in the Context of Renaissance Poetics and Modern Criticism', in *The Reader in the Text: Essays on Audience and Interpretation,* edited by Susan R. Suleiman and Inge Crosman (Princeton: Princeton University Press, 1980), 264–91.

we are the ones that should be 'couchez'. To unambiguously 'coucher' Plato's writing is, on one level, to play the role of God, to 'interpreter ses ouvrages' instead of letting oneself be 'read' in His Book of Nature.

Scepticism and Sexuality

It is not simply what these 'interpretes' do that is problematic; it is also what they refuse to do. Many of the issues Montaigne has with this type of re-reading could also be considered to result from interpretive nonconformity to sceptical methods, be they Pyrrhonian or Platonic, so dear to Montaigne in this essay.[15] In what could be considered a kind of Platonic scepticism, certitude and human intellectual 'puissance' do not exist:

> où il escrit selon soy, (Platon) ne prescrit rien à certes.
>
> (p. 492)

> Croyons nous que Platon, luy qui a eu ses conceptions si celestes, et si grande accointance à la divinité, que le surnom luy en est demeuré, ait estimé que l'homme, cette pauvre creature, eut rien en luy applicable à cette incomprehensible puissance?
>
> (p. 498)

A single, sexual, 'puissant' certitude stands in marked opposition with Platonic methodology and is one more way in which the 'interpretes', by rejecting this methodology, act anachronistically.[16]

But more importantly than reading Plato non-Platonically, the re-readings in question are problematic because they refuse to 'suspend judgment' about ancient sexuality, i.e. to employ sceptical methodology as coded by Sextus Empiricus.[17] In his *Outlines of Scepticism* and in Henri

---

[15]   Various schools of ancient 'scepticism' besides those of Plato ('Academic scepticism') and Sextus ('Empirical scepticism') influenced Montaigne, especially the 'New Academy' represented by Cicero's *Academica*. On the influence of this brand of scepticism, see Elaine Limbrick, 'Was Montaigne Really a Pyrrhonian?', *Bibliothèque d'Humanisme et Renaissance*, 39 (1977), 67–80. Unable to locate a direct connection to the topic at hand, I have not taken this brand of scepticism into account here.

[16]   Whether Plato can be considered a 'sceptic', however, is difficult to say. Montaigne writes, for example: 'Au demeurant, les uns ont estimé Plato dogmatiste; les autres, dubitateur; les autres, en certaines choses l'un, et en certaines choses l'autre' (p. 489).

[17]   The issue of Montaigne's scepticism, or his 'Pyrrhonism', is complicated and the bibliography extensive. The classic source is Richard H. Popkin, *The History of Scepticism from Erasmus to Spinoza* (Berkeley: University of California Press, 1979), pp. 42–65. See also Charles Larmore, 'Scepticism', in *The Cambridge History of Sev-*

RE-READING PLATONIC SEXUALITY

Estienne's famous and influential 1562 Latin translation of the text that Montaigne almost surely worked from, a methodology is posited through the famous ten modes, by which we can arrive at suspension of judgment 'through the opposition of things'.[18] Dogmatists are the implicit group Sextus is attacking for thinking 'they have discovered the truth' (p. 3), especially of what is good or bad 'by nature'. The cultural juxtaposition relevant here corresponds to the tenth mode, 'which especially bears on ethics' (p. 37) and is composed of five separate but related elements:

> The tenth mode is the one depending on persuasions and customs and laws and beliefs in myth and dogmatic suppositions.
>
> (p. 37)
>
> Decimus vero modus ad moralia maxime spectat: quippe qui sit ex institutis & consuetudinibus & legibus, fabulosisque persuasionibus ac dogmaticis opinionibus.[19]
>
> (p. 41)

---

enteenth-Century Philosophy, volume II, edited by Daniel Garber and Michael Ayers (Cambridge: Cambridge University Press, 1998), 1145–92. For a recent critique of traditional views on Montaigne's scepticism (especially Montaigne's supposed 'crise sceptique'), see Gérard Defaux, 'Montaigne, la vie, les livres: naissance d'un philosophe sceptique et "impremedité"', *MLN*, 117, 4 (2002), 780–807. The essay builds on his earlier essay 'Montaigne chez les sceptiques: essai de mise au point', *French Forum*, 23, 2 (1998), 147–66.

[18] Sextus Empiricus, *Outlines of Scepticism*, edited by Julia Annas and Jonathan Barnes (Cambridge: Cambridge University Press, 2000), p. 11. Further English references to Sextus Empiricus are to this edition. As Montaigne is assumed to have done, I have examined Henri Estienne's 1562 Latin edition of Sextus Empiricus, *Sexti Philosophi pyrrhoniarum hypotyposeon libri III* (Geneva). All Latin references in my text are to this edition. On the influence of Estienne's translation of Sextus's text in the late Renaissance, see Luciano Floridi, *Sextus Empiricus: The Transmission and Recovery of Pyrrhonism* (Oxford: Oxford University Press, 2002), pp. 72–7. On parallels between Montaigne's 'Apologie' and Estienne's Latin introduction, see Floyd Gray, 'Montaigne's Pyrrhonism', in *O Un Amy! Essays on Montaigne in Honor of Donald M. Frame*, edited by Raymond La Charité (Lexington, KY: French Forum, 1977), 118–36.

[19] Bury translates the five categories as 'rules of conduct, habits, laws, legendary beliefs, and dogmatic conceptions'. Estienne's Latin 'institutum' would suggest something more deeply rooted than Bury's 'rules of conduct'. 'Persuasions' perhaps comes closer to the solidity of the term implied by Estienne's definition of the term as 'electio vitae'. See Sextus Empiricus, *Outlines of Pyrrhonism*, trans. R. G. Bury (London: William Heinemann, 1955), p. 85. Montaigne suggests his own approximate version of these five categories in the 'Apologie': 'inclinations naturelles', 'impulsion et contrainte des passions', 'constitutions des loix', 'coustumes', and 'tradition des arts' (p. 485).

112

These five categories are systematically juxtaposed to each other, and to themselves, in order to create permutations of every possible opposition. Thus, in his first example, he compares law and custom ('there is a law against adultery, but with us it is a custom not to have sex with a woman in public', p. 37), and he compares custom to custom ('some of the Ethiopians tattoo their babies, while we do not', p. 38). It is well known that Montaigne implicitly and explicitly employs this oppositional methodology throughout the essay and that he routinely moves toward what he calls a 'surcreance et suspension de jugement' (p. 485).[20] This sceptical approach to epistemology pertains, in particular, to questions of identity in the *Essais*, as William Hamlin has discussed within the context of ethnography and cultural identity.[21] By continually performing cross-cultural comparisons of elements of the tenth mode, one should suspend judgment about what is 'natural' and realise the inherent relativity of culture. Because Montaigne's discussion of reading inserts itself within the larger context of 'la diversité d'opinions' (p. 565), it performs an inherent juxtaposition of two cultural contexts, of 'mœurs licites' and 'illicites', in the same way that Montaigne famously compares the cultural contexts of the New World and the Old World in 'Des Cannibales'. This cross-cultural approach to ancient homosexuality is also reminiscent of the well known discussion of ancient pederasty in 'De l'amitié', which began in the a *couche* as nothing but a simple cross-cultural comparison between ancient Greece and 'our' culture: 'Et cet'autre licence Grecque est justement abhorrée par nos mœurs' (p. 185). In these two cases of comparing sexual 'mœurs' (as in Estienne's tenth mode, which concerns 'moralia'), juxtaposing customs and laws is particularly important, but all five of Sextus's categories, with the exception of myth, are somehow implicit in the comparison.

But not only is sceptical methodology present in the ethnographic juxtaposition of sexual mores: in his explication of the tenth mode, Sextus includes actual examples of 'homosexual acts'. Opposing custom to law means that 'we say that in Persia homosexual acts are customary [*consuetudinem esse uti venere mascula*], while in Rome they are forbidden by law' (p. 38). Also, he opposes law to belief in myth: 'the poets represent the gods as committing adultery and indulging in homosexual acts [*praeposteram venerem*], while with us the law forbids these things' (p. 40).

20   See, for example, Popkin, p. 50.
21   See William M. Hamlin, 'On Continuities between Skepticism and Early Ethnography; or, Montaigne's Providential Diversity', *The Sixteenth Century Journal*, 31 (Summer 2000), 361–79.

Indeed, homosexuality appears central to Sextus's attempt to suspend judgment in this mode and to show that no custom is inherently natural or virtuous. In the chapter entitled 'Is Anything by Nature Good, Bad, or Indifferent?' (III. xxiii), where Sextus's larger goal is to show that '[n]othing…is by nature good' (p. 191) in opposition to the dogmatists, homosexuality appears in the discussion of virtue and the good. Implicitly employing his tenth mode, Sextus contrasts custom and custom, and law and custom:

> Among us, for instance, homosexual sex is shameful [*turpe…mascula venere vti*] — or rather, has actually been deemed illegal — but among the Germani, they say, it is not shameful and is quite normal [*turpe non est, sed unum ex iis quae vsu recepta sunt*]. It is said that among the Thebans in the old days it was not thought shameful, and that Meriones the Cretan was so called to hint at this Cretan custom [*consuetudinis*]. And some refer to this the ardent friendship [*ardentem amorem*] of Achilles for Patroclus. What wonder, when Cynic philosophers and the followers of Zeno of Citium and Cleanthes and Chrysippus say that it is indifferent?[22]
>
> (p. 196)

Sextus's goal is to keep anything from being considered as 'good or bad by nature' so as to produce tranquillity through 'equipollence' in the mind of the true sceptic (p. 10). Only without judgment, and thus without preconceived ideas of what is natural, can inner peace be found. Interestingly, examples of cultural approaches to various forms of homosexuality play a role in that goal: since homosexuality has been considered *contra naturam* — even in Rome, where Sextus may have been writing — it occupies a natural position for the dismantling of the concept of the natural.[23] Homosexuality might also be included because

---

[22]   Estienne, p. 179. According to Bury, the 'Germani' do not refer to the 'Germans', but to 'a Persian tribe', recalling the earlier quotation about Persian homosexual acts. See Bury, p. 460, note c.

[23]   On homosexuality as *contra naturam* in ancient Rome, see Craig A. Williams, *Roman Homosexuality: Ideologies of Masculinity in Classical Antiquity* (New York: Oxford University Press, 1999), pp. 234–44. Williams comments briefly on Sextus Empiricus's remark on homosexuality as illegal in Rome: 'this cannot refer to all sexual acts between males, but must instead refer to sexual acts with freeborn males, in other words, to certain acts of *stuprum*' (p. 314). Williams points out the distinction in mainstream Roman culture between male/male act and desire, the latter not coded as unnatural (p. 242–3). On sodomy and homosexuality as *contra naturam* in ancient Greece, see Dover, pp. 165–70; in Christian theology, see Mark D. Jordan, *The Invention of Sodomy in Christian Theology* (Chicago: The University of Chicago Press, 1997), pp. 34, 94–9, 110–1, 126–7, 144–9. See also John Boswell, *Christianity, Social*

the sceptical method requires some 'extreme' examples of cultural mores in order to break down judgment. If Sextus compared different types of bread in two cultures, for example, the concept of the natural would hardly be broken down, but to compare cultural attitudes toward something like cannibalism aids in his goal. Ironically, then, cultural assumptions of homosexuality as contrary to nature and as extreme permit, or even require, the inclusion of same-sex sexuality in the process of breaking down judgment and assumptions about the natural.

Montaigne's 'interpretes' are readerly manifestations of the 'dogmagtistes' who 'sont portez, ou par la coustume de leur païs, ou par l'institution des parens, ou par rencontre...voire le plus souvent avant l'aage de discretion, à telle ou telle opinion' (p. 484). In addition, they 'n'ont pris le visage de l'asseurance que pour avoir meilleure mine' (p. 487), and they do not conform to Montaigne's discussion of the sceptics (p. 482–7), whom he considers superior to the dogmatists. Their problem is their refusal to read sceptically. To read an ancient text monologically in the Renaissance inherently evokes cultural juxtaposition: coming from one culture, readers and their mores are confronted with a writer and another culture, and are juxtaposed with them. To read out Platonic sexuality is the antithesis of this ethnographic juxtaposition as one's own cultural context is assumed to be superior, and perhaps even natural, and as judgment is not suspended. Montaigne's 'interpretes' would be sexuality dogmatists unable to leave a fixed heteronormative reading context for another sexual context. They are unable to take part in the aspect of Montaigne's scepticism that consists in, as Ann Hartle articulates it, 'the refusal to simply dismiss what is not familiar, what is not immediately recognized as being like us'.[24] The repetition of the reading act and the interpretive 'asseurance' fabricate a humanist heteronormative identity for the reader whose sexual dogmatism is not and cannot be put into question.

One of the problems, then, with these dogmatic 'interpretes' is their assurance of a 'naturelle puissance' in their hermeneutics. For Montaigne, no given thing in the world is believed 'par les hommes d'un consentement universel' and 'ce, qu'il ne se void aucune proposition qui ne soit

Tolerance, and Homosexuality (Chicago: The University of Chicago Press, 1980), pp. 11–15, 159–61, 201–2, 303–32.
[24] See Ann Hartle, 'Montaigne's Scepticism', *Montaigne Studies*, 12 (2000), p. 86. The context of the discussion of Plato in the essay (pp. 567–9) implies that, for Montaigne, sexuality in a larger sense is closely related to this type of cultural relativity and 'ethnography' (as it is in Sextus).

RE-READING PLATONIC SEXUALITY

debatue et controverse entre nous, ou qui ne le puisse estre, montre bien que nostre jugement naturel ne saisit pas bien clairement ce qu'il saisit' (p. 545). Particularly in the 'Apologie', Montaigne sees that he apprehends 'par quelque autre moyen que par une *naturelle puissance* qui soit en moy et en tous les hommes' (p. 545, my emphasis). There is also nothing 'natural' about reading techniques, which are always 'impuissant' because they are culturally coded and not trans-cultural or trans-historical. For Montaigne, '[i]l est croyable qu'il y a des loix naturelles, comme il se voit ès autres creatures; mais en nous elles sont perdues' (p. 564), and as a result, the reading act is never a natural 'law', nor are the heteronormative 'mœurs' that inform them. Consequently, monologic reading becomes coded as unnatural act, taking the place of the traditional association of homosexual acts as *contra naturam*.

In the 'Apologie', the non-naturalness of non-interactive re-reading is implied by images related to 'giving birth' to texts.[25] For Montaigne, nature and generation are closely related ('[l]a generation est la principale des actions naturelles', p. 449), but textual generation is impossible without 'la grace de Dieu' (p. 424): 'nos imaginations et discours...ont quelque corps, mais c'est une masse informe, sans façon et sans jour, si la foy et grace de Dieu n'y sont joinctes' (p. 425). Though one may be interpreting along with a Christian 'cours des choses', the reader cannot create a 'discours humain' or an interpretation capable of 'life' all alone. As the mother provided only the matter to the child, the 'interprete' cannot conceive a child without God's textual paternity. In fact, he can only infect the innocent matter with his 'venin' and as a mere human, can only create 'matiere lourde et sterile' (p. 424). The interpreter's infertile reading can only 'give birth' to falsity: 'En la parole la plus nette, pure et parfaicte qui puisse estre, combien de faucité et de mensonge a lon fait naistre?' (p. 569). Giving birth — the natural act par excellence — is dissociated from the act of reading out, and consequently attempts to re-read Plato are unable to establish naturalness by reading out the unnaturalness of same-sex sexuality. From this perspective, these readers do not follow Christian scepticism, which requires that because of the difficulty of knowing, we turn ourselves over to God's 'Book of Nature' and let Him play the role of 'natural' interpreter who reveals his 'readings' when he pleases. In His

---

[25] On this child/text metaphor in a larger sense, see Richard L. Regosin, *Montaigne's Unruly Brood: Textual Engendering and the Challenge to Paternal Authority* (Berkeley: University of California Press, 1996).

Book, unlike in theirs, the diversity of customs should not be read out since they stand as proof of God's presence.[26] Ironically, it is Socrates, in the famous 'sage homme' metaphor, who is linked with birthing in the essay. Like midwives who 'en prenant ce mestier de faire engendrer les autres, quittent le mestier d'engendrer', Socrates 'par le tiltre de sage homme que les dieux lui ont deferé, s'est aussi desfaict, en son amour virile et mentale, de la faculté d'enfanter' (p. 489). By giving up bearing children, Socrates becomes linked with the process of birthing, and by extension with nature.[27] For though he may give up physical birth, he is still the ultimate parent of thought because he realises and accepts that he knows nothing.[28] But this link to birth is partially because he gives it up 'en son amour virile'. His perceived homosexuality becomes one reason for his tie to the birthing process, and Socratic sexuality, far from 'contra naturam', is one reason that he alone gives true birth. Playing with the metaphor, in which the most natural birth is non-physical, Montaigne also mentions in the same passage that ten philosophical sects 'were born' ('dix sectes diverses nasquirent') from Plato (p. 489). The Academy's metaphorical fertility is opposed to the interpreters' sterility because the latter refuse to 'not know' as they read the ancients.

Montaigne himself, unlike the 'interpretes', follows many of the traits of the ideal sceptic in his writing. If Sextus's goal is to de-naturalise, to suspend judgment, and to show that there is no good or bad, Montaigne at least partially suspends judgment about homosexuality. In his study of homosexuality in the *Essais*, William Beck hypothesises that Montaigne's additions, especially to 'De l'amitié', reveal a more tolerant attitude toward homosexuality than those made in the first *couche*.[29] Indeed, the fa-

---

[26] On cultural diversity and the Book of Nature, see Hamlin, p. 376.
[27] On Socrates as linked to nature within the context of interpretation, see Richard L. Regosin, 'The Boundaries of Interpretation: Self, Text, Contexts in Montaigne's *Essays*', in *Renaissance Re-readings: Intertext and Context*, edited by Maryanne Cline Horowitz et al. (Urbana: University of Illinois Press, 1988), 18–32.
[28] See Regosin, *Montaigne's Unruly Brood,* pp. 207–10. Regosin is interested in the relation between gender and Montaigne's remarks on Socrates.
[29] William J. Beck, 'The Obscure Montaigne: The Quotation, the Addition, and the Footnote', *College Language Association Journal*, 34 (1990), 228–52. Beck also points out that 'the additions made in the 1588 text and in the Bordeaux copy to his original text are manifestly more personal, bolder, and more revelatory of his thoughts and feelings' (p. 232). Beck notes the possibility that Montaigne's travels to Rome may have changed his attitude toward contemporary homosexuality (pp. 248–9). On this passage in the 'Apologie' and its relation to irony in the 'Apologie', see Daniel

mous passage from 'De l'amitié' on 'licence grecque', part of the c *couche*, spends much of its time presenting the positive aspects of Greek sexuality. This may very well be true, and the discussion from the 'Apologie' (also in the c *couche*) would correspond to a growing tolerance for Greek pederasty in a time when Montaigne was reading more Plato. It would also explain Montaigne's seeming neutrality here with respect to sexuality: his attitude could imply some kind of sceptical tranquillity vis-à-vis ancient sexuality, as his Pyrrhonian scepticism and his reading of Plato converge.[30]

Yet I think it would be difficult to argue that Montaigne has truly suspended judgment, based on the evidence here and the implications of sceptical methodology. Other nearby examples of the cultural relativity of sexual customs, such as brothels (p. 568) and Diogenes' public masturbation (p. 569), are described in an explicitly non-judgmental light. Despite the well known scepticism of the essay, critics have remarked that Montaigne does not systematically take sceptical methodology to its full conclusion.[31] There is no guarantee, quite simply, that the sceptical method leads to its desired result, and even the most die-hard Pyrrhonian scepticist in the end should live within the day-to-day confines of one's own laws and culture, a position that Montaigne affirms. If Montaigne claims to assume 'le choix d'autry' (p. 553) and to remain 'en l'assiette où Dieu m'a mis' (p. 553),[32] he presumably also takes on at least some of the

---

Ménager, 'L'Ironie dans l'*Apologie*', in *Montaigne*: Apologie de Raimond Sebond, *De la* Theologia *à la* Théologie, edited by Claude Blum (Paris: Champion, 1990), 247–60. Ménager sees this passage as proof of Montaigne's irony. For him, 'Montaigne admire et critique la lecture qu'il rapporte' (p. 255).

[30] On the role of the brands of scepticism that influenced Montaigne in his later life, see Limbrick, who argues that 'at the end of his life Montaigne distinctly favoured and adhered to Socratic scepticism' (pp. 68–9) and remarks that after 1580 there is 'no trace of any borrowing from Sextus Empiricus in the *Essais*' (p. 69). Frederick Kellermann discusses Montaigne's reading of Plato late in his life and 'his growing affection for Socrates between 1580 and 1588' (p. 308). See 'Montaigne, Reader of Plato', *Comparative Literature*, 8, 4 (Autumn 1956), 307–22. Villey writes that 'c'est surtout après 1588 que Montaigne a lu Platon' (194). See also Elaine Limbrick, 'Montaigne and Socrates', *Renaissance and Reformation*, 9, 2 (1973), 46–57. For a statistical approach to the presence of Plato in the *Essais*, see Edouard Simon, 'Montaigne et Platon', *Bulletin de la Société des Amis de Montaigne*, 35–36 (Jan.–June 1994), 97–104. Of all the essays, Plato is the most cited and borrowed from in the 'Apologie' (Simon, p. 102).

[31] See Hamlin, p. 374 and his note 39 for references.

[32] For a similar idea, see also p. 562. On this sceptical move, see Popkin, pp. 49–50.

'mœurs' that abhor homosexuality (as he explicitly does in 'De l'amitié'). And despite his interrogation of customs, Montaigne at times leaves himself a judgmental out, as if to suspend judgment systematically would be anti-sceptical and imply some kind of doctrinal truth. If 'les diverses mœurs et fantasies aux miennes ne me desplaisent pas tant comme elles m'instruisent' (p. 496), it is possible that some 'mœurs' might still 'displease' him, even as they instruct him.

In addition, the very methodology that Montaigne employs maintains these 'mœurs' as distant. Focusing on the reading act in the first place, and distinguishing between past and present meanings, has the effect of keeping the acts in the classical world. With the sexual act located well in the past, it cannot become any kind of transhistorical and/or transcultural identity. Homosexuality might fit the definition of what Montaigne calls an extreme cultural 'usage' that can be found somewhere: 'il n'est rien…si extreme qui ne se trouve receu par l'usage de quelque nation', including 'licence à toutes sortes de voluptez' (p. 564). But these particular 'usages' are elsewhere in time or space. If he were to collect numerous examples of such 'usages' from many 'nations', past and present, east and west, 'our' culture and others, homosexuality might cease to be a simple 'usage' and appear stable and coherent. In addition, Montaigne does not evoke a form of homosexual 'persuasion' in his juxtapositions nor does he allow for what he calls 'inclinations naturelles', focusing only on 'constitutions des loix et des coustumes' and 'la tradition des arts' (p. 485). The extremity, inextricably linked with foreign culture, is always elsewhere as our 'mœurs' serve only as points of contrast to the sexual foreignness and as aspects of homosexuality in the essayist's own culture (such as those related to Henri III) are absent from direct juxtaposition.

In so doing, Montaigne follows Sextus, whose remarks on homosexuality could be considered to betray a similar hidden intolerance. He, too, selects examples of homosexuality as cultural 'custom' or 'usage' ('consuetudo' (p. 41)), which he defines as 'a common acceptance by a number of people of a certain way of acting, transgressors of which are not necessarily punished' (p. 37). All of Sextus' examples distance homosexuality, placing them far away in time and/or space or in the mythological realm. This approach follows his more general methodology, in which examples should be 'furthest removed from the usage of life'.[33] The only

---

[33]   Bury, p. 315. As the sceptic should take such examples for philosophical use, he should on the other hand live within his cultural context: 'it is, I think, sufficient to conduct one's life empirically and undogmatically in accordance with the rules and beliefs that are commonly accepted' (Bury, p. 315).

relation between homosexuality and his culture, his 'usage of life', is the illegality or shamefulness of sodomy 'amongst us'.[34] Homosexuality is never linked to the category of juxtaposition that Sextus reserves for what comes closest to what we might call identity: 'persuasion' — what Estienne translates as 'institutum' (p. 41) — does not figure in, since as 'a choice of life [*electio vitae*] or of a way of acting practised by one person or by many' (p. 37), it would imply a solidity for same-sex sexuality. Indeed, the word choice related to sexuality refers to male/male sexuality as only sexual, not as identity based: 'homosexual acts' (p. 38) ['venere mascula' (p. 42) and 'praeposteram venerem' (p. 43)], or 'homosexual sex' (p. 196) ['mascula venere' (p. 179)]. Homosexuality exists, then, only as isolated, cultural coding: a priori, sceptical methodology cannot allow it to exist beyond separate and disparate instances, nor can it permit connections between various manifestations of homosexuality (e.g. custom with persuasion). For Sextus — or Montaigne — to do so would gesture toward a sense of same-sex universality and toward the implication that homosexual groupings are approaching the natural. Since the method consists of comparing good to bad, one cultural manifestation of sexuality to its legal or cultural interdiction, same-sex sexuality can only remain fragmented and thus not natural, even as it is shown to be not unnatural.

'Putting Plato to Bed': Textual/Sexual Dialogue

Montaigne may not push his scepticism to the limit in the area of sexuality, but he does create another tool to denaturalise the interpreter's hermeneutic normativity. Because Montaigne's focus here is reading and not sexuality, a sceptically inflected juxtaposition between two cultural contexts cannot remain a simple binary opposition since for the essayist, ancient text and reader interact in a more dynamic way than in the methodology outlined in Sextus. Renaissance reader and ancient context are not simply compared to each other in a discrete, ethnographic way. As a result, Montaigne moves beyond the classical sceptical framework and displays the failure of monologic readings of Platonic sexuality. His description of doing what I will call 'putting Plato to bed' implies that this type of anachronistic interpretation opens up a liminal space where re-reading becomes a site of struggle, and where the reading act does not simply reaffirm a heteronormative hermeneutic but destabilises it, implying the im-

---

[34]   For Bury, 'amongst us' 'means 'amongst the Greeks' and refers in special to the laws or customs of Athens' (p. 460, note b).

possibility of simply constituting identity through the reading act.[35] In this liminal space, a binary opposition between reader and textual meaning gives way to an interest in the relation between the two, as evidenced by the suggestive verbs denoting an interpretive relationship ('Chacun...le couche', 'On le promeine et l'insere', 'le differente lon', 'On faict desad-voüer'). In this way, Montaigne moves away from the opposition technique to create a permeable membrane between ancient sexual custom and Renaissance reading custom, where each custom influences the other. Despite attempts to create a normative hermeneutic, this interpretive identity is undermined by the very thing meant to construct it. In this revised reading act, the writer's subjectivity cannot ultimately be effaced, cannot be made to 'walk and talk', and the reader's normativity cannot simply be affirmed. The approach to reading in this context corresponds to Montaigne's larger ideas on the subject, as Richard Regosin explains in his study of reading: 'If the *Essais* both affirm and undermine the status of the writer as subject, they also affirm and undermine the status of the reader as subject.'[36] Simply put, the subject of Platonic homosexuality cannot be read out as the status of the subjectivity of the reader is undermined. Montaigne reinscribes Platonic sexuality in the 'esprit de l'interprete', undermining its attempts to distance itself from the Platonic 'esprit'. The attempt to read out fails, as it turns into a reading in, not of heteronormativity but of the repressed or censured object.

The ambiguity of the language in Montaigne's discussion implies that text and reader exist together in a grey area. The treatment of reading practices, the use of 'costé' ('Chacun...le couche du costé qu'il le veut') refers to the reading of a text neither 'selon' nor 'au contraire de la [forme]' of an author (p. 570), suggesting a middle space created by the interpretive process. In this space, the choice of 'coucher' gestures to the literal sense of the verb: the reader — or the culture that reads — desires to transform Platonic sexuality to contemporary mores ('le couche du

---

[35]   Iser defines a 'liminal space' of interpretation that 'demarcates both the subject matter and the register from one another'. For Iser, this space 'does not belong to either but is opened up by interpretation itself'. See Wolfgang Iser, *The Range of Interpretation* (New York: Columbia University Press, 2000), p. 6. Relations between reader response theory and Montaigne have been treated in Bauschatz; Hope H. Glidden, 'Recouping the Text: The Theory and Practice of Reading', *L'Esprit Createur*, 21 (Summer 1981), 25–36; Richard L. Regosin, 'Conceptions of the Text and the Generation(s) of Meaning: Montaigne's *Essais* and the Place(s) of the Reader', *Journal of Medieval and Renaissance Studies*, 15 (Spring 1985), 101–14. I am particularly indebted to Regosin's study here.

[36]   Regosin, 'Conceptions of the Text', p. 113.

costé qu'il le veut') or chooses to 'put him to bed' with a woman or by himself, in short to transform same-sex sexuality. But even so, sexuality reasserts itself like a repressed 'memory' in Montaigne's description, as the language of interpretation itself evokes sexuality.

Montaigne's use of 'costé' may also refer to the touchy issue of seating positions at the end of the *Symposium* (222C–223C).[37] Having repeatedly attempted to seduce Socrates, Alcibiades again attempts seduction, in part by placing himself between Socrates and the younger and more beautiful Agathon, in order to divide the two of them. Socrates and Agathon resist as the latter tells the former: 'I will come and sit by your side' (p. 241). Socrates will not let the seduction take place, in part so that he can praise Agathon, the neighbour sitting on his right side. Agathon arises to take his place on Socrates' right side to represent his most favoured male status. Putting Socrates to bed 'du costé qu'il le veut' would also be a question of whether Socrates is positioned next to Agathon, with whom there is no possibility of sexual relations, or next to Alcibiades with whom at least such a possibility exists, and thus a question of whether homoeroticism is represented corporally. That the seduction scene from the *Symposium* was a problem for Ficino, who simply cut it from his *Commentary on Plato's* Symposium *on Love*, would help explain why Montaigne gestures toward the issue.[38]

The opening sentence of Montaigne's discussion ('Voyez demener et agiter Platon') likewise turns these readers back on themselves. It is unclear whether the sentence refers to a Plato before or after interpretation takes place. On the one hand, especially when the sense of 'demener' as trembling from love is taken into account,[39] this description of the shaking

---

[37] See Plato, *Symposium*, trans. W. R. M. Lamb (Cambridge: Harvard University Press, 1925), pp. 240–4.

[38] Ficino cuts the seduction scene and adds a section that praises Socrates as teacher. On these revisions to the original text, see Marsilio Ficino, *Commentary on Plato's* Symposium *on Love*, edited by Sears Jayne (Woodstock: Spring Publications, 1985), p. 9. However, as Jayne points out, this last section of the *Symposium* (215B–223D) was 'notorious (as one of the bawdy passages of Greek literature) throughout the Middle Ages, even when the text of the dialogue itself was not known' (p. 9). Montaigne's use of 'costé' may also be a reference to the sexual connotation of the Latin equivalent *latus*. Adams writes that the word 'is often vaguely suggestive of the male genitalia'. See J. N. Adams, *The Latin Sexual Vocabulary* (Baltimore: The Johns Hopkins University Press, 1982), p. 49.

[39] Baïf, for instance, uses the verb to talk about the tremblings of love: 'Plaindre donc je me doy / D'Amour, qui vous et moy si fierement demeine.' Cited in Huguet, volume II, p. 782.

Plato refers to eroticism and corresponds to other descriptions of the erotic excesses of the Academy in the *Essais*. The 'reproche de Decaear-chus à Platon mesme', for example, reveals 'combien la plus saine phi-losophie souffre de licences esloignées de l'usage commun et excessives' (p. 567). And if '[t]out le mouvement du monde se resoult et rend à cet accouplage' (p. 835), even Plato is subject to this 'accouplage'. Socrates gives 'preceptes' in order to 'instruire les courtisanes', and Montaigne asks rhetorically: 'Que veulent pretendre les descriptions si estendues et vives en Platon, des amours de son temps plus hardies' (p. 835). On the other hand, however, 'Voyez demener et agiter Platon' suggests the act of interpretation. Previously, Montaigne had referred to the interpretive act as one of shaking: 'Nombre d'esprits, le [the author] belutans et secouans, en exprimeront quantité de formes' (p. 570). In this scenario, when the critic moves Plato around by re-reading him and by making him 'speak' — as in the secondary sense of 'demener' — his or her own interpretive 'agitations' are channelled into the act of interpretation.

This indeterminacy destabilises the separation between interpretation and sexuality, as 'les descriptions si estendues et vives' that the 'inter-prete' is attempting to read out create a kind of interpretive *enargeia* that feeds off the sexual energy of the original text and, unable to be repressed, is transferred not into a new text, but into 'l'esprit de l'interprete'.[40] The visual language that Montaigne employs (e.g. 'coucher', 'promeine', 'vivement') suggests that the humanist and rhetorical goal of finding transhistorical aspects of an ancient text (here, Platonic sexuality) is at least partially successful since the language evokes an image of intensity that transcends the mere meaning of the words. In short, the repressed work takes on an energy of its own, an energy transferred metonymically into the vigour of the reader: 'Tout cela vifvement et puissamment, autant qu'est puissant et vif l'esprit de l'interprete' (p. 571). That the critic doth protest too much implies an undermining excess in the re-reading process, an excess no longer about Plato, but about the identity of the interpreter who cannot maintain sexual juxtaposition as two discrete categories. In-stead of producing a stable re-reading of an ancient text, the reader be-comes the text to be read, and his or her identity as reader opens to being read and thus undermined, in the same way as such readers attempt to un-

---

[40]   On *enargeia* in Montaigne, see Gerard Paul Sharpling, 'Towards a Rhetoric of Experience: The Role of *Enargeia* in the *Essays* of Montaigne', *Rhetorica*, 20 (Spring 2002), 173–92. On the 'translative energies of the word', see Glyn P. Norton, *The Ide-ology and Language of Translation in Renaissance France and their Humanist Ante-cedents* (Geneva: Droz, 1984), esp. 259–322.

dermine the original text. In the end, it is Montaigne that does the 'couching', by relying on two senses of the word, as the attempts of the interpreter to distance Plato are re-read from the essayist's point of view. The interpreter's vivacity and 'puissance' result in part from a lack of sceptical methodology in reading. In his chapter 'What is the Aim of Scepticism?' (I. xii), Sextus Empiricus writes:

> Those who hold the opinion that things are good or bad by nature are perpetually troubled....But those who make no determination about what is good and bad by nature neither avoid nor pursue anything with intensity; and hence they are tranquil.
>
> (p. 10)

Or, as Montaigne explains in similar terms in the 'Apologie':

> cette assiette de leur jugement, droicte et inflexible, recevant tous objets sans application et consentement, les achemine à leur Ataraxie, qui est une condition de vie paisible, rassise, exempte des agitations que nous recevons par l'impression de l'opinion et science que nous pensons avoir des choses.
>
> (p. 483)

Maintaining 'opinion' leads to, among other things, 'les desirs immoderez' and 'la desobeissance' (p. 483). In this case, the interpreter internally and unwillingly 'disobeys' the reading self. The 'interprete' moves and shakes precisely because of an impossibility of moving out of a cultural context in which withholding judgment about something considered 'bad by nature' does not take place.

Though Montaigne does not elaborate on this force of mind, the description of interpretation, where the end result is different from the stated intent, functions similarly to other processes that create something other than what they begin with, as in the areas of sexuality, censorship, religion, and memory. In 'Sur des vers de Virgile' (III. 5), for instance, Montaigne presents his theory of 'l'action genitale': 'moins nous en exhalons en parole, d'autant nous avons loy d'en grossir la pensée', or '[n]'en va-il pas comme en matiere de livres, qui se rendent d'autant plus venaux et publiques de ce qu'ils sont supprimez?' (p. 825). Montaigne explains in the 'Apologie' that Catholicism has a similar effect as repression and censorship; it attempts to hide vice, but its actual effect is quite the opposite: 'Nostre religion est faicte pour extirper les vices; elle les couvre, les nourrit, les incite' (p. 421). And in his discussion of the functioning of memory as selective, 'la memoire nous represente non pas ce que nous choisissons, mais ce qui luy plaist. Voire il n'est rien qui imprime si vivement

quelque chose en nostre souvenance que le desir de l'oublier' (p. 474).
Like memory, religiously inflected re-reading aims to 'forget' 'les mœurs
licites' of sexuality, but in the end it has the opposite effect. This notion of
an active forgetting is particularly suited to this discussion, especially
given the sense of 'coucher' as 'to commit to memory'. But censorship,
sexuality, religion, and memory all merge in the concept of Platonic sexuality as the text comes alive and reacts to the reading act, in a model of
reading in which reading out sexuality produces a reverse mechanism that
resembles sexuality itself in its functioning.

I might also say that Montaigne imposes his own brand of scepticism
on the familiar, following his often repeated model in which the strange
becomes part of the familiar, or the far-away becomes not so far after
all.[41] In this approach, the classical issue of suspending judgment is
peripheral to that of creating visibility. The complicated issue of how the
essayist judges or does not judge Platonic sexuality loses its importance to
the fact that Montaigne's scepticism consists of not letting something
seemingly strange or foreign, or 'against nature', be effaced as he forces it
to be taken into account against the will of those who resist doing so.

Still, the strange remains the minority position as the ancient text can
only become present through the concept of reading and can only disrupt
the familiar. In this sense, Montaigne relies on early modern homosexuality's disruptiveness in order to make his point about reading, and explains
why homosexuality appears within the context of reading. What Jonathan
Goldberg calls the 'deontologizing effect' of sodomy pertains here to the
disruption of reading ontologically, of reading as if the ancients were like
the moderns.[42] The disruptive potential of reading ontologically is realised
in the interpreter, but it should not be viewed as disruption *tout court*. For
the interpreting act and Platonic sexuality overlap, as Plato and the re-
reader have something in common and as the failed re-reading act comes
to resemble, at least partially, the repressed sexual act. The homosexuality
in Plato dove-tails, for example, remarkably well with the rhetoric of early
modern male friendship (including Montaigne's), and can be difficult to
extricate from it. As Mario Digangi writes, 'homoerotic practices in the
Renaissance were not always considered "sexual deviance", but could be
aspects of the most "straight" social relations'.[43] In the end, then, the act

---

[41] For a full reading of this model of scepticism, see Hartle, 'Montaigne's Scepticism'.
[42] Goldberg, p. 20.
[43] *Homosexuality in Early Modern Drama* (Cambridge: Cambridge University
Press, 1997), p. 13.

of reading Plato locates its reader both inside and outside heteronormativity, simultaneously disrupted and normative, somewhere between the unstable identities of heteronormativity and non-heteronormativity.

6

Betwixt and Between:
Hermaphroditism and Masculinity

John O'Brien

Passing through Vitry-le-François in September of 1580, Montaigne saw a strange sight:

> ... je peuz voir un homme que l'Evesque de Soissons avoit nommé Germain en confirmation, lequel tous les habitans de là ont cogneu et veu fille, jusques à l'aage de vingt deux ans, nommée Marie. Il estoit à cett'heure-là fort barbu, et vieil, et point marié. Faisant, dict-il, quelque effort en sautant, ses membres virils se produisirent: et est encore en usage, entre les filles de là, une chanson, par laquelle elles s'entradvertissent de ne faire point de grandes enjambées, de peur de devenir garçons, comme Marie Germain.[1]

In the version of the story that appears in book I of the *Essais*, Montaigne is an eyewitness. In the version that appears in the *Journal de voyage*, he is not: Marie Germain is away in the village when Montaigne visits. But the differences these two seemingly insignificant points of detail articulate have extensive implications for the views that Montaigne is presenting of this phenomenon. Indeed, in 'De la force de l'imagination', the essayist glosses the incident in this way:

> Ce n'est pas tant de merveille, que cette sorte d'accident se rencontre frequent: car si l'imagination peut en telles choses, elle est si continuellement et si vigoureusement attachée à ce subject, que, pour n'avoir si souvent à rechoir en mesme pensée et aspreté de desir, elle a meilleur compte d'incorporer, une fois pour toutes, cette virile partie aux filles.[2]

---

[1] *Les Essais de Michel de Montaigne*, ed. Pierre Villey and V.-L. Saulnier (Paris: Presses Universitaires de France, 1965), I. 21, p. 99. For this incident, see Patricia Parker, 'Gender Ideology, Gender Change: The Case of Marie Germain', *Critical Inquiry* 19 (1993), 337–64.
[2] I. 21, p. 99.

The point is twofold: a comment on the contemporary medical debate concerning the doubleness of sexuality within the human being, each gender vying for prominence,[3] and a comment on the role of the imagination in fabricating or fantasising male sexual organs in girls.[4] The true hermaphrodite might be less of a freak phenomenon than is commonly thought, Montaigne implies; in which case, the miraculous or prodigious attributes that are predicated of it are themselves the effect of the imagination:

> Il est vray semblable que le principal credit des miracles, des visions, des enchantemens et de tels effects extraordinaires, vienne de la puissance de l'imagination agissant principalement contre les ames du vulgaire, plus molles. On leur a si fort saisi la creance, qu'ils pensent voir ce qu'ils ne voyent pas.[5]

The ordinary observer sees what is not there to be seen; the essayist has seen Marie Germain — an old man with a bushy beard — but does not guarantee what he has not seen for himself, Marie Germain's change of gender.

The entry in the *Journal de voyage* looks at this phenomenon from a different angle. The story of Marie Germain is the last of three, all of which Montaigne knows only by report, and of these the second is probably the most important. It is the story of a hanging, the hanging of a certain Mary, one of a group of seven or eight girls who have engaged in cross-dressing and decide to pass themselves off as male. Mary had fallen in love with a local girl from Vitry and had been condemned to death 'pour des inventions illicites à supplir au defaut de son sexe'.[6] Floyd Gray may well be right in interpreting this key phrase as a reference to prosthetic sexual devices.[7] By contrast with the natural if hidden genitalia of Marie Germain, Mary has supplied what Nature has not provided; he is

---

[3]   Stephen Greenblatt, 'Friction and Fiction', in *Shakespearean Negotiations: The Circulation of Social Energy in Renaissance England* (Oxford: Clarendon Press, 1992), pp. 78–9; Thomas Laqueur, *Making Sex: Body and Gender from the Greeks to Freud* (Cambridge, MA: Harvard University Press, 1990), pp. 126–8.

[4]   On the disruptive, transformative power of the imagination, see John O'Brien, 'Reasoning with the Senses: The Humanist Imagination', *South Central Review*, 10/2 (1993), pp. 3–19, esp. pp. 11–13.

[5]   Montaigne, *Essais*, I. 21, p. 99.

[6]   Michel de Montaigne, *Journal du voyage de Michel de Montaigne en Italie, Par la Suisse & l'Allemagne, en 1580 & 1581* (Rome and Paris: Le Jay, 1774), p. 7.

[7]   Floyd Gray, *Gender, Rhetoric and Print Culture in French Renaissance Writing* (Cambridge: Cambridge University Press, 2000), p. 143.

a *contrefaçon*, a copy that is a counterfeit. For that counterfeiting, an out-
rage against Nature, he must be destroyed.

However, it is not just to defend a principle of moral philosophy, important though that is, that Mary must die and conversely that Marie Germain is allowed to live. The larger context of these stories exhibits a net-
work of half-hidden discourses and authorities that are implicated in these
cases of *merveilleux*. The most visible is medical opinion. The version of
the anecdote about Marie Germain given in the *Journal de voyage* expressly refers to the entry on this matter in Ambroise Paré's *Des monstres
et prodiges*.[8] At a slightly later date, the physician Jacques Duval, who
similarly refers to Paré's account of the Marie Germain case, was engaged
to examine another hermaphrodite, Marin le Marcis, and left a detailed
discussion of it in his book on the topic.[9] Beyond medical opinion and the
empirical phenomena it set itself to investigate and assess, religious sanc-
tion also came into play. In Montaigne's essay I. 21, it is the bishop of
Soissons who gives Germain his name at confirmation; in the *Journal de
voyage*, it is the Cardinal de Lenoncourt, as bishop of Chalons, who gives
Germain this name once his sexual identity has been revealed.[10] In one
case, ecclesiastical authority pre-empts the discovery; in the other, it licences it.

A significant detail in the story of Marie Germain reveals one probable reason for his survival: he had never married. In other instances of
gender change, the attempt by the person concerned to live as male with
female or to marry her directly triggers the intervention of the civil
authorities and the legal system. Jones and Stallybrass justifiably emphasise that it is better to start from legal rather than medical definitions of

---

[8]   Montaigne, *Journal de voyage*, p. 7; Ambroise Paré, *Des monstres et prodiges*,
ed. Jean Céard (Geneva: Droz, 1971), pp. 29–30.
[9]   Jacques Duval, *Des hermaphrodits, accouchemens des femmes, et traitement qui
est requis pour les releuer en santé, & bien éleuer leurs enfans* (Rouen: Geuffroy,
1612); Greenblatt, 'Friction and Fiction', pp. 73–86, contested by Ruth Gilbert, *Early
Modern Hermaphrodites: Sex and Other Stories* (Basingstoke: Palgrave, 2002),
pp. 44–6. For excellent surveys of the topic, see Lorraine Daston and Katherine Park,
'Hermaphrodites in Renaissance France', *Critical Matrix*, 1/5 (1985), 1–19, and 'The
Hermaphrodite and the Order of Nature: Sexual Ambiguity in Early Modern France',
in *Premodern Sexualities*, ed. Louise Fradenburg and Carla Freccero (New York and
London: Routledge, 1996), pp. 117–36. For a recent study of Duval, see Joseph Harris,
'"La force du tact": Representing the Taboo Body in Jacques Duval's *Traité des
hermaphrodits (1612)*', *French Studies*, 57/2 (2003), pp. 311–22.
[10]   Montaigne, *Essais*, I. 21, p. 99 and *Journal de voyage*, p. 7.

the early-modern hermaphrodite for an understanding of gender.[11] Jacques Duval had indeed been specifically commissioned by the authorities in Rouen to conduct a physical examination of Marin le Marcis as a result of the trial proceedings and was instrumental in securing Le Marcis's acquittal from a death sentence, although the terms of the acquittal were hardly lenient: Le Marcis was ordered to wear women's clothes until the age of 25 and forbidden to live with either sex during that time.[12] The story of Mary from the *Journal de voyage* usefully confirms and enhances these lessons: his prosthetic addition to his body at once contravenes Nature's work in distinguishing between the sexes and mocks Nature's work in supplying the correct tools for procreation. These natural laws in turn double up as legal criteria, providing for the individuation of the sexes and for their 'proper' hierarchy and function, as well as for securing property and inheritance rights (to which hermaphrodites were equally entitled in sixteenth- and seventeenth-century law). Gender crossing is one thing; feigning marriage is another, inasmuch as it apes and thereby threatens the very basis of legal and social regulation. As Ruth Gilbert puts it, it is not so much the embodiment of hermaphroditism that causes the problem, as its enactment.[13] Mary is thus not just a counterfeit in law and Nature. He is an imposter. As such, he is not essentially different from that Renaissance imposter *par excellence*, Arnaud du Tilh. It seems no coincidence that Du Verdier, who gives a lengthy account of Arnaud's imposture in his *Diverses Leçons*, directly precedes it with a parallel account of an 'estrange transformation d'vne fille en masle' in contemporary Portugal,[14] before stipulating the grounds on which Arnaud was convicted: 'imposture' and 'fausseté' are the first two, 'suposition de nom & de personne' another, 'sacrilege' against the sanctity of marriage another.[15] In Duval's account, Le Marcis has likewise 'vsurpé le nom...d'homme' and tried to cover his sin 'du manteau du sacré mariage: en quoy elle à violé nature,

[11] Ann Rosalind Jones and Peter Stallybrass, 'Fetishizing Gender: Constructing the Hermaphrodite in Renaissance Europe', in *Body Guards: The Cultural Politics of Gender Ambiguity*, ed. Julia Epstein and Kristina Straub (New York and London: Routledge, 1991), p. 88.
[12] Duval, *Des hermaphrodits*, p. 441; Greenblatt, 'Friction and Fiction', p. 74, translates 'habiter avec' as 'to have sexual relations with', while Daston and Park, art. cit., p. 124, translate: 'to use neither set of genitals for sex'. These are both alternative possibilities.
[13] Gilbert, *Early Modern Hermaphrodites*, p. 26.
[14] Antoine Du Verdier, *Les Diverses Leçons d'Antoine du Verdier S. de Vaupriuaz*, 2 vols (Lyon: Soubron, 1592), I. 313–15.
[15] Du Verdier, *Diverses Leçons*, p. 317.

offensé l'honnesteté publique, deceu l'Eglise, prophané ses saincts sacrements'.[16] In all instances analysed so far, a wondrous and horrifying transformation occurs: Arnaud transmutates into Martin Guerre through impersonation;[17] Mary, Marin, and Marie Germain transmutate into another version of themselves and, at least in the case of Mary and Marin Le Marcis, hope to pass off before the law, as they have before Nature, the impersonations wrought by art.

Gender-switching, hermaphroditic enactment, impostures, impersonations: late Renaissance popular and semi-popular literature is full of such stories that aroused titillated fascination in an avid public. The existence and widespread distribution of such tales point to an uncomfortable fact: the attempt by the authorities to deal with marginal sexualities and to keep them marginal is outstripped by the sheer volume of popular interest they sustain, accompanied by an uneasy sense that such sexualities overwhelm the neat categorisation official discourse and legal process endeavour jointly to impose upon them.[18] Yet the problem is not restricted to one type of discursive, para-literary publication in the medical and legal spheres. For the simple fact of late French Renaissance culture is that the hermaphroditic *prodigieux* is perceived to be located in the figure of the king; it is held to be a component feature of the character of the monarch and in a very particular sense of the institution of monarchy. In this central section of my paper, I shall seek not to come to a truth about the personality of Henri III, but to show how it is caught up in the systems of representation of Renaissance sexuality. Henri III is far from being the

---

[16]   Duval, *Des hermaphrodits*, p. 397.

[17]   Cf. the interesting series of analogies drawn in the liminary poem to the *Histoire admirable d'vn faulx & supposé mary, aduenue en Languedoc, l'an mil cinq cens soixante* (Paris: Sertenas, 1561), f. [A^v]: 'Les transformations d'Ouide merueilleuses / Tous les enchantemens & l'ensorcellerie, / Toutes illusions, toute la tromperie, /... / Si tu lis cest escript ne te sembleront riens / Apres le faux mary....'

[18]   Jones and Stallybrass, 'Fetishizing Gender', p. 90, point out that Renaissance hermaphrodites had the legal right to inherit and leave bequests, as well as to choose their gender according to their prevailing sexual characteristics. Contravention of this gender choice brought retribution, however: cf. Duval, op. cit., p. 302: 'A telles personnes les loix, & prudents Magistrats instrumens energiques d'icelles, commandent choisir l'vn ou l'autre sexe. Sçavoir est celuy auquel la titillation & mouvement de nature s'incline & eschauffe d'auantage. Apres l'auoir esleu ils deffendent bien expressement, d'outrepasser les rites coustumiers, & vsages d'iceluy, pour fuir les abus qui pourroyent estre commis tant par tels corps monstrueux, que sous pretexte d'iceux. Et s'ils cognoissent que quelque contrauention ait esté commise à leurs sentences & arrests, ils punissent les delinquants, voire mesme de mort, comme d'vn crime capital.'

paradigm of all such systems of sexuality — we have already seen that other types have their location and specific form in sixteenth-century French culture — but he is nevertheless the index of one particularly powerful and functionally important strand that tangles together conflicting images and political propaganda, rhetoric, and polemic, and constitutes evidence of disturbance and upheaval in the image of the king as an emblem of a traditional masculinity.

A short article by Denis Richet offers an incisive assessment of the stages by which attitudes towards Henri III have evolved since his assassination. Crucially refusing to separate historiography from legend, Richet examines, first, the emergence of the 'légende noire' of Henri III, then the resurgence of interest in the Valois during the nineteenth century, centring especially on the Queen Mother, and finally the current rehabilitation of Henri III associated with the names of Pierre Chevalier, Jean-Marie Constant, and Jacqueline Boucher.[19] It was of course Boucher who, in her monumental thesis, felt obliged to dispel suppositions surrounding the king's sexuality, making of him a *galant* only a little less *vert* than Henri IV.[20] Such redressing of the balance is an historical necessity and, by implication for Richet, an inevitability. Yet it neglects Richet's fundamental insight — that it is impossible fully to disentangle historiography from legend. Hermaphroditism is arguably the point of intersection between the two. Dubois observes that whereas this term is a purely technical one in the medical teratology of the age, in sixteenth-century politics it is a pejorative expression, occurring most famously in book 2 of D'Aubigné's *Les Tragiques*, where the poet contrasts restraint and self-control with

> ...les hermaphrodits, monstres effeminez,
> Corrompus, bourdeliers, et qui estoyent mieux nez
> Pour valets des putains que seigneurs sur les hommes.[21]

---

[19] Denis Richet, 'Henri III dans l'historiographie et dans la légende', in *Henri III et son temps*, ed. Robert Sauzet (Paris: Vrin, 1992), pp. 13–20. Richet is referring to Pierre Chevalier, *Henri III, roi shakespearien* (Paris: Fayard, 1985); Jean-Marie Constant, *Les Guise* (Paris: Hachette, 1984); and Jacqueline Boucher, *Société et mentalités autour de Henri III*, 4 vols (Lille: Atelier de Reproduction des Thèses, 1981). Constant's more recent work, *La Ligue* (Paris: Fayard, 1996), pp. 81–107, also deals with Henri sympathetically.

[20] Boucher, *Société et mentalités*, pp. 109–15. Cf. Chevalier, *Henri III*, pp. 441–6.

[21] D'Aubigné, *Les Tragiques*, in *Œuvres*, ed. Henri Weber, Jacques Bailbé and Marguerite Soulié (Paris: Gallimard, 1969), *Princes*, vv. 667–9; [Artus Thomas], *L'Isle des hermaphrodites*, ed. C.-G. Dubois (Geneva: Droz, 1996), pp. 9, 12.

Short as it is, this quotation illustrates two of the three principles that Ruth Gilbert connects with the appearance of the hermaphrodite in political contexts: excess and imbalance — corresponding here to sexual libertinism — and 'ineffectual, or compromised, masculine power', a characteristic present in the word 'effeminez'.[22] The hermaphrodite is the figure that allows moral, ideological, and political boundaries to be marked out by embodying in that figure that which exceeds those boundaries (effeminacy) as well as that which fails to live up to expectation (political impotence and inadequacy). Simultaneously *au-delà* and *en-deçà* of traditional categories and demarcations, the political hermaphrodite is both double and between, to adapt slightly the phrase used by Daston and Park.[23]

The *Isle des hermaphrodites*, published by Artus Thomas in 1605, reinforces but also expands on these characteristics. Interpreted at the time as satirising the court of Henri III (Fig. 15), this work has been read more recently as an attack, more generally, on dandyism and worldly vanity.[24] Dubois rightly points out that specifics are hard to come by in the *Isle*: 'tout est occulté par une couverture allégorique ou symbolique.'[25] Yet for all that the work peddles a stereotype, albeit a potent and politically acute one, certain salient features emerge: alongside sexual licence, and the preference for pleasure over religion, there is an emphasis on masquerade and disguise, dress and appearance, all within a framework that, from the outset, views hermaphroditic activity in histrionic terms:

> Le monde est un bouffon, l'homme une comedie,
> L'un porte la marotte, et l'autre est la follie.[26]

The quotation, adapted from Petronius's 'fere totus mundus exerceat histrioniam', and reinforced by other references to 'ce grand theatre',[27] in-

---

22   Gilbert, *Early Modern Hermaphrodites*, p. 126.

23   Daston and Park, art. cit., p. 118.

24   Guy Poirier, *L'Homosexualité dans l'imaginaire de la Renaissance* (Paris: Champion, 1996), pp. 157–9, discusses the work in relation to the court of Henri III; Gray, *Gender*, p. 145, sees it as a 'satire of aristocratic dandyism'; Dubois, p. 21, describes it as a work that 'rassemble les divers attributs de la vanité et de l'esprit mondain'.

25   [Thomas], *L'Isle des hermaphrodites*, p. 23.

26   [Thomas], *L'Isle des hermaphrodites*, p. [53].

27   [Thomas], *L'Isle des hermaphrodites*, p. 54. On this fragment from Petronius, see the sources quoted in *Petronii Arbitri Satyricon* (Paris: Pattison, 1587), p. 112, particularly John of Salibury's *Policraticus*, III, chap. 10, 'De mundana Comœdia vel Tragœdia', where the dictum is cited in two slightly different forms. Cf. also Montaigne, *Essais*, III. 8, p. 1011: 'La plus part de nos vacations sont farcesques. *Mundus*

evitably brings to mind known characteristics of the late sixteenth-century French court: speaking of their 'vision théâtrale de l'existence humaine', Jacqueline Boucher adds, 'l'idée que le monde était un théâtre fut souvent exprimée autour des derniers Valois'.[28] The self-proclaiming theatricality of the court mirrors the histrionic sense of existence and is part of a series of reversals that characterise the last Valois monarch and his followers: an emphasis, in particular, on *paraître*, spectacle, ostentation, and display, ranging from sumptuous costumes and banquets to religious and secular processions, combined with a hyperbolical devotional fervour and spirituality, all serving to underscore the violent juxtaposition of usually separate activities.

Of that violent juxtaposition, royal hermaphroditism is the extreme but logical development. In confirmation of Gilbert's analyses, we could infer that anxiety about the current political situation is displaced onto the fantasised symbolic body of the king and his court, which is construed in line with contemporary fascination with, and revulsion from, the hermaphrodite. The theatre of the court is perceived as a stage for the transgressive enacting or performing of hermaphroditism, in much the same way that Mary or Marin Le Marcis transgessively enact their hermaphroditism, with the result that contemporary propoganda, both *ligueur* and Protestant, seize on this idea to conflate the disconcerting reversal of court practices with ontological inversion and sexual perversion. That conflation is itself facilitated by a profound modification that occurs within the very notion of the hermaphrodite: it was a commonplace of hermaphrodite discourse that the hermaphrodite commonly emerged by the transformation of female into male, the weaker into the stronger, the subservient into the dominant.[29] Courtly hermaphrodites, in the form of the *mignons* and their royal master, moved in the opposite direction, as D'Aubigné's telltale term 'effeminez' indicates, thus enacting a further change within an already overdetermined figure. The iconography of this troubled period likewise enables us to picture those changes precisely. The image of royal androgyny embodied in the Fontainebleau portrait of François Ier (Fig. 16)

---

universus exercet histrioniam. Il faut jouer deuement nostre rolle, mais comme rolle d'un personnage emprunté.'

[28] Boucher, *Société et mentalités*, p. 1149, and ibid. for other examples (La Noue, Boaistuau, Du Bartas).

[29] See Gray, *Gender*, pp. 142–3, and n. 28, p. 200; Du Verdier, *Diverses Leçons*, p. 315: '... s'en ensuit par necessaire consequence que ceste transmutation s'entend de fille en masle & non de genre masculin en feminin. La raison est, que la nature aiouste tousiours, sans iamais diminuer, elle pousse tousiours hors & onques ne retient, encline ordinairement vers la chose plus digne & non iamais vers l'indigne.'

is an image of the king as the ideal combination of martial vigour and balanced wisdom, invested with all the potent attributes that classical mythology can provide.[30] The corresponding image of his grandson, Henri III (Fig. 17), has no such all-inclusive, comprehensive purpose.[31] It is a portrait of pure *bigarrure*, suffused with negative overtones, a picture of a monarch wavering uncertainly and multiply between too many identities, and none. In place of a permissibly diverse royal symbolism, the picture of Henri III gives back a diffuse, shattered image — or an overcrowded one, which amounts to the same.

Always a signifier of something beyond its physical existence, hermaphroditism becomes the focus and the vehicle for the expression of the progressive erosion and final *éclatement* of royal authority that Henri III experiences. At the same time, the notion of gender performance undergoes a transformation in the pamphlet war of the 1580s; as Denis Crouzet has shown, there is a transfer of actual violence to a theatre of words: 'un champ de bataille est le théâtre qui se crée dans la lecture', 'une guerre est donnée à lire et à imaginer à celui qui lit'.[32] And against the ambiguities of royal hermaphroditism is set the 'normative' masculinity and, by implication, sexuality of that supreme exemplar of the French warrior caste, Henri de Lorraine, duc de Guise. In the final section of this paper, I turn to depictions of the two Henris, monarch and peer, in a representative sample of the historical writing of the period, while endeavouring not to lose sight of Richet's dictum that it is impossible fully to separate historiography from legend. None of the historians to be discussed deals expressly with the question of hermaphroditism; but arguably their accounts are shot through by half-submerged anxieties and allusions that inflect and sometimes deflect the narrative as they attempt to reinscribe gender disturbance in constitutional terms. In all these writers, there is evidence of the

---

[30]   Cf. Raymond B. Waddington, 'The Bisexual Portrait of François Ier: Fontainebleau, Castiglione, and the Tone of Courtly Mythology', in *Playing with Gender: A Renaissance Pursuit*, ed. Jean R. Brink et al. (Urbana and Chicago: University of Illinois Press, 1991), pp. 99–132.

[31]   The image is contained in Keith Cameron's *Henri III: A Malignant or Maligned King? (Aspects of the Satirical Iconography of Henri de Valois)* (Exeter: University of Exeter Press, 1978), p. 79, and in Martine Tissier de Mallerais et al., *La Tragédie de Blois: quatre siècles de polémique autour de l'assassinat du duc de Guise* (Blois: Conservation du Château et des Musées, 1988), p. 140.

[32]   Denis Crouzet, 'Le Règne de Henri III et la violence collective', in Sauzet, *Henri III et son temps*, p. 219; cf. loc. cit., Crouzet's characterisation of this phase of the religious struggle as a 'théâtre imaginaire sur lequel les adversaires luttent avec l'aide des mots'.

double-that-divides, to re-phrase Ruth Gilbert's characterisation of the political hermaphrodite:[33] actual brothers (such as Henri and Louis de Guise), rival fellow kings related by marriage (Henri III and Henri de Navarre), adversaries that share the same name (Henri de Guise, Henri de Valois, Henri de Navarre), all contenders for a kingdom that is divided by the very rhetorical figure that describes its ruler.

As an index, therefore, of this relationship between the last Valois king of France and the man he mockingly referred to as 'le roi de Paris', we may examine the assessments made by three historians of the Blois assassinations, the moment of paroxysm of violent words and violent deeds. The first of these historians is also one of the most colourful: Pierre Matthieu, the vehement *ligueur* turned official historiographer of Henri IV, was the author of the 1589 *Guisiade* before he produced his *Histoire des derniers troubles de France*. In Matthieu's hands, the murder of Guise elicits a five-page comparison in his *Histoire* between the Duke and Julius Caesar; conducted in close point-by-point detail, it is plainly modelled on Plutarch's parallel lives, as is made clear by Matthieu's initial allusion to Camillus and Themistocles, Numa and Lycurgus, Scipio and Epaminondas, Marcellus and Pelopidas, Pompey and Agesilaus, and Sulla and Lysander.[34] The death of Guise is for Matthieu a turning point of history and he devotes considerably more space to the careful elaboration of the Caesar–Guise parallel than he does to the assassination of Henri III, which gains official expressions of mourning with accompanying epitaphic verse, but with little assessment of his virtues and vices.[35] This is not, however, negligence or omission, but part of a careful compositional strategy, for an analysis of the King's character has already been made much earlier, no doubt in order to avoid directly invidious comparisons. Henri III emerges from that earlier analysis as an essentially religious man, determined to eradicate heresy. Yet the terms of the analysis highlight the obsessive nature of the monarch's policy:

> En vn mot, il viuoit plus en Capucin qu'en Roy, il n'aimoit plus la guerre, sa diane estoit le chant des Feuillantains, son champ de bataille vn cloistre, sa cuirasse vn sac de Penitent, il ne viuoit plus que cloüé & attaché au

[33] Gilbert, *Early Modern Hermaphrodites*, p. 126.
[34] [Pierre Matthieu], *Histoire des derniers troubles de France*, 2 vols (n.p., 1606), I. ff. 159ʳ–162ʳ.
[35] [Matthieu], op. cit., II. ff. 7ᵛ–8ᵛ. The short assessment that there is recalls closely that of Du Haillan: '...il craignoit Dieu, & n'avoit d'autre volonté que d'auancer la Religion Catholique, reformer les abus & maluersations de ses Officiers, en toutes les charges de son Royaume, aymoit les lettres, & aduançoit les gens d'esprit.'

Crucifix, & s'il viuoit, ce n'estoit plus luy qui viuoit, c'estoit Iesus-Christ
qui viuoit en luy.[36]

The closing reference to *Galatians* 2. 20 crowns the picture of the monarch whose field of conflict is now inward, personal, devotional. The traditional masculine attributes of the monarch are twisted and deflected into the image of spiritual combat in the battleground of the soul. That picture of the unwarlike king is reinforced by other details a little later, which Matthieu draws from André Maillard's *Le Francophile*, first published, he informs us, in Chartres in 1591:

> Il s'ennuya bien tost de la guerre, & comme sa nature estoit molle, coulante, & delicate, son esprit foible, rauallé, & mal patient de peine, & toutes ses complexions inegales, plus diuisees & basses que guerrieres, il recherchoit la vie tranquille & le repos. Ainsi bien tost il se tourna de tout point aux nopces & aux danses...[37]

Softness, delicacy, weakness, a liking for weddings and dance: the text describes the effeminate hermaphrodite without using the term, but by constructing the King's character in binary opposition to the conventional view of the warrior. This stands in marked contrast to the depiction of Guise. It stands also in contradistinction to the destiny that God has marked out for Henri de Navarre after the murder of Guise:

> ...de spectateur qu'il [Henri de Navarre] estoit, [Dieu] le met sur le theatre, comme celuy qui à l'improuiste par accidens ny craints, ny preueus, ny esperez, deuoit non representer vne Royauté de Comedie, mais le vray & legitime office de Roy.[38]

The theatricality of court life, with its performance of gender ambiguity, is dismissed as a comedy when compared to the theatre of action in which Henri de Navarre's career will be played out. Of the three Henris — the monarch, the peer and the Protestant — only the last will be for Matthieu the true symbiosis of the warrior and the king, of Mars and Minerva; if Henri III is the hermaphrodite, Henri IV will become the royal androgyne, the spiritual and iconographical heir of François Ier.

---

[36]   [Matthieu], op. cit., I. f. 14[r].
[37]   [Matthieu], op. cit., I. f. 14[r]; [André Maillart], *Le Francophile ... contre les conspirations du Roy d'Espagne, du Pape & des rebelles de France* (n.p., 1606), p. 41.
[38]   [Matthieu], op. cit., I. f. 157[v].

The two remaining historians add particular colour to Matthieu's detailed account. Bernard Girard du Haillan, a friend and neighbour of Montaigne, became the official historian of Henri III when the latter was still duke of Anjou. Du Haillan's reputation stemmed from his *De l'estat et succez des affaires de France*, which first appeared in 1570, and which categorises and justifies the constitutional status of France viewed as an historical and political entity that has developed according to identifiable criteria. Although the principle of kingship underlies this structure and its development, the system of *De l'estat* is perfectly abstract; following the convention of not dealing with contemporary history, it sets itself the task of explaining the French constitution as it stands. It is thus not an express defence of any particular king, but implies a defence of kingship based on historical principles. More explicit assessment is to be found in Du Haillan's *Histoire generale des Roys de France*. First published in 1576, this work went through numerous editions to keep pace with historical change. Of the three historians, Du Haillan is the most sparing of details of the murder of Guise:

> Le Duc sort du Conseil pour trauerser en la chambre du cabinet: & comme il leue d'vne main la tapisserie pour entrer, on le charge à coups d'espees, de poignards, de pertuisanes: non toutefois: auec tant de violence, qu'il ne monstrast aux assassins les derniers efforts d'vne inuincible vaillance en vn magnanime courage.[39]

This matter-of-fact narrative is immediately followed by a character sketch of the Duke:

> Ainsi vesquit, ainsi mourut Henri de Lorraine Duc de Guise, Prince digne certes des premiers rangs entre les Princes, beau, grand, haut à proportion, amiable de face, grand de courage, prompt à l'execution de ses entreprises: populaire, dissimulé, mais par ses façons exterieures couurant auec sagesse les secrets de son ame, bon mesnager & du temps & de l'occasion, rusé en stratagemes, caressant ses soldats, honorant ses Capitaines. Mais Prince qui par ambition extreme a flaistri le plus beau de ses loüanges. Factieux, vanteur, vain à croire les Astrologues qui l'asseuroyent de sa grandeur, d'vn changement de famille en la Royauté, haut à la main, ne pouuant sousmettre ses esperances mesme à ceux desquels il en deuoit esperer l'aduance, voulant par son inclination donner à cognoistre qu'il estoit né non pour obeïr, mais pour commander, & à ce desseing, disposant dés ses

---

[39]   Bernard Girard Du Haillan, *Histoire generale des Roys de France*, 2 vols (Paris: Petit-pas and Sonnius, 1627), II. 570.

premieres actions les esprits des François, à croire qu'il auoit des parties
propres à faire vn estrange changement au Royaume.[40]

Contrast that with the corresponding character sketch of Henri III after his
assassination in 1589:

> Prince debonnaire & docile, courtois, accort, disert, graue, mais de facile
> accez: deuotieux, aimant les lettres, auançant les gens d'esprit, liberal re-
> munerateur des hommes de merite, desireux de reformation és abus &
> maluersations de ses Officiers: amy de paix, capable de conseil.[41]

As with Matthieu, the portrait of Guise is a portrait of the warrior, the embodiment of the masculine ideals that were traditionally held up for admiration and emulation: he is 'd'vne inuincible vaillance', he possesses 'vn
magnanime courage', and he is 'bon mesnager & du temps & de
l'occasion, rusé en stratagemes, caressant ses soldats, honorant ses Capitaines'. He is above all born to lead, not to obey. And despite the condemnation of the Duke's ambition, the historian cannot resist the admiration
he feels, imparting an abiding impression of strength of character that
Barnavi and Descimon associate with the desired ideal of the king in the
popular imagination: 'le modèle du roi chevalier, du guerrier victorieux
plus épris d'exercices physiques que de choses de l'esprit dominait encore
les consciences.'[42] It is nonetheless precisely these 'choses de l'esprit' that
predominate in Du Haillan's carefully-worded picture of the well-
intentioned, devout, and benevolent scholar who just happened to be King
of France. Guise is automatically what Henri III, despite early promise,
had failed to become; warlike incompetence, personal inadequacy, and
political impotence are the marks of the hermaphrodite, a term that is
never mentioned, but is everywhere implicit in the contrast Du Haillan
makes.

That contrast is further intensified by the perspective that Du Haillan
constantly introduces into his account of the reign of his royal patron: the
vocabulary of tragedy, that describes at one and the same time the Blois
assassinations ('le dernier acte de la tragedie'), Henri III's own role as a
player in it ('s'en ensuiuoit le dernier acte de ceste tragedie du Roy'), and,
connecting the two, the larger catastrophe that is engulfing France ('le

---

[40] Du Haillan, op. cit., pp. 570–1.
[41] Du Haillan, op. cit., p. 582.
[42] Elie Barnavi and Robert Descimon, *La Sainte Ligue, le juge et la potence: l'assassinat du président Brisson (15 novembre 1591)* (Paris: Hachette, 1985), pp. 39–40.

Roy regarde ceste piteuse tragedie qui se ioüe sur le teatre de son Estat').[43] History is converted into drama, solidifying into actual event the pantomime that the King's enemies regarded him as playing (epitomised by Matthieu's 'Royauté de Comedie'). Thus Du Haillan stages his writing of history as an inevitable antagonism between two major political players, an antithesis that never resolves itself into a complementarity or synthesis, but anticipates a fateful outcome that in turn confirms the train of events as tragic in the dramatic as well as the political sense. In this way, Du Haillan at least implicitly refutes the charges of levity and nonchalance that were brought against Henri III; his King is a tragic actor, caught up in a situation of which he is the victim as much as the protagonist. '...le théâtre...était l'expression de la vie réelle', writes Jacqueline Boucher, 'et il n'existait pas de séparation entre ceux qui jouaient et ceux qui regardaient.'[44]

Jean de Serres, the probable author of *Histoire des choses memorables auenues en France*, was no true admirer of Henri III and no admirer at all of the Queen Mother and the Duc de Guise, whom he regarded as being in league. De Serres adds nonetheless a further dimension to this story of confraternal conflict. His *Histoire*, a fifty-year chronicle of French history from 1547 to 1597, contains one of the most detailed accounts of Guise's death, which partly results from the Duke's own hubris (although De Serres never has recourse to the theatrical or tragic image). But by way of motivating the King's decision to have Guise killed, De Serres supplies details not found elsewhere:

> D'auantage, le Duc auoit tellement pourueu à ses affaires, qu'il se tenoit pour maistre du chasteau de Blois, & de la personne du Roy, n'y ayant porte, salle, ni cabinet, dont il n'eust les clefs, auec appareil & prouision d'armes, vtiles aux exploits de guerre, que l'on trouua puis apres. Ses gens enuironnoyent le Roy: & quant aux compagnies d'ordonnances establies pour demeurer autour de Blois, durant les Estats, le Duc les licentia, iusques à exempter par lettres signees de sa main & seellees du seau de ses armes les habitans de Romorantin, de receuoir vne compagnie, & defendre bien expres au Commissaire general des viures, de leur demander aucunes munitions pour icelle compagnie ou autre.[45]

---

[43] Du Haillan, op. cit., pp. 570, 568, 577.

[44] Boucher, *Société et mentalités*, p. 1148. Cf. Montaigne, *Essais*, III. 12, p. 1046: 'Si cherchons nous avidement de recognoistre en ombre mesme et en la fable des Theatres la montre des jeux tragiques de l'humaine fortune.'

[45] [Jean de Serres], *Histoire des choses memorables auenues en France* (n.p., 1599), p. 674.

140

As De Serres goes on to say in the conclusion of his chapter on Henri III, the King is no longer master in his own house; he has found the door closed on him, 'et ceux qu'il auoit trop supportez en infinies sortes, establis en sa place'.[46] Expelled from what might accommodate him politically and generically, and condemned as an imposter by the League, he finds his place usurped by one who wields power with greater authority than he could ever muster. The impersonator has indeed effectively seized control and become the King, just as Arnaud du Tilh became Martin Guerre. De Serres expresses puzzlement that Henri III did not strike down the impersonator at once. He does not see that Guise represented the masculine that in the eyes of his subjects Henri had singularly failed to be; that in effect the two Henris were the intertwined halves of one contradictory being, as surely inseparable as the plural identities of Marie Germain, Mary, and Marin Le Marcis; and that in finally destroying Guise, Henri III would equally bring destruction upon himself. The last act in the tragedy of this King is that he cannot survive existentially as the political hermaphrodite he has become.

Ever a notable observer of the empirical data around him, Montaigne records in essay II. 30 his encounter with a monstrous child, whose congenital deformation is akin to that of Siamese twins.[47] His essay on this topic first appeared in 1580, but he pondered its significance throughout his career. In the earliest version of his essay, he offered an expressly political interpretation of the phenomenon:

> Ce double corps et ces membres divers, se rapportans à une seule teste, pourroient bien fournir de favorable prognostique au Roy de maintenir sous l'union de ses loix ces pars et pieces diverses de nostre estat;...[48]

Montaigne's words recognise the political situation as hopelessly entangled, with each side dependent on the other for its existence, as with political adversaries that feed off each other. Almost immediately, however, this explanation is qualified:

---

46   [De Serres], op. cit., p. 703.
47   Cf. Jean Céard, *La Nature et les prodiges: l'insolite au XVIe siècle*, revised edition (Geneva: Droz, 1996), pp. 432–44. For a reading of this episode from a complementary standpoint to my own, see Wes Williams, 'Some Monsters: Montaigne, Heliodorus, and Some Others', in *Self and Other in Sixteenth-Century France*, Proceedings of the Seventh Cambridge French Renaissance Colloquium, 7–9 July 2001, ed. Kathryn Banks and Philip Ford (Cambridge: Cambridge French Colloquia, 2004), pp. 154–7.
48   Montaigne, *Essais*, II. 30, p. 713.

...mais de peur que l'evenement ne le démente, il vaut mieux le laisser passer devant, car il n'est que de deviner en choses faictes.[49]

Historical event might not correspond to the allegorical interpretation derived from the figure; and in 1588, in confirmation of his own final comment, Montaigne quotes Epimenides' dictum that 'il devinoit à reculons'. After 1588, even the benefit of hindsight seems insecure to Montaigne and he offers two further interpretations of the strange sight. The first considers 'monstres' to be both a misnomer and a category mistake: in a deliberately provocative remark, he declares that their meaning is known only to God, adding that 'est à croire que cette figure qui nous estonne, se rapporte et tient à quelque autre figure de mesme genre inconnu à l'homme'.[50] Human ignorance misnames what it in any cases misrecognises; certain knowledge in this matter is not possible. Consistent with his Sceptical position on such questions, Montaigne thus implicitly proposes acknowledgement of the limitations of our understanding of this natural phenomenon and suspension of judgment about its significance. His second explanation moves in a complementary direction:

Nous apelons contre nature ce qui advient contre coustume: rien n'est que selon elle, quel qu'il soit. Que cette raison universelle et naturelle chasse de nous l'erreur et l'estonnement que la nouvelleté nous apporte.[51]

Where the first explanation places definitive understanding beyond the boundaries of human cognition, the second locates it as a cultural phenomenon, a matter of custom. The thrust of the argument has shifted, but the ultimate message remains the same: to judge, to classify on the basis of 'estonnement' is no less to commit intellectual error. Caution, restraint, reservation of judgment: these are the reactions that such 'nouvelleté' should inspire. Its mystery is not thereby dissolved; but the human mind becomes less brashly assertive in claiming to understand and interpret it.

If it is true to its etymology, the *monstre*, the *monstrum*, ought at the very least to portend something, and preferably declare it, show it. But what? D'Aubigné had been in no doubt: court hermaphrodites were 'monstres effeminez', creatures whose effeminacy was tangible proof of degeneracy, implying a renunciation of masculine domination and authority, a sapping of vital spirits, a decadent mutation into weakness. Montaigne's reflection, in parallel circumstances, on the whole process of constructing,

---

[49]   Id., ibid.
[50]   Id., ibid.
[51]   Id., ibid.

deriving or imposing meaning on portentous signifiers is contrastingly an instructive reminder that to read history through the figure, as I have been attempting to do here, is to deal not with a universal token fluidly commutable and malleably exchangeable in all contexts, but to confront a densely-layered puzzle that invites yet resists full explanation. Hermaphrodite is perhaps at best a name for an enigma, a name supplied in default of any other more suitable — because there is nothing suitable — to cover the doublenesses and mixtures, the too much and the not quite, the betwixt and between, that are all at once gendered, sexualised, cultural, and politico-historical. 'Figure porte absence et présence': forty years after Genette adopted Pascal's phrase as his motto,[52] the figure of the Renaissance hermaphrodite challenges us to understand what that motto might mean.

---

[52]   To *Figures I* (Paris: Seuil, 1966).

Fig. 15, 'Portrait satyrique d'Henry III',
[Artus Thomas], *Isle des hermaphrodites* (1605)

Fig. 16, Niccolò Bellin, *François Ier*
(Cliché Bibliothèque nationale de France, Paris)

Fig. 17, 'Portrait monstrüeux et allegorique d'Henri III'

7

Masculinité et virilité: récits d'un roi sans enfant

Guy Poirier

La stérilité est encore aujourd'hui une tragédie pour de nombreux couples. L'impossibilité d'engendrer entraîne remises en question et souffrances; l'intérêt de la science pour la question n'est d'ailleurs pas, à notre avis, gratuit. Il s'agit bien d'une entrave à la perpétuation de l'espèce que l'être humain ne saurait tolérer. Les enjeux de la stérilité à la Renaissance n'étaient pas moins grands. Les croyances diverses quant à la conception, qu'elles soient religieuses ou pseudo-scientifiques, n'offraient que peu de réponses aux angoisses des couples frappés par le destin. L'on ne peut que tenter d'imaginer les affres que devaient affronter les jeunes mariés s'ils ne parvenaient à assurer une progéniture. Dans une société où la famille noble était bien plus qu'une simple unité familiale, la survie, mais également la sécurité et le pouvoir, appartenaient aux maisonnées unies et nombreuses. Le système de favoritisme qu'ont dû développer les derniers Valois, et notamment Henri III, n'est certainement pas étranger aux difficultés rencontrées par une famille dont les enfants mâles succombaient à différentes maladies lorsqu'ils n'étaient encore que de jeunes adultes.[1]

Si c'est bien l'histoire de la représentation du roi Henri III qui nous intéresse dans le présent chapitre, il nous faut rappeler que même si les torts étaient partagés, la responsabilité de l'infertilité d'un couple était le plus souvent assumée par la femme. Dans le cas de Catherine de Médicis, par exemple, la répudiation avait été envisagée par François Ier et son fils. Robert Knecht, rapportant les propos de l'ambassadeur vénitien Contarini, rappelle que le roi changea d'avis lorsque l'épouse du dauphin aurait déclaré '[...] qu'elle ne lui causerait pas d'ennuis, elle était prête à entrer au couvent ou à devenir l'une des compagnes de la dame qui aurait assez de

---

[1]   Voir notamment à ce propos l'excellent ouvrage de Nicolas Le Roux: *La Faveur du Roi: mignons et courtisans au temps des derniers Valois* (Paris: Champ Vallon, 2000), et notamment le chapitre 3, 'La Naissance de la majesté'.

chance pour épouser son mari'.[2] Il était cependant assez évident, dans le cas de Catherine, que le dauphin n'était pas à l'origine de cette stérilité. Le futur Henri II avait ainsi eu une aventure, en 1537, dans le Piémont, avec la fille de l'un de ses écuyers. Cette dernière donna naissance à une fille, qui fut légitimée sous le nom de Diane de France.[3] Catherine n'avait donc plus qu'à se soumettre et à suivre les conseils de ses médecins et, dit-on, de sa dame d'honneur, Catherine de Gondi.

Même si une première grossesse inattendue mit fin aux inquiétudes de la famille royale après dix ans de mariage, Catherine de Médicis, ayant échappé à la répudiation, fut d'autant plus sensible aux difficultés que rencontra sa belle-fille, Louise de Lorraine. L'âge (elle avait vingt-deux ans) et la beauté de Louise '[...] faisaient espérer qu'elle donnerait bientôt des héritiers à la couronne'.[4] Selon Jacqueline Boucher, la reine fut effectivement enceinte dans les mois qui suivirent son mariage, mais tomba malade. Les médecines qu'on lui administra lui firent faire une fausse couche au troisième mois de sa grossesse.[5] Ce qui peut paraître surprenant, dans cette histoire, c'est que la cour semble avoir ignoré cet incident, et que c'est Henri III qui fut rapidement soupçonné d'impuissance: 'La cour avait sur Louise une opinion mitigée. Au fond sa vertu gênait. On lui reprocha d'être sans enfant, attribuant d'ailleurs au Roi cette stérilité.'[6] On aurait d'ailleurs suggéré à la reine de prendre un amant, et Saint-Luc aurait voulu jouer ce rôle. Le Duc d'Alençon, toujours selon Jacqueline Boucher, aurait également tenté sa chance auprès de l'épouse de son frère... S'entremêlent donc, dans les récits de stérilité du couple royal, avis médicaux, croyances et anecdotes.

Il faut dire que la liste des raisons devant expliquer la stérilité du roi est longue. Ce dernier fut soupçonné d'avoir contracté une maladie vénérienne[7] et de s'intéresser aux autres femmes de la cour et aux religieuses. Si Henri III avait des maîtresses, il ne les fréquentait que de façon éphémère;[8] la chronique retiendra cependant son goût pour les couvents, comme le rappellent certaines pièces satiriques citées par Pierre de

2   Robert Knecht, *Catherine de Médicis* (Bruxelles: Le Cri, 2003), p. 43.
3   Ibid., p. 43.
4   Jacqueline Boucher, *Deux épouses et reines à la fin du XVIᵉ siècle: Louise de Lorraine et Marguerite de France* (Saint-Étienne: Publications de l'Université de Saint-Étienne, 1995), p. 34
5   Ibid., p. 125.
6   Ibid., p. 130.
7   Ibid., p. 134.
8   Ibid., pp. 126–27.

L'Estoile.[9] Pierre Chevallier citant Renieri, explique que le roi, en 1580, subit un examen et que l'on découvrit qu'il avait: 'la verge tordue vers le bas, de sorte qu'il ne peut émettre le sperme dans la matrice, et pour cette raison les médecins ont décidé de la fendre plus haut.'[10] En 1584, les envoyés vénitiens auraient noté la grande nervosité du roi et on lui aurait suggéré de boire du lait d'ânesse; il transmettait alors 'la semence pendant le coït avec plus de rapidité qu'il ne le faut pour pouvoir engendrer'.[11]

Le discours médical de l'époque nous apporte quelques éclaircissements sur les connaissances gynécologiques liées à l'impuissance. Ambroise Paré élabore la description de certaines causes naturelles et accidentelles de la stérilité. Du côté des causes naturelles, Paré note l'insuffisance de la semence, ou trop chaude ou trop froide, ou trop sèche, ou humide et fluide. L'âge est un élément important. Les vieilles gens et les jeunes 'en trop bas aage' n'ont pas la qualité de semence adéquate (trop fluide et humide). Un autre facteur rend également la semence 'indelebile, indigeste et corrompuë', et c'est le coït trop fréquent. Le diagnostic que les médecins du roi nous transmirent s'inscrit donc bien dans les croyances de l'époque quant à la stérilité de l'homme. La 'fluidité de la semence' pouvait s'expliquer par le jeune âge du souverain. La fréquence du coït, en revanche, laisserait entendre, comme nous le verrons par ailleurs, que le roi faisait preuve d'une certaine lascivité.[12]

La température de la semence est aussi importante dans le processus de génération; trop froide ou trop chaude, elle peut devenir inféconde, ou engendrer 'plutost une femelle qu'un masle'. Certaines maladies ou interventions chirurgicales provoquent la stérilité chez l'homme: l'incision de la pierre, une plaie derrière les oreilles 'qui aura coupé certains rameaux des veines et arteres jugulaires', empêchant l'esprit animal et la matière de passer du cerveau aux testicules. D'autres malformations anatomiques s'ajoutent alors à la liste: verge trop courte ou énorme, point de trou au bout de la verge, paralysie particulière de la verge, et verge tordue! En conclusion, Ambroise Paré ajoute aux vices de conformation certains éléments liés à l'alimentation.[13] D'autres 'défauts et maléfices' retiennent

---

[9]   Cf. Guy Poirier, *L'Homosexualité dans l'imaginaire de la Renaissance* (Paris: Champion, 1996), p. 149.

[10]   Pierre Chevallier, *Henri III* (Paris: Fayard, 1985), p. 375.

[11]   Pierre Chevallier, op. cit., p. 375, passage cité par Pierre Chevallier sans indication de note.

[12]   Ambroise Paré, *Les Œuvres* (Lyon: Veuve de Claude Rigaud et Claude Obert, 1633), p. 722.

[13]   'Bref, les causes de l'impuissance d'engendrer viennent ou du default de suffisante et bonne nourriture, comme on void es ectiques, emaciez et cachectiques, ou

finalement l'attention du chirurgien du roi. Le charme des aiguillettes apparaît dans sa liste, mais également les ravages que peut exercer la grosse vérole que nous appelons aujourd'hui la syphilis:

> Car aucuns perdent un œil, et souvent les deux [...] autres perdent le cultiveur du champ de nature humaine, de façon qu'ils demeurent apres steriles...[14]

Selon Pierre Chevallier et Jacqueline Boucher, le roi possédait un exemplaire, relié à ses armes, du *Liber prior de morbis mulierum* d'Hippocrate publié en 1585. Même s'il ne lisait que très mal le latin, il aurait pu aussi consulter à partir de 1587 la traduction de Jean Liebault du *Thresor des remedes secrets pour les maladies des femmes*.[15] Malgré son titre, cette publication traite longuement de la stérilité chez l'homme. Le chapitre sur la 'curation de sterilité' commence donc par le passage suivant:

> Si donc l'homme et la femme sont de temperament egal, distemperé toutesfois, seroit bon, ou ne les avoir point conjoincts ensemble, ou si les loix de Dieu le pouvoient permettre, les separer. Mais d'autant que Dieu, l'honneur, et la raison defendent telle separation: au lieu de les separer, faudra par regime de vie et tous autres moyens changer leur naturel semblable, et les rendre de contraire et dissemblable temperature l'un à l'autre.[16]

L'harmonie entre les contraires décrite par Marinelli nous permet d'envisager qu'en plus des causes anatomiques, d'autres raisons pouvaient alors expliquer la stérilité. Marinelli indique ainsi que l'impuissance à procréer dérive de ce que nous appellerions aujourd'hui nos fantasmes:

> Ce qu'advient coustumierement, quand nos esprits, cogitations, et pensees sont occupees à autres besongnes, comme à la contemplation des choses divines, à quelque bonne estude, à quelque trafic et marchandise: lesquelles vacations divertissent et attirent du tout à soy les desirs et affections de l'esprit.[17]

---

d'intemperies comme en ceux qui sont trop chauds ou trop froids, ou de vice de conformation [...]'; ibid., p. 723.
[14]   Ibid., p. 519.
[15]   Paris: Jacques du Puys, 1587.
[16]   Ibid., pp. 195–96.
[17]   Ibid., p. 97.

MASCULINITÉ ET VIRILITÉ

Le parallèle avec la crise religieuse qu'a traversée Henri III à partir de 1582 est assez paradoxal. Si Henri, probablement sur le conseil de ses confesseurs, amorça un rapprochement de la reine Louise[18] à partir de 1586, l'on ne peut que rester songeur sur ce qu'était devenue sa 'gaillardise'. Marinelli indique bien que la seconde cause d'impuissance, chez l'homme, survient lorsque la 'gaillardise' qu'il devrait éprouver à l'approche de la personne est bloquée par 'quelque phantasie ou imagination':

> L'autre, quand la personne à l'heure mesme qu'elle veut satisfaire à sa concupiscence, se represente en l'esprit quelque phantasie ou imagination, qui luy fait perdre et oublier la volonté de passer plus outre, et executer gaillardement son entreprise: ou, quant à ceste heure mesme là luy survient à l'improviste quelque craincte d'ailleurs: quelque honte et vergongne de sa compagnie: Car il advient le plus souvent que celuy qui a quelque vergongne de la femme avec laquelle il veut habiter, perd soudain toute sa concupiscence encor qu'il l'aime et desire ardemment.[19]

Est-ce que l'imagination du roi aurait été en quelque sorte bloquée par ce que représentait désormais sa vie conjugale? C'est du moins ce que semblent avoir perçu les courtisans.

Le *Registre-journal* de Pierre de L'Estoile offre des indications précieuses quant aux différentes pratiques du couple royal souhaitant avoir un enfant. Alors que le mémorialiste note, dans un premier temps, qu'il s'agit de superstitions,[20] il va pourtant relever de façon systématique les manifestations publiques du roi et de la reine: pèlerinages, processions, séjours aux bains. L'on pourrait même croire que le roi et la reine, au cours de ces années 1579 à 1584, ne se montrent publiquement qu'à ces occasions... Même si le roi traverse une période dépressive pendant l'année 1582, le couple royal se consacre activement aux exercices de pénitence devant lui permettre d'engendrer. On compte ainsi deux pèlerinages à Chartres, l'un en janvier et l'autre en juin, une cérémonie du jubilé à

---

[18] Cf. Jacqueline Boucher, *Deux épouses et reines*, op. cit., p. 143.
[19] Giovanni Marinelli, *Thresor des remedes secrets pour les maladies des femmes [...]*, op. cit., p. 97.
[20] 'Superstitions. — Le vendredi 23ᵉ janvier, le Roy alla à Olinville se baingner et purger. Le semblable fit la Roine sa femme, qu'il laissa à Paris. Puis alla faire sa feste de Chandeleur en l'église de Chartres, et ses vœux et prieres à la belle Dame; et y prist deux chemises de Nostre-Dame de Chartres, une pour luy, l'autre pour la Roine sa femme. Ce qu'aiant fait, il revinst à Paris, coucher avec elle, en esperance de lui faire un Enfant, par la grace de Dieu et de ses chemises' (Pierre de L'Estoile, *Registre-journal du règne de Henri III*, tome III (Genève: Droz, 1997), p. 22).

151

Paris, en mars, et une procession générale, en décembre, avec les reliques de la Sainte-Chapelle et la châsse de Sainte-Geneviève. Toujours dans le but d'avoir un enfant, la reine fréquente les bains au mois d'août. L'année suivante, la reine va à Notre-Dame de Liesse en janvier, puis le roi et la reine se rendent à pied, le lendemain de Pâques, à Chartres. La même année, des rumeurs se répandent après les processions de la semaine sainte organisées par les mignons transformés en pénitents. Une série de quatrains gaillards et scatologiques, qui furent barrés du manuscrit A du *Registre-Journal*, et qui n'apparaissent pas dans le manuscrit B,[21] sont tout de même parvenus jusqu'à nous. Selon L'Estoile, ces pièces furent 'faites et semées' à la suite des processions et des flagellations. Il souligne également que ces manifestations pénitentielles publiques étaient les 'signes certains d'un grand orage prest à tumber sur un Estat'.[22] Les satires représentent les Pénitents 'accouplés deux à deux', se couvrant le visage afin de ne pas reconnaître les 'bougres et les bougerons'. Au moins cinq allusions aux pratiques contre nature et à l'impuissance sont faites. Au quatrain V, cette dernière est ainsi décrite:

> Le Roy s'est rendu penitent,
> Pource que des enfans il n'a.
> Mais, entendez pourquoi cela:
> C'est à cause qu'à peine il tend.[23]

Des pièces font aussi allusion aux dévotions du roi et de la reine à Notre-Dame, laissant entendre que ces pratiques permettaient au roi de se rapprocher de ses 'enfants', c'est-à-dire de ses mignons:

> Il a choisi la Bonne Dame
> Pour la patrone de ses vœux:
> Mais il aime mieux, sur mon ame,
> Un jeune fils aux blonds cheveux.

> Il ne faut s'esbahir si le grand Roy des Gaules
> A du nom de ses fils ses mignons adopté;
> C'est bien raison, puisque ce pere ils ont porté,
> Comme Ænée fit le sien, sur leurs dos et espaules.[24]

---

[21]   Voir note 1, p. 80, Pierre de L'Estoile, *Registre-journal du règne de Henri III*, t. IV (Genève: Droz, 2000).
[22]   Ibid., p. 80.
[23]   Ibid., p. 81.
[24]   Ibid., pp. 81 et 82.

Et, finalement, une strophe est attribuée à un bouffon de la cour et fait de nouveau référence aux actes contre nature qui seraient commis par un roi dont la semence est versée au mauvais endroit:

> Quatrains faits par Jan Sibiloth
>
> Comment! n'est-ce pas grand pitié
> Qu'un si beau roiaume se perde,
> Versant, sous l'ombre d'amitié,
> Le sang roial dedans la merde![25]

L'impuissance du roi est donc associée, dans ces sonnets, à l'amitié contre nature qu'il éprouve pour ses mignons. Il faut cependant saisir le rapport qu'établissent les polémistes entre l'incapacité de procréer du roi et la perte de dignité du sang royal. Il s'agit de dénoncer une nouvelle pratique qui rompt avec la tradition d'assurer une lignée et la perpétuation de l'ordre dans une société de l'Ancien Régime, tout en cherchant à camoufler ces lois nouvelles sous des pratiques religieuses (les processions de pénitents) et de favoritisme (les mignons entourant et assurant le pouvoir du roi). Du coup, L'Estoile change de ton. Dans l'entrée du *Registre-journal* qui suit, un paragraphe décrit ainsi les 'Voyages du Roy et de la Roine pour avoir enfans':

> L'onziesme jour d'avril, qui estoit le lendemain de Pasques, le Roy avec la Roine son espouse partirent de Paris à pied et allerent à Chartres, et de Chartres à Cleri, faire leurs prieres et offrandes à la Belle Dame reverée solemnellement ès eglises desdits lieux, à ce que, par son intercession, il pleust à Dieu leur donner la masle lignée que tant ils desiroient. D'où ils furent de retour à Paris, le 24ᵉ dudit mois, tous deux bien las et aians les plantes des pieds bien ampoullés d'avoir fait tant de chemin à pied.[26]

L'on voit dans quelle mesure le mémorialiste semble maintenant se moquer des pratiques du souverain auxquelles on ne croit plus vraiment. Le roi releva cependant la tête, notamment lorsque l'on crut, comme en décembre 1586, que la reine était enceinte.[27] Ces quelques espoirs purent

---

[25] Ibid., p. 83.

[26] Ibid., p. 88.

[27] 'Courte joie au Roy. — Au commencement de decembre, le Roy s'en alla faire sa neufvaine à Nostre Dame de Chartres, et estant revenu à Paris, s'en alla droit aux Capussins faire sa penitence et des prieres à Dieu pour le remercier de ce que la Roine estoit grosse, comme il en avoit pris l'opinion: laquelle, au bout de trois ou quatre jours, se trouva fausse, à son grand regret et desplaisir, joie et contentement de ceux de

restaurer pour de brefs moments l'image du souverain, mais elle poursuivait irrémédiablement sa chute. De moine, il devint ainsi pervers et se métamorphosa en Sardanapale.[28] Agrippa d'Aubigné n'aura alors plus qu'à procéder à l'amalgame, dans son *Histoire universelle,* attribuant aux actes contre nature du souverain sa perte de courage:

> Vous oyiez dire tout haut, que depuis que ce Prince s'estoit prostitué à l'amour contre nature, mesme avoit tourné ses voluptez à patir au lieu d'agir, on cottoit la perte du courage qu'on avoit veu à Monsieur avant la naissance de telles enormitez.[29]

Lorsque le discours polémique donnera la parole à la reine, elle ne pourra alors que confirmer les dires de la populace:

> [...] je vous confesse que, me sentant un jour desesperée de l'insolente et impudique vie de mon mari, je fus quasi preparée de mettre mon amour au Guisard, par les menées du Cardinal et de ceste preude femme la Mirande...[30]

Il faut préciser que le roi, en octroyant ses faveurs à ses mignons et à ses archimignons, donnait indirectement le ton à la polémique. Ses tentatives officielles de faire du duc de Joyeuse un membre de sa famille en lui faisant épouser sa belle-sœur alors que son propre frère était toujours vivant en est l'exemple le plus probant. La promotion des archimignons devint ainsi non plus uniquement un exemple de la faveur du roi, mais bien celle d'un phantasme qui obnubila l'intelligence du souverain.

Les noces du duc de Joyeuse, en 1581, expriment bien le type de rapport nouveau qui pouvait être perçu entre le roi et ses favoris. Des poètes comme Joachim Blanchon n'hésiteront pas à englober dans une thématique néoplatonicienne et solaire, habituellement réservée au souverain, un duc de Joyeuse s'élevant à la grandeur de l'Astre du Jour:

---

la Ligue, qui n'apprehendoient rien au monde tant que cela' (Pierre de L'Estoile, *Registre-Journal du règne de Henri III,* tome V (Genève: Droz, 2001), p. 208).

[28] Cf. ibid, p. 198 (juillet 1585): 'Voila comme, par l'artifice de Madame la Ligue, la premiere pointe de l'amour du Roy estant desja emoussée au cœur du peuple, qui ne parloit plus de lui qu'avec toute sorte de mespris, et comme d'un Sardanapale et d'un prince faineant, enyvré de luxe, ouvroit la porte par ses pasquils à des monopoles et conjurations contre le Prince.'

[29] Agrippa d'Aubigné, *Histoire universelle,* tome VI (Genève: Droz, 1992), (année 1585), p. 208.

[30] Pierre de L'Estoile, op. cit., t. V, p. 345.

MASCULINITÉ ET VIRILITÉ

A Monseigneur le duc de Joyeuse

Comme l'Astre du Jour vostre front nous redore,
D'infinité d'esclairs, et de raiz Gracieux,
Orné du plus parfait des Tresors precieux
Que l'Immortalité ait en reserve encore.

Le Sainct Nepveu d'Athlas, Ambassadeur du Ciel,
Vous donna le plus doux du plus doux de son Miel,
Mais sa vive Vertu, et Pallas sa Prudence.

Et tant qué le Soleil au Monde regnera,
D'un Laurier tousjours Vert en vous, Coronnera,
Tant vostre honneur paroist en vulgaire evidence.[31]

L'on retrouve également, cette fois-ci dans les *Mélanges* publiés en 1584 à Lyon par Jacques de Romieu, d'autres allusions au duc de Joyeuse, et notamment un anagramme sur la naissance du duc en Vivarais. Le poète insiste sur la beauté et la vaillance de l'archimignon qu'il dit venir des dieux et qui imprègnent le 'visage de la France'.

Pierre de L'Estoile a recueilli un certain nombre de pièces irrévéren- cieuses à propos du mariage du duc de Joyeuse. Dans un 'Pasquil Courti- zan' de 1581, le faste des noces et les mariages contre nature de la famille et des proches du roi sont condamnés:

Car ce n'est pas tant seullement
Pour ce nouveau Duc de Joieuse
Et pour sa gentille amoureuse,
C'est pour le Roi, c'est pour sa Mere,
C'est pour sa Femme, pour son Frere,
Pour leurs Mignons et pour leurs Gens,
Et brief pour tous les courtizans,
Dont les uns enhui se marient
Et les autres se remarient.
Mais ce sont mariages tels,
Qu'on ne vid jamais de pareils:
Un homme à l'autre se marie,
Et la Femme à l'autre s'allie,
Brouillans ensemble les ordures
De leurs deux semblables natures.[32]

---

[31]   Joachim Blanchon, *Les Premieres Œuvres poetiques de Joachim Blanchon, Au treschrestien Henry III, roy de France et de Pologne* (Paris: Thomas Perier, 1583), p. 273.
[32]   Pierre de L'Estoile, *Registre-journal du regne de Henri III*, t. III, éd. cit., p. 171.

Si, dans la suite du 'pasquil', des couples de mignons et de nobles sont formés puis déformés,[33] une 'Suitte' est donnée à cette pièce où alors apparaissent les personnages mythologiques des ballets et des pastorales de l'époque. Tout laisse donc présumer que le premier pas vers une mise en fiction des mignons, devenus personnages d'un récit licencieux, est maintenant franchi:

> Tu ne vis jamais tant de choses
> Qui dedans Paris sont encloses!
> Les Dieux, les Nimphes, les Driades,
> Satyres, Tritons et Naiades
> Y ont visité nostre Roy,
> Qui avecques ses Ganimedes
> Les a receus en bel arroy.
> Que ce sont de beaux compagnons
> Que le Roy et tous ses mignons!
> Ils ont le visage un peu palle,
> Mais sont-ils Femelle ou Masle?
> Car ils servent tous d'un mestier,
> La Valette est bien en quartier,
> Et le plus aimé, ce dit-on;
> Il est un peu bougre et poltron:
> Sont-ce belles qualités
> Pour estre entre les deités?[34]

Divinités mineures, liées à la pastorale mais également à la priapée, les mignons font désormais partie d'un univers où réalité et satire ne font plus qu'un. Ce nouveau monde fantasmatique possède des lois qui lui sont propres et des procédés de reproductions nouveaux. Le roi s'allie désormais à ses mignons: 'Ainsi que font les hannetons!' La cour devient le théâtre de pratiques de socialité des plus imaginatives:

> Mais que veux-tu que je te die?
> Il n'y a plus que Vilanie!
> Et pour te le faire plus court,
> Tous les François de nostre Court,
> Tant du Conseil que de l'espée,
> Prennent trestous à la Pippée,
> Tant les Masles que les Femelles,
> Larrons, Maquereaux, Maquerelles,

---

[33] Saint-Luc avec La Valette, le Cardinal de Guise avec Antraguet, Do avec Ville-quier, etc.
[34] Pierre de L'Estoile, *Registre-journal du regne de Henri III*, t. III, pp. 180–81.

MASCULINITÉ ET VIRILITÉ

> Bougres, Putains, et Bougerons:
> Au demeurant, bons Compagnons.
> Chacun en son art est habille.[35]

Cette mise en place d'une nouvelle mécanique des rapports courtisans visait certainement une dénonciation des pratiques de favoritisme, mais l'on pourrait également croire, si l'on adopte une perspective historique, que l'on assiste déjà à des mises en scène bien rodées. S'il était trop tôt, à la fin des années 1570, pour élaborer une vision dynamique du roi dépravé, les années quatre-vingt permirent l'élaboration d'œuvres à la trame fictionnelle plus complexe.

* * *

Le *Songe creux envoye à Henry de Valoys par un Parisien* publié en 1589 correspond bien à cette transformation du 'pasquil' en récit.[36] Dans cette description d'une cour imaginaire, le roi, après avoir banni les vénérables doctes, institue un 'venerable college de maquereaux et maquerelles'. La prostitution devient affaire d'institution, à la cour, alors que le roi se fait servir par des femmes nues. Le polémiste y voit le signe d'une morale de plus en plus dissolue:

> [...] afin que par ce moyen son peuple avec plus grande liberté, fut provoqué à lasciveté et paillardise.[37]

Ce récit du songe du roi s'éloigne cependant des clichés jusqu'à maintenant identifiés, dont celui de la confusion des sexes. Nous assistons plutôt à un commentaire sur le travestissement anatomique:

> [...] il estoit toutesfois si effeminé, qu'il se fardoit ainsi que les femmes, et pour mieux les imiter s'accoustroit de leurs habits, et contrefaisoit leurs gestes et contenances, et desiroit entre les plus delicats souhaits d'estre transformé en femme, afin d'esprouver les delices du sexe feminin [...][38]

Ce souhait de transformation, que l'on peut évidemment rattacher à l'histoire d'Héliogabale, se double d'une volonté dite diabolique, par le

---

[35] Ibid., p. 184.
[36] Voir aussi, à ce propos, la récente édition critique publiée par Keith Cameron de la *Vie et faits notables de Henry de Valois* (Paris: Champion, 2003).
[37] *Songe creux envoye à Henry de Valoys par un Parisien* (Paris: Anthoine du Breuil, 1589), p. 8.
[38] Ibid., pp. 8–9.

157

polémiste, mais que nous jugerions aujourd'hui purement médicale, de
transformer la physiologie de son corps:

> [...] ce diable incarné se persuada une chose, qu'il n'y a esprit maling qui
> s'en fust peu aviser, car ainsi qu'un peché attire l'autre, il fantastiqua en
> son esprit que par artifice il pourroit estre transformé en forme, et pour
> mieux executer son diabolique vouloir, il fit congreger tous les plus ex-
> cellens chirurgiens, Medecins et Philosophes de son temps, et leur permit
> luy cauteriser le corps, et faire toutes les ouvertures et plaies qu'ils vou-
> droient, pourveu qu'ils le rendissent apte à se conjoindre avec l'homme.[39]

La volonté de s'unir à un autre homme repousse le corps du souverain
vers une zone incertaine entre le féminin et le masculin. Il est d'ailleurs
assez ironique que les médecins, qui avaient été appelés à la rescousse par
le couple royal, deviennent soudainement les complices des perversions
du roi. Le lecteur n'est donc pas surpris outre mesure lorsqu'il se rend
compte, quelques lignes plus loin, que le stratagème visait à transformer
Henri en femme:

> [...] a la persuasion duquel ils le decoupperent en plusieurs endroits, et le
> chastrerent. Mais il demeura en fin par la permission de Dieu, inutile en
> tous les deux sexes.[40]

Le souverain se retrouve finalement avec un corps émasculé, ayant perdu
tous ses attributs, et toujours incapable d'assurer la lignée royale. Devenu
'inutile en tous les deux sexes', le narrateur n'abandonne la figure du dernier Valois que pour la resituer à la fin d'une longue chronologie des ty-
rans pervers: Hercule, Alexandre le Grand, mais aussi Popiel, roi de
Pologne.

* * *

Agrippa d'Aubigné, à cause de son talent ou de sa popularité auprès de
l'élite, demeure le 'champion' de la mise en image de Henri III. Ce qui le
distingue de ses prédécesseurs, c'est le fait qu'il procède à l'utilisation
conjointe de la littérature et de l'histoire afin de tracer le portrait du dernier Valois. Autant les *Tragiques* intègrent, par exemple, l'histoire de

---

[39]   Ibid., p. 9.
[40]   Ibid., p. 9.

Henri III à une écriture de l'affect, autant l'*Histoire universelle* fait de notre roi un personnage subissant le poids de son destin.[41]

Dans les *Princes*, une véritable biographie romancée de Henri III est livrée au lecteur avide d'anecdotes. Dans l'appel lancé aux Polonais, d'Aubigné suggère que les 'Sarmates' ont finalement élu un roi dont ils ignoraient à peu près tout:

> Ha! si vous eussiez eu certaine conoissance
> D'un feminin sanglant, abattu d'impuissance,
> Si vous n'eussiez ouy mentir les seducteurs
> Qui pour luy se rendoyent mercenaires flatteurs,
> Ou ceux qui vous faisant un cruel tyran doux,
> Et un poltron vaillant, deschargerent en vous
> Le faix qui leur pesoit: vous n'eussiez voulu mettre
> Vos loix, vostre couronne, et les droits et le sceptre
> En ces impures mains.[42]

D'Aubigné n'éprouve aucune réticence à associer la féminité et l'impuissance du roi à la thématique du sang. Gisèle Mathieu-Castellani le précisait d'ailleurs dans son étude des thèmes amoureux, rappelant que le sang, dans la poésie de D'Aubigné, était à la fois 'signe visible de la cruauté de la nature féminine [...] et seul apaisement au désir brûlant'.[43] La figure du roi se féminise donc très tôt, dans son œuvre, et occupe, dans l'imaginaire du poète, la place de la femme et d'une cruelle maîtresse. L'hypothèse se confirme quelques lignes plus loin lorsqu'impuissance et féminité font l'objet d'un échange au sein de la famille royale. La reine mère et Henri vont jusqu'à troquer leur identité sexuelle:

> Encor la tyrannie est un peu supportable
> Qu'un lustre de vertu fait paroistre agreable.
> Bien heureux les Romains qui avoyent les Cesars
> Pour tyrans, amateurs des armes et des arts:
> Mais mal-heureux celui qui vit esclave infame
> Sous une femme hommace et sous un homme femme![44]

---

[41] Nous remercions Jacqueline Boucher de nous avoir transmis un résumé de son article sur les anecdotes à propos de Henri III dans l'œuvre d'Agrippa d'Aubigné qui sera publié dans la revue *Albineana* 16.

[42] Agrippa d'Aubigné, *Les Tragiques*, in *Œuvres*, éd. de Henri Weber (Paris: Gallimard, 1969), p. 71.

[43] Gisèle Mathieu-Castellani, *Les Thèmes amoureux dans la poésie française (1570–1600)* (Paris: Klincksieck, 1975), p. 341.

[44] Agrippa d'Aubigné, *Les Tragiques,* éd. cit., p. 72.

Dans la suite des portraits royaux esquissés par d'Aubigné, Charles IX devient le chasseur sanguinaire se plaisant à tuer cruellement animaux et sujets, et Henri III rejoint de nouveau la sphère sémantique de Sardanapale et du travestissement. Examinons de plus près ce passage des *Tragiques*:

> L'autre fut mieux instruit à juger des atours
> Des putains de sa cour, et, plus propre aux amours,
> Le geste effeminé, l'œil d'un Sardanapale:
> Si bien qu'un jour des Rois ce douteux animal,
> Sans cervelle, sans front, parut tel en son bal.
> De cordons emperlez sa chevelure pleine,
> Sous un bonnet sans bord fait à l'italienne,
> Faisoit deux arcs voutez; son menton pinceté,
> Son visage de blanc et de rouge empasté,
> Son chef tout empoudré nous monstrerent ridee,
> En la place d'un Roy, une putain fardee.[45]

Le thème du fard peut à la fois s'intégrer à une suite de métaphores du mal[46] et à un processus de 'désymagination'. Ce dernier procédé, visant un dévoilement progressif de l'objet, à la manière du sculpteur dégageant peu à peu son œuvre de la pierre, consiste en un nettoyage de l'image:

> En somme, l'image procède par soustraction et défalcation des déchets et scories qui la rongent en surface; elle surgit par frottage et abrasion comme la désincrustation du modèle intérieur ainsi libéré de la gangue externe qui l''incarcère' et le défigure.[47]

Le fard qui voile le modèle intérieur, le naturel du prince, ce sont également les vêtements, monstrueux, semblables à son amour:

> Pensez quel beau spectacle, et comm'il fit bon voir
> Ce prince avec un busc, un corps de satin noir
> Couppé à l'espagnolle, où, des dechicquetures,
> Sortoyent des passements et des blanches tireures;

---

[45] Agrippa d'Aubigné, éd. cit., p. 72

[46] 'Si l'on se penche sur la poétique propre à d'Aubigné, on sait que sa réflexion assez peu théorique passe par une multiplicité de métaphores très concrètes et sensuelles: dire le mal, c'est dire le masque, le fard, le travesti, l'ordure, le vol, le meurtre, le sang, l'inversion, etc.'; voir Marie-Madeleine Fragonard, 'Agrippa d'Aubigné et Henri III', in *Henri III et son temps*, pp. 52–53.

[47] Olivier Pot, 'Les Tableaux des *Tragiques* ou le paradoxe de l'image', in *Poétiques d'Aubigné* (Genève: Droz, 1999), p. 122.

Et, affin que l'habit s'entresuivist de rang,
Il monstroit des manchons gauffrez de satin blanc,
D'autres manches encor qui s'estendoyent fendues,
Et puis jusques aux pieds d'autres manches perdues.
Pour nouveau parement il porta tout ce jour
Cet habit monstrueux, pareil à son amour:
Si qu'au premier abord chacun estoit en peine
S'il voyoit un Roy femme ou bien un homme Reyne.[48]

L'habit monstrueux, tout comme la lubricité et la volupté, étouffent
l'esprit du roi, son âme et son courage. Il n'agit donc plus qu'en suivant
son instinct, destructeur dans la mesure où l'impuissant s'attaque à des
enfants qu'il ne peut avoir:

Pour s'eschauffer sur eux en la fleur de leurs ans,
Incitant son amour autre que naturelle
Aux uns par la beauté et par la grace belle,
Autres par l'entregent, autres par la valeur,
Et la vertu au vice haste ce lasche cœur.[49]

Bien entendu, toutes ces mises en scène sont camouflées, et c'est à cet
exercice de transformation de la véritable nature du roi que D'Aubigné
revient en abordant la question des mignons et en soulignant comment le
roi, ce nouveau Néron, a ainsi pu devenir 'androgame':

On a des noms nouveaux et des nouvelles formes
Pour croistre et déguiser ces passetemps enormes
Promettre et menacer, biens et tourmens nouveaux
Pressent, forcent, aprés les lasches macquereaux.
    Nous avons veu cela, et avons veu encore
Un Neron marié avec son Pytagore,
Lequel, ayant fini ses faveurs et ses jours,
Traine encor au tombeau le cœur et les amours
De nostre Roy en dueil, qui, de ses aigres plaintes,
Tesmoigne ses ardeurs n'avoir pas esté feintes.
Signé du sang de d'O, son privé macquereau;
Disons, comme l'on dit à Neron l'androgame:
Que ton pere jamais n'eust conu d'autre femme!

Dans la suite des 'Princes', de nombreuses allusions aux mignons
s'inspirent des satires antiques; le poète emprunte à Juvénal des vers sca-

---

[48]   Agrippa d'Aubigné, éd. cit., p. 72.
[49]   Agrippa d'Aubigné, éd. cit., p. 73.

tologiques qui demeurent peut-être l'allusion la plus intéressante à l'opprobre lancé contre les pratiques courtisanes:

> Je reviens à ce siecle où nos mignons vieillis,
> A leur dernier mestier vouëz et accueillis,
> Pipent les jeunes gens, les gagnent, les courtisent;
> Eux, autresfois produicts, à la fin les produisent,
> Faisans, plus advisez, moins glorieux que toy,
> Par le cul d'un coquin chemin au cœur d'un Roy.[50]

Des anecdotes liées au comportement moral du roi sont également rapportées dans l'*Histoire universelle*. Dans l'épisode de la sarbacane, Saint-Luc aurait fait croire au roi qu'un ange s'adressait à lui et condamnait son péché.[51] C'est cependant à partir de 1585 que D'Aubigné fait directement allusion aux comportements 'actif' et 'passif' du roi. Jodelle avait bien entendu déjà abordé la question de l'arrière-vénus, en 1573, mais D'Aubigné s'exprime en utilisant les termes 'Vénus active' et 'Vénus passive'. La nomenclature utilisée, d'inspiration médicale, s'accompagne d'ailleurs de commentaires à propos de l'un des mignons qui aurait contracté chancres et maladies vénériennes 'gaignees par le derriere'.[52]

Ces passages rappelant la transformation des pratiques sexuelles du roi se doublent également d'un constat de mort clinique. A l'année 1585, l'auteur de l'*Histoire universelle* précise que 'le feu estoit mort au foyer de son cœur, et tous ces soufflets n'en faisoyent voler que de la cendre'.[53]

---

[50]   Agrippa d'Aubigné, éd. cit., p. 85.
[51]   '[...] un jour prenant Arques (depuis appelé Joyeuse) à part, ils entreprirent avec le conseil de la Dame de Rets de percer un cabinet, et de faire couler par la ruelle du lict, entre la contenance et le rideau, une sarbatane d'airain, par le moyen de laquelle ils vouloyent contrefaire un Ange et faire couler en l'aureille de ce Roi des menaces du Ciel et quelques terreurs encontre son peché. Ils entreprenoyent cela sur un esprit affoibli par gibotteries, par songes estranges, et terreurs ordinaires, qui le faisoyent cacher sous les licts, cercher les basses voutes du Louvre au moindre tonnerre qu'il ayoit' (Agrippa d'Aubigné, *Histoire universelle*, tome VI (Livre IX, chap. XV), p. 70).
[52]   A propos du pamphlet *Advertissement des catholiques Anglois aux françois catholiques de 1586*, où '[...] resveillans tous les noms odieux que les gens de bien lisent à regret dans les histoires Romaines, et notamment attaquent un des mignons de quelques chancres et maladies veneriennes, gaignees par le derriere, traictees et en fin gueries par le Medecin Miron, qui estant mal content, donnoit tels advertissements' (Agrippa d'Aubigné, *Histoire universelle*, t. VI, livre X, chap. VII, pp. 174–75).
[53]   Agrippa d'Aubigné, *Histoire universelle*, t. VI, pp. 207–8.

La cause de cet évanouissement de la personnalité du souverain? Les pratiques de l'amour contre nature:

> Vous oyiez dire tout haut, que depuis que ce Prince s'estoit prostitué à l'amour contre nature, mesme avoit tourné ses voluptez à patir au lieu d'agir, on cottoit la perte du courage qu'on avoit veu à Monsieur avant la naissance de telles enormitez.[54]

Dans la *Confession du Sieur de Sancy*, D'Aubigné parlera de fantaisie, alors que le roi passe de celle 'd'agent en celle de patient'.[55] Il précisera que le souverain devint alors si 'timide qu'il craignoit mesme les vents'.

C'est aussi à partir de cette époque que d'Aubigné offre des commentaires sur le maniérisme se développant à la cour. Pensons par exemple à l'engouement de Henri III pour les petits chiens, ou encore le plaisir qu'il éprouvait à effectuer des découpages, ces enluminures où de jeunes capitaines étaient représentés en Saint-Jérôme ou en cordeliers.[56]

* * *

Nous avons tenté de démontrer, dans le présent chapitre, que la stérilité du couple royal, sous Henri III, n'était pas une donnée négligeable dans l'élaboration de la polémique contre le roi. Même si stérilité du couple et efféminement ne participaient pas, à l'époque, d'une relation de cause à effet, il est tout de même remarquable que la satire contre le roi effectua des amalgames qui laissent non pas uniquement croire que Henri n'était pas capable de procréer naturellement, mais que ses capacités de procréateur s'exerçaient avec ses mignons qui devenaient ses acolytes et ses enfants. Cette nouvelle famille excluait la reine, mais intégrait, par le biais

---

[54] Ibid., p. 208.

[55] Agrippa d'Aubigné, *Œuvres*, p. 608.

[56] En 1586: 'Il lui prit un goust excessif d'amasser et de nourrir une telle quantité de petits chiens de Lyon, qu'en une grande sterilité et destruction de finances, il en fit un estat, qui montoit plus de cent mille escus par an. [...] Ceste despense en fut suivie d'une autre, asçavoir des enluminures qu'il faisoit couper par les livres du temps passé et les achetoit au pris du vendeur, et puis on fit une grande recerche des enlumineurs par les mains desquels le Roi faisoit enluminer ses heures de portraits des personnes qu'il aimoit violemment, et lesquelles, estans peintes au naturel, il faisoit drapper et habiller en saincts et en sainctes, et les plus aimees en Nostre-Dame. [...] De là nous vismes toute la Cour pleine de ses presens: entre ceux-là, nous avons veu des plus excellens jeunes Capitaines de nostre aage peints en S. Hierosme et en Cordeliers dès le premier desir de leur frequentation' (Agrippa d'Aubigné, *Histoire universelle*, tome VII, Livre onzième, chapitre XII, pp. 95–96).

d'un échange des sexes, la reine mère, tête dirigeante de la famille royale depuis la mort de Henri II.

Le contrôle de l'information quant à la situation réelle du couple royal s'avère cependant un mystère. Si les ambassadeurs étaient au courant des tragédies qui touchaient la vie intime du couple, les auteurs de pamphlets, un Agrippa d'Aubigné ou même un Pierre de L'Estoile, n'avaient qu'une connaissance approximative de la situation. L'on peut également se demander pourquoi Henri était montré du doigt, dans toute cette affaire, alors que l'on ne mettait pas en cause, du moins publiquement, la reine Louise. Était-ce justement parce qu'elle était liée au clan Lorraine-Guise?[57] Si Agrippa d'Aubigné avait pu quant à lui impliquer la reine, il ne le fit pas. C'est bien toujours Henri, travesti, qui nourrit l'imaginaire du poète et qui se subtilisera même à la figure obsessionnelle de l'amante cruelle.

Les différentes pièces que nous avons analysées ont également permis d'explorer les images liées aux rapports sexualisés entre le roi, ses mignons, et les pénitents. L'accouplement des hommes du roi suscitent le sarcasme et le rire d'autant plus qu'ils apparaissent semblables aux yeux de la foule sous leur sac de pénitents ou portant leurs riches vêtements. N'oublions d'ailleurs pas que même s'il est plus facile de tourner en ridicule un groupe qu'un seul individu, y parvenir multiplie le pouvoir des mots. Même si nous ne pouvons parler de discours raciste ou homophobe, à l'époque, le pamphlet et l'imprimé ont exploité la généralisation et l'amalgame. Le *Registre-journal* de Pierre de L'Estoile permet également de constater que le roi n'était 'vu', par la populace, qu'à de rares occasions. Les images les plus fortes viennent alors de ces instantanés qui ne se juxtaposent parfois que difficilement. Si le roi et la reine se rendent à Chartres pendant la période pascale, par exemple, L'Estoile n'hésite pas à souligner que le roi et ses mignons avaient participé de façon bruyante au carnaval. Comment alors bien saisir les comportements paradoxaux du souverain? La mise en récit de ces épisodes par la polémique favorisera donc la création d'une fiction intercalaire reliant de façon fantasmatique les 'représentations' du roi et de ses mignons.

Des 'pasquils semés' dans Paris aux songes imaginés et recyclés par Agrippa d'Aubigné en images baroques, les récits du roi sans enfant n'en sont qu'au début d'une longue chaîne d'emprunts intertextuels et de recyclages littéraires.[58] Ils seront, d'ailleurs, au début du XVIIe siècle, confondus avec la satire libertine contre le monde des courtisans. Henri III, qui

---

[57] Jacqueline Boucher, op. cit., p. 55.
[58] Cf. Guy Poirier, monographie en préparation.

était malheureusement demeuré impuissant face à la stérilité de son couple, engendra contre son gré un nombre impressionnant de récits satiriques transfigurant sa personne.

8

Men Are From Mars:
Jean de Sponde's Homeric Heroes
and Vision of Just French Leaders

Marc Bizer

In the preface to his commentary on Homer's *Iliad* and *Odyssey*, Jean de Sponde informs the French King Henri de Navarre that Homer's poetry is of utmost relevance to governing his country in both peace and war.[1] If Sponde remains true to his word, one can expect the *Iliad* in particular to be rich in examples of leadership, for it is rife with heroes who also happen to be kings. We will see that Sponde finds in Homer lessons applicable not only to the French king but also to those who serve him — or whose sense of justice places them in opposition to royal authority, a subject of particular relevance to a Huguenot such as Sponde writing during the Wars of Religion. Indeed, he uses Homer's warriors to offer a critical perspective on the French monarchy and on his period in general. Since leaders are by definition men in both ancient Greek and contemporary French societies, Sponde's observations amount to a consistent characterisation and critique of the behaviour of male leadership. By carefully analysing his remarks on the conduct of Agamemnon, Hector, Achilles, Nestor, and Odysseus, I hope to demonstrate that he is guided by a vision of a well-balanced, less bellicose man; the conduct of Sponde's ideal ruler in turn serves as a model for his subjects who strive to make their actions consistent with those of their wise, just, peace-loving king.

The pedagogical point of departure of this enterprise consists in enumerating the many heroes of the Homeric epics. Specifically, Sponde uses these exemplary men to impress upon the king what he calls the two 'pil-

---

[1] *Homeri quae extant omnia... Perpetuis item iustisque in Iliada simul & Odysseam Io. Spondani Mauleonensis commentariis* (Bâle: Eusebius Episcopus, 1583): 'Siue enim belli siue etiam pacis negotia administres, habet Maiestas tua quod in utroque Homeri uolumine à suis occupationibus alienum non reperiat' (f. a2ᵛ). A little later, Sponde writes in his introduction: 'Ecce Homerus tuus utramque partem ita persequitur, ut eum demum finem spectasse uideatur, quò Regibus digna omnia scriberet' (ibid.).

167

lars of the royal condition':[2] prudence (*prudentia*) and valour (*fortitudo*, or sometimes *virtus*). However, the term 'fortitudo' is followed by the word 'nimirum' in Sponde's introductory phrase, suggesting some reluctance on Sponde's part to give it an importance equal to that of *prudentia*. This is borne out in the commentary, for although Sponde tells Henry that the entire *Iliad* is devoted to demonstrating *fortitudo*,[3] Sponde himself seems to have relatively little to say about it and tends to concentrate on *prudentia*.[4] He does begin by stating that this virtue is best exemplified in Achilles and unequalled at any later time, except by his majesty himself.[5] The point, of course, in evoking the valiant deeds of such great heroes is that nothing inspires *fortitudo* more.[6]

Since Achilles does relatively little fighting, one tends to find remarks about the valour of other heroes. If, for example, we turn to the face-off between Hector and Ajax in Book VII of the *Iliad*, Sponde comments that exchanging threats has considerable efficacy in driving 'generosi et fortes viri', noble and brave men, to acts of manliness ('ad uirtutem exacuendam'), just as a lion whips itself with its tail.[7] Sponde adds that we should devote considerable attention to Ajax's speech to Hector in this scene.[8] When Hector taunts Ajax by asking him whether

---

[2] 'Fortitudo nimirùm & Prudentia tutissima sunt esse Regii status columina' (ibid.).

[3] 'Primùm tota Ilias integrum est & perpetuum FORTITUDINIS speculum...' (ibid.).

[4] Curiously, though, perhaps more so in the *Iliad* than in the *Odyssey*, despite the fact that he finds the *Odyssey* richer in examples. 'Quod idem de Prudentiæ, quam Rege dignam uirtutem dixi, tum præceptis tum exemplis intelligi uolo. Quæ licet in Iliade passim disseminentur, at peculiare Odysseæ uolumen uberius & copiosius complectitur...' (f. a3ʳ).

[5] 'Primùm tota Ilias integrum est & perpetuum FORTITUDINIS speculum uel in solo Achille, quem ita informauit, ut ei parem, si Maiestatem tuam excepero, sequentia secula neminem protulerint' (f. a2ᵛ).

[6] 'Enimuerò quid Hectoras, quid Agamemnonas, quid Menelaos, quid Aiaces, quid Diomedes, quid Idomeneos, quid Nestoras, quid Menestheos, quid Vlysses & reliquos Heroas clarissimos commemorem, in quibus luculenta fortium uirorum effigies ita ad uiuum expressa est, ut nihil exactius à mortalitate excogitari possit?... Nulla enim alia re solet fortitudo magis excitari, quàm fortium uirorum commemoratione' (f. a3ʳ).

[7] 'quæ plerunque comminationes continet, qualis ista Aiacis & Hectoris, nullam aliam ob causam, nisi quòd non exiguam efficacitatem habent uerba ad uirtutem exacuendam & excitandam, quibus, non secus ac leo caudæ stimulo, generosi & fortes uiri utuntur' (VII. 226, p. 124).

[8] 'Attendenda est autem Aiacis oratio' (VII. 226, p. 124).

Achilles' absence has made him bolder, Ajax replies that the strength of the army and the princes does not reside in Achilles alone, but also in others who do not trail Achilles in bravery (*uirtus*) and courage.[9] Thus by lauding Ajax's modesty, Sponde is emphasising the value of common effort over individual accomplishment.[10]

While Sponde makes clear that both *fortitudo* and *prudentia* are necessary for a military leader,[11] one cannot be certain that kings must absolutely possess *fortitudo*. *Prudentia*, on the other hand, is declared to be a 'Rege digna uirtus',[12] but it is also a quintessentially human quality.[13] In the *Iliad*, Sponde happens to define *prudentia* succinctly in a comment made when Achilles formulates acerbic criticism of king Agamemnon, whose messengers have arrived with the order to take Briseis away. Achilles tells them: 'Truly he raves in his destructive mind, and knows not how to look at the same time both before and after' (I. 343), which prompts Sponde to elaborate: 'It is precisely the essence of the prudent man to consider both the antecedents and the consequences of a course of action.'[14] Agamemnon would seem to be an anti-model at this point.

Achilles is not the only character to point out Agamemnon's lack of prudence; prudent Odysseus does so in Book XIV, where Agamemnon again urges flight from Troy (he first did it in Book II). In the passage in question, Odysseus directly calls him an 'accursed man' (XIV. 84) and comments bitterly: 'I wish that you were in command of some other, inglorious army, and not king over us, to whom Zeus has given, from youth

---

[9]   'docet leuem esse illam causam, neque totius exercitus robur & præsertim procerum in uno Achille consistere, adesse quoque alios, qui Hectoris uirtuti & audaciæ non cedant' (ibid.).

[10]   'Quod modestè ab Aiace enuntiatum est: quia non sibi soli laudem illam tribuit Hectori resistendi, quasi sibi ut præstantissimo illæ partes demandatæ sint, sed & eam sibi cum multis alijs prætereà communem' (ibid.).

[11]   'Egregij ducis duas necessarias uirtutes Prudentiam & Fortitudinem indicat, quæ si in eum concurrant, nihil deest illi quod ad bellorum confectionem desideret' (I. 258, p. 14).

[12]   'Quod idem de Prudentiæ, quam Rege dignam uirtutem dixi, tum præceptis tum exemplis intelligi uolo' (p. 4).

[13]   'id propriè homini donatum est, in quo uiget pars illa præstantissimi rationis, qua euentus & consequentiæ, denique omnes negotiorum περιστάσεις expenduntur' (X. 18, p. 175). Note the use of the word 'homo' (human being) in 'id propriè homini donatum est', rather than 'uir'; as we shall see, however, Sponde generally has men in mind.

[14]   'Est enim prudentis uiri, principia & causas rerum uidere, earumque progressus, & quasi antecessiones non ignorare, similitudines comparare, & rebus præsentibus adiungere atque annectere futuras' (p. 18).

right up to age, to wind the skein of gruesome wars till we perish, every
man of us' (XIV. 84–9). Sponde limits his own observations to remarking
that Odysseus urges Agamemnon to keep quiet, lest the other soldiers
make fun of this speech unworthy of a 'vir integer' and a leader of the
people.[15]

Perhaps conscious of the necessity of highlighting some prudent behaviour in Agamemnon, Sponde nevertheless declares at the beginning of
Book X that nothing takes Agamemnon by surprise, which is the height of
prudence.[16] For Sponde, there is also reason for praise in the very same
passage when, unable to sleep because of worry, Agamemnon decides to
go to Nestor 'in the hope that he might contrive with him some incompa-
rable device that would serve to ward off evil from all the Danaans' (X.
18). Thus is it prudent for a king to defer to another who is more prudent
than he. This episode involving sleepless Agamemnon contrasts interestingly with sleepy Odysseus in the bag of winds episode, in book X of the
Odyssey: here Sponde directly reproaches Odysseus with imprudence, for
dozing and being unable to stop his crew from opening the bag of winds
at a precise moment when he should have been more vigilant.[17] In a sense,
Odysseus is more at fault than his crew members, for he gave them a
chance to be led astray.[18] It is clearly imprudent for leaders to be sleeping
on the job.

Nestor has precisely this fine ability to weigh causes and effects. In-
deed, Nestor had begged Agamemnon to let go of his anger towards
Achilles, so that the Greeks would not lose their most valuable warrior.[19]
What makes Nestor truly unique is that he unites prudence with great ex-

---

[15] 'Silentium Agamemnoni Vlysses indicit, ne si hoc consilium intellexerint cæteri
Græci, Regem irrideant, ex cuius ore tam insulsa oratio exciderit, indigna uiro integro,
idque populi Principe' (XIV. 90, p. 264).

[16] 'Notandum est Agamemnonem nihil inconsultò aggredi, quod summæ est in eo
prudentiae' (X. 18, p. 175).

[17] 'Exitus tamen docuit, quàm imprudenter hoc fecerit. Ita solent oculatissimi interdum cæcutire, & res, quæ maiorem uigilantiam postulant, somniculosiùs gerere' (X.
31, p. 132).

[18] 'Hoc enim ipsi magis est uertendum uitio, quàm ipsis socijs, quòd aliorum
moderatoris negligentia ansam peccandi subditis exhibeat' (ibid.).

[19] 'Hac Achillis commendatione ostendit Nestor, quanto sit Græcis ille præsidio, ut
etiam hoc pacto ipsum Agamemnoni anteponere uideatur, cùm nihil tale de eo præ-
dicet: itaque tacitè quodammodo Agamemnonem ad iræ remissionem excitat, quasi
isto belli propugnaculo ipse idem carere non possit' (I. 284, p. 15).

perience ('magna rerum experientia') and eloquence ('persuadendi facultas').[20]

According to Sponde, Odysseus's prudence is also derived from experience. Commenting on the beginning of the *Odyssey* where it is mentioned, 'Many were the men whose cities he saw and whose minds he learned' (I. 3), Sponde declares that the most prudent heroes of the Ancients had travelled through faraway lands.[21] Like Montaigne in 'De l'institution des enfans', Sponde furthermore states that travel, which brings one into contact with other peoples and cultures, can really help one acquire prudence.[22] Indeed, comparisons with other cultures bring knowledge that sole familiarity with one's own country cannot possibly supply.[23] Sponde concludes by observing that Odysseus is said to have become more prudent through exposure to the customs and minds of many men.[24]

It is interesting to note that, despite the occasionally severe misogyny of Sponde's commentary, he can apply male standards of behaviour to women. For example, when in book I Agamemnon expresses his regret that he has to give up Chryseis, the Loeb translation reads: 'I would far rather keep her at home. For in fact I prefer her to Clytemnestra, my wedded wife, since she is in no way inferior to her, either in form or in stature, or in mind, or in handiwork' (I. 115). Perhaps aware of the scandalous nature of Agamemnon's preference, Sponde interprets this remark as an appreciation not of that part of her body but of her prudence ('Per φρένας non partem illam corporis, sed prudentiam,' p. 8).[25]

---

[20]   'Præterea hoc Nestori fuit peculiare, ut eloquentia polleret, quam cum summa prudentia coniunctam habebat, cui accedebat magna rerum experientia, quibus omnibus tota ferè persuadendi facultas continetur' (X. 57, p. 176).

[21]   'Prudentissimi heroës apud ueteres sunt existimati, qui in longinquas regiones peregrinati fuissent' (*Od.* I. 3, p. 2). Sponde cites the example of famous men who enriched their own cultures with the customs and laws they had learned in foreign lands: 'immò ab exteris regionibus optimi Rerumpublicarum moderatores in patriam suam elegantes mores ac leges inuexerunt, ut Lycurgus, Solon, ipsique adeò Romani, ut docent satis historiæ.'

[22]   'Nos uerò aliud sentimus, & non mediocre ad prudentiam comparandam auxilium uariarum gentium mores cognitos arbitramur' (ibid.).

[23]   'sic unica patria omnium rerum sufficientem notitiam suppeditare non potest, quæ proinde nobis est aliunde comparanda' (ibid.).

[24]   'Aliter ergo se gessit Vlysses, qui non solùm urbes, sed etiam mores ac ingenia hominum multorum nouit, unde factus dicitur longè prudentior' (ibid.).

[25]   It is true however, that he also interprets the praise of her ἔργα to mean that she is devoted to household duties, 'administrandæ rei familiaris studiosa'. More interestingly, Anne Dacier, writing her own commentary more than a century later than

Sponde offers some very direct comparisons between heroes in terms of *virtus*, *consilium/prudentia* (wisdom), and *fortitudo* that establish a hierarchy among the Greek heroes. For example, Sponde declares that Nestor and Odysseus surpass both Agamemnon and Achilles in prudence and valour.[26] On the one hand, Sponde declares Odysseus is even superior to Nestor in terms of these dual virtues, because he has Nestor's wisdom and courage, but is a better warrior.[27] On the other, Agamemnon, of course, is not in the same league as Achilles in terms of valour and so places last in the ranking.[28]

Prudentia has an important role to play as a check on anger, which can erupt as dangerous violence. Indeed, when Homeric heroes get angry, their ire can often be at war, so to speak, with prudence. For example, there comes a point in Book I where Achilles is on the verge of killing Agamemnon, and Athena is sent down from Olympus to discourage him from doing so. Sponde discusses this crisis as a struggle between 'ratio' and 'pars irascibilis'.[29] Sponde concludes that *ratio* is to be imitated, *ira* to be fled.[30] It is Achilles' uncontrollable rage that leads him to call Agamemnon 'dog-face' in the course of the quarrel, for example. Sponde comments here that he shows a lack of respect for his superior, and since Agamemnon demonstrates his moral superiority by not responding in

---

Sponde, finds Agamemnon's preference for his mistress over his wife to be outrageous and unjustifiable for any reason: while normally insisting much more than Sponde on the respect due a king, on this occasion she supports Achilles' accusation of insolence by remarking: 'Qu'y a-t-il de plus impudent que l'aveu public d'une passion si injuste & si insensée?', *L'Iliade d'Homère, traduite en françois, avec des remarques*, trans. Madame Anne Dacier (1699; repr. Paris: Rigaud, 1719), I. 291.

[26] 'Ab utraque ergo uirtute Nestor utrumque heroa Achillem & Agamemnonem commendat... Vterque porrò consilij facultate Nestori & Vlyssi subsidebat' (I. 258, p. 14).

[27] 'Prudentia & Fortitudine: quibus & Nestorem ipsum antecellit, qui optimus quidem erat consiliarius, sed non æquipollens bellator' (II. 272, p. 35).

[28] 'Etenim non poterat Agamemnon iurè in fortitudinis Achillis societatem uenire, quia ipso longè erat inferior' (I. 258, p. 14).

[29] 'Certamen istud in Achille fuit Rationis & partis irascibilis. Illa iræ moderationem suadebat: hæc ad uindictam stimulabat. Exitus quoque certaminis duplex fuit. Nam ab Ira primùm Ratio superata est: deinde à Ratione Ira. Rationem enim per Mineruam liceat allegoricè interpretari' (I. 189, p. 11). While some, such as Christiane Deloince-Louette, maintain that Sponde is absolutely opposed to allegorical interpretation, it is precisely at this spot in the commentary that he wants to take Athena allegorically as Reason. See her *Sponde, commentateur d'Homère* (Paris: Champion, 2001), p. 46 and *passim*.

[30] 'Hoc postremum nobis imitandum est, alterum uerò fugiendum' (ibid.).

kind, Sponde concludes that he is more modest.[31] Sponde adds here that one must be careful about choosing what to follow (i.e. imitate) and what to flee, noting that the 'lex honestatis' needs to be heeded at all times,[32] and later that it is never a good idea to speak violently or angrily.[33]

In book IX, when Phoenix is making a last attempt to persuade Achilles to return to battle, Nestor tells the story of Meleager's wrath that brought misfortune to the Curetes. Sponde remarks that even the most prudent men can be overcome by rage.[34] The consequences that arise when this happens to a king are terrifying: thus, when ever-prudent Nestor tells Agamemnon at the beginning of Book IX, 'A clanless, lawless, heartless man is one who loves the horror of war among his own people' (ll. 63-4), Sponde adds ominously that he who incites to civil war carries a heavy responsibility for violating and destroying the very fabric of civil society.[35]

Sponde analyses this comment on the role of the ruler in fomenting civil war by explaining that Greek society consists of both the public and the private, and that the Homeric term ἀφρήτωρ, 'clanless', refers to the public side while ἀνέστιος, 'heartless', refers to the private. The middle

---

[31] 'In hac autem Achillis oratione iracundi hominis status satis exprimitur, docemurque, eum qui se impetui & furori iræ concesserit, effrænem ore fieri, sine superiorum reuerentia, quam idcircò Regi Achilles non præstat, iniuriosas in eum contumelias effutiens, his uerbis... & paulò post κυνώρην ['dog face'] appellat, cùm eum uerbis alioqui non lacessisset contumeliosis Agamemnon solo uocabulo ἐκπαγλότατε usus, pro quo longè acerbiora Achilles rependit. Agamemnon itaque ea in re modestior fuit' (I. 151, p. 9). A century later, Dacier voices much stronger condemnation of Achilles' conduct: for her, Sponde 'dans le personnage d'Achille veut nous donner le caractere d'un homme colere, emporté, enfin d'un homme vicieux, & dont les mœurs sont moralement mauvaises' (p. 297), and insists that Homer teaches us that 'il n'y a ni naissance ni valeur, en un mot rien qui puisse dispenser ceux qui leur sont soumis, de leur rendre le respect & l'obeissance qu'ils leur doivent' (p. 304).

[32] 'Sic in ista μιμητικῇ διηγήσει, ut appellat Plato, uidendum est cautè quid sequamur, quid fugiamus, ne nobis loquentium authoritas ipsa honestatis lege sit antiquior' (I. 151, p. 9).

[33] 'Quippe consentaneum est, nihil per iram & uehementiam rectè dici' (I. 223, p. 12).

[34] 'quasi dicat Phoenix: Tu quidem Achilles huic Melagro similis es, quòd ira sis incensus: sed non est adeò hoc in uobis uituperandum, cùm affectus ille soleat etiam prudentissimos quosque inuadere, quod etiam nescio quem salem reconditum habere uidetur, quasi dicat, mirum non esse, si Achilles, quem iuuenilis ætas prudentem esse adhuc non patitur, eadem perturbatione conflictetur' (IX. 553, p. 170).

[35] 'ut animus Agamemnonis remollescat in Achillem: quia docet quibus criminibus se obliget, qui bella intestina concitat & fouet, nimirum ut omnia iura & uincula societatis humanæ uiolet & perfringat' (IX. 63, p. 152).

term ἀθέμιστος, denoting lawlessness and injustice, occurs when someone believes himself so much in the right that he inflicts harm on others.[36] This leads to civil war, fought between people who normally are held together by what is fair and just.[37] It is hardly surprising, then, that in another passage, 'bellicosus' appears to be opposed to 'prudens'.[38] In book I, Sponde had commented on how difficult it is for one friend to help settle the strife between two others; he is bound to alienate one of them. Nestor's prudent ('prudenter', p. 15) solution is not to take any sides.[39] Nestor thus displays great civic-mindedness by trying to reconcile Agamemnon with Achilles and resolve their violent quarrel.[40] Finally, as if the pertinence of this passage for the contemporary situation in France were not already clear, Sponde concludes his long note by lamenting that there is currently nobody in France who would listen to 'this Nestor'.[41]

The analysis of the quarrel as being based on a conflict between private interest and public welfare actually represents an important leitmotiv in Sponde's commentary, one that is also a criterion of evaluation of Ho-

---

[36]   'Ea societas autem duplex est: publica, & priuata. Illa per ἀφρήτωρ, hæc per ἀνέστιος explicatur. ἀθέμιστον autem eum intelligit, qui sibi tantum iuris assumit, ut alijs iniuriam inferat: quod fit in bellis ciuilibus ubi illi inter se bella gerunt, qui se mutuo ciuilitatis nexu complecti debuerant, quod erat æquum & iustum. Est enim æquitas societatum omnium uinculum firmissimum' (ibid.).

[37]   'quod fit in bellis ciuilibus ubi illi inter se bella gerunt, qui se mutuo ciuilitatis nexu complecti debuerant, quod erat æquum & iustum' (ibid.). For Sponde, fairness or justice is the strongest bond of all societies: 'Est enim æquitas societatum omnium uinculum firmissimum' (ibid.).

[38]   Where he speaks of 'huius Concilij personae, quia ex uiris prudentibus & bellicosissimis conflatum est' (XIV. 107, p. 264).

[39]   'Difficillimè amicorum lites à tertio quodam amico componuntur: quia si in unius gratiam magis propendere uideatur, alterius odium incurrit. Ideò Biantem scribit Plutarchus arbitrium inter duos amicos olim recusasse. Prudenter itaque Nestor duorum istorum heroum dissidium sedare nititur, unius non magis quàm alterius partes amplexatus' (I. 275, p. 15).

[40]   However, Sponde also states that the faculty of anger has not been placed in us in vain, on the condition that it be used with moderation: 'Sed non existimo frustrà à natura insitam hanc irascendi facultatem, cuius moderatus potest esse usus' (I. 189, p. 11). Thus Athena does not want Achilles not to feel his anger, but to give into it less. Anger tempered by prudence serves Odysseus well in the *Odyssey*, because he refrains from stabbing the Cyclops on impulse (they would otherwise have been sealed in the cave) (see IX. 302, p. 124), but of course he cannot resist taunting the Cyclops once they are sailing away, and almost causes the destruction of the entire crew. This is not mentioned by Sponde.

[41]   'De sola infelici Gallia nunc loquor, in qua nullus est qui Nestorem hunc exaudiat, ut de pietatis nostræ præceptis conticescam' (p. 152).

meric heroes. Indeed, Sponde's reaction to individual heroes is determined to a considerable extent by their *generositas*, which can be defined as the ability to put the public good (*publicum commodum*) above narrow self-interest. Sponde's analysis of the quarrel between Achilles and Agamemnon in book I is largely based on this principle. For example, at least initially, Sponde praises Achilles as 'publici commodi studiosus'[42] when he offers to protect the seer Calchas; fear of Agamemnon's ire prevents Calchas from speaking his mind as to the cause of the Greeks' calamity, because this means returning Chryseis to her father, a priest of Apollo, from whom she was taken by Agamemnon. Sponde seizes this opportunity to comment that, in his own day, innumerable Calchases are kept from the king's delicate ears (I. 85, p. 7) since so many are looking to protect him from hearing unpleasant truths.[43] There is thus a suggestion here that *generositas* in a king implies the ability to listen, and heed, advice contrary to his personal interests. Sponde acknowledges nevertheless that there are many Achilles willing to oppose the 'furor' of kings.

Much of the argument between Achilles and Agamemnon is analysed in terms of the conflict between personal and public interest. Sponde supports Achilles' position, pointing out that by the consensus of the people and kings it is not right to take back what has already been distributed;[44] the commentary also paraphrases the Greek hero's argument that he is fighting this war for the king and has nothing against the Trojans.[45] Sponde enlarges this idea by stating that he who favours his own interests rather than his soldiers' runs the risk of alienating them.[46] Sponde sides with Achilles when he states that it is unfair for him to bear the brunt of tumultuous battle and yet receive a lesser gift than Agamemnon, whom he

---

[42]   'Ita publici commodi studiosus est Achilles, ut illius procurandi gratia audenti animo esse iubeat Calchantem, quem timor Agamemnoniæ potestatis prohibebat liberè sententiam suam de causa Grecorum calamitatis exponere' (I. 85, p. 7).

[43]   'Non ita se gerunt hodie, qui Calchantas innumeros potiùs repellunt, quàm ut eorum libera oratione delicatulas regum aures offendi patiantur' (ibid.).

[44]   'quia nimirum semel unicuique distributa totius populi & Regum consensu non poterant rectè sine tumultu aut summa iniquitate repeti' (I. 126, p. 8).

[45]   'Vt doceat Achilles, se Agamemnonis gratia hoc bellum confecisse, ostendit, nihil se iniuriarum à Troianis accepisse, quod eum ad arma impulerit' (I. 155, p. 9).

[46]   'Etenim ea ratione fit, ut cùm ipse magis proprijs quàm militum commodis studeat, imò cum ipsorum militum dispendio faciat, compendium eorum animos à se alienet, ut de Achille contingit' (I. 152, p. 9).

goes so far as to call 'otiosus'.[47] However, even Agamemnon has his moments of *generositas*: in book X, Sponde praises the sleepless, anxious king for prudently deciding to consult Nestor, and he emphasises that a model king, an 'egregium Regis exemplum', is one who worries more about his soldiers' condition than about his private, domestic affairs.[48]

Most importantly, Sponde sees in these passages in Homer the question of the proper manner of dealing with wrongful and unjust kings.[49] When Sponde complains that, in his time, innumerable seers like Calchas were being turned away from the delicate ears of the king, he also claims that there were nevertheless many Achilles who would resist their madness, 'generosè', he adds, because they defend what is right.[50] For Sponde, Achilles' example demonstrates not only that the first line of resistance is with words,[51] but also that it is much better to use words than force.[52] Despite his condemnation of Achilles' own selfish behaviour in asking his mother Thetis to help the Trojans and bring destruction on the Greeks (I. 407–13), Sponde presents him almost as a sort of model conscientious objector who has the patience that 'probi viri' must show 'ad iniurias tolerandas', since he, the most valiant of the Greeks, does not lift a finger when his prize is taken away.[53] The principle of fairness permits

---

[47] 'Eam tamen symmetriam inter Græcos seruari in prædæ distributione hoc loco Achilles conqueritur, quasi sibi, cui totum penè belli negotium incumbit, non minus quam otioso Agamemnoni tribuendum sit' (I. 165, p. 9).

[48] 'ubi notandum est egregium Regis exemplum, qui de suis tantoperè angatur, & non minus, immò magis de illorum statu, quàm de proprijs ac domesticis negotijs sit sollicitus' (X. 88, p. 178).

[49] In his commentary, Sponde thus raises an important issue in Protestant thought of his time, namely the duty of resistance to lawful authority. See chapter 7 in vol. 2 of Quentin Skinner's *The Foundations of Modern Political Thought* (Cambridge, New York: Cambridge University Press, 1978), 189–238.

[50] '...neque desunt tamen Achilles multi, qui se illorum furori generosè opponant' (I. 85, p. 7).

[51] 'Sanè iniuriosis & iniquis regibus sic primùm uerbis resisti interdum posse opinor, id tamen modestiùs longè faciendum, quàm Achilles exemplo suo doceat. Grauiter enim & οὐ κατ' αἶσαν Agamemnoni conuitiatur, cùm nos reuerentiam, quæ reipsa maioribus exhiberi debet, uerbis quoque præstandam esse existimemur' (I. 211, p. 12).

[52] 'melius esse uerbis quàm ui cum Agamemnone contendere, quod reuerà longè etiam melius erat' (I. 217, p. 12).

[53] 'Egregium est patientiæ exemplum, quæ ad iniurias tolerandas uiros probos præditos esse decet. Ecce enim Achilles uir alioqui Græcorum omnium fortissimus' (I. 388, p. 17). Sponde also writes, 'tamen imitando procul dubio est illa Achillis modestia, ijs qui alienæ subditi sunt potestati' (ibid.).

us to oppose injustice at all levels. When Agamemnon's heralds arrive to take Briseis, Achilles tells them that he does not hold them responsible for the king's wrongdoing, but Sponde wonders whether one should obey the servants carrying out a king's unjust order,[54] and concludes that if one may resist the king himself in many civil affairs ('civilibus negotiis'), we can shake the yoke of his emissaries as well if they are making an unjust demand.[55]

The character that best incarnates *generositas* for Sponde is Hector, a model of civic-mindedness and virility (p. 30). Sponde's remarks in Book VI are unequivocal. Commenting on the passage where Hector states that he will go to Paris and try to bring him to reason, Sponde marvels that he engages in the defence of his city in such an 'iniqua causa'.[56] Furthermore, Sponde admires Hector's complete devotion to kingdom and country.[57] About one hundred and twenty lines later, after Hector declares to Helen (in the Loeb translation), 'For I shall go home to see my servants, my dear wife, and my infant son; for I know not if anymore I shall return home to them again...' (VI. 365, p. 113), Sponde declares succinctly that Hector is so concerned with public affairs that he puts them before personal matters (31), and adds that Homer without a doubt was proposing Hector as a model of a man devoted to his country ('ubi sine dubio Poeta exemplum hominis Reipublicae studiosi proposuit'), 'quod omnino imitatione dignum est'. In book XV, Sponde declares: 'patriae studiosissimus fuit Hector.' In Hector, love of one's country supersedes love of one's wife and children (XV. 496, p. 286), and Sponde seems to add almost wistfully that in days of yore there were not a few outstanding men who put public interests first.[58]

As we have seen, Sponde does not see the Homeric heroes as uniformly valiant, prudent, or selfless. Indeed, he seems to welcome this kind of imperfection. While he notes that the Stoics might find shameful the

---

[54]   'Vbi non exigua agitari potest quæstio, Vtrum rectè à subditis iniustum quippiam præcipientibus Regibus obediatur in rebus Politicis' (I. 327, p. 17).
[55]   'Tamen modestè de ea statuendum puto: quia si in plerisque ciuilibus negotijs ipsi Regi resisti potest, possumus etiam illorum mandatorum, si qua iniqua sunt, iugum aliquando excutere' (ibid.).
[56]   'Ex hoc loco constat, quanto odio sit Alexandrum Hector prosecutus, quòd illius causa tot malis regnum Troianum conflictetur, & tamen mirum est, quòd illius etiam propugnationem in tam iniqua causa susceperit' (VI. 281, p. 111).
[57]   'Scilicet fraternus etiam amor, qui uix totus ob occasionem quantumuis grauem deperit, & studium regni & patriæ, facti iniustitiam obtenebrarunt' (VI. 281, p. 111).
[58]   'Patriæ enim charitas una reliquas omnes charitates uincit, fueruntque non pauci uiri præstantissimi, qui sua omnia commoda publico postposuerunt' (VI. 365, p. 113).

177

image of a king tormented by worry for his troops, he declares: 'let them understand that the Homeric men are not made of stone or horn, but are human beings.'[59] Indeed, Sponde also opposes Socrates (and Plato) on the subject of tears. Although it may be a dishonour for valiant men such as Achilles to be seen crying *in public* (he distances himself from the others when Briseis is led away so as to be able to cry in private), Sponde takes issue with the third book of Plato's *Republic* in which it is said that tears, typical of 'mulierculae' and little boys, are unworthy of 'viri fortes'.[60] He even cites the proverb according to which men that cry are good.[61]

In the preface to his commentary on the *Iliad* and the *Odyssey*, Jean de Sponde reassured Henri de Navarre that he would find Homer's epic to be of utmost relevance. By studying the conduct of Homer's famous heroes, the king should be able to perfect, as it were, his royal role. One is hardly surprised to find that the two pillars of the royal condition are the rather traditional *prudentia* and *fortitudo*, yet for Sponde, neither of these qualities is particularly meaningful in a hero unless he also has *generositas*, an ability to put his country first. This criterion of truly heroic behaviour gives rise to considerable ambivalence on the part of the commentator toward Agamemnon in particular, mainly because he occasionally demonstrates such selfish and unjust behaviour. Conversely, it is the Greek king's subjects who most frequently seem to be models of selflessness. Yet Sponde may question the point of blind devotion: while Hector may be the paragon of the royal subject who devotes himself completely to the service of his king, Sponde seems to marvel that he does so for such an ill-justified cause. In the world of the *Iliad*, where war is seen as being motivated in general by rulers' private interests to the utter disregard of others, *generositas* can also become the basis for resisting the abuse of royal authority. Thus Achilles offers to protect the seer Calchas, fearful that king Agamemnon will not want to hear the truth, or Nestor desper-

---

[59]   'Vbi Stoici quidam in suas ἀναισθησίας leges peccatum clamitarent, qui his perturbationibus Regem illum conflictari uideant. Sed intelligant illi homines Homericos non esse saxeos aut fibris corneis, nec in rebus humanis humanam naturam exuere' (X. 10, p. 175).

[60]   'Videntur tamen uiro eoque forti, qualis est Achilles Homericus, indignæ lachrymæ, & muliercularum potiùs aut puerorum mollities redolere. Vnde sic est Plato 3. de Repub. locutus [3 line quotation from the *Republic*]. Itaque, hoc Achillis dedecus Poeta texit, cùm eum à reliquorum cœtu separat, turpe enim fuisset eum, qui armis non uincebatur, sic ab ista perturbatione uinci, unde poterat fortitudini suæ non leuem maculam inurere' (I. 348–9, p. 18).

[61]   'Lachrymarum profusio animi est facilis & mitis, unde prouerbio uiri lachrymabiles boni appellati sunt' (ibid.).

ately tries to ease Agamemnon's anger toward Achilles, declaring that only the worst kind of king loves to see violent conflict between his subjects. Both of these examples of *generositas* prompt the commentator Sponde to draw parallels with the current situation in France. Sponde cautiously avoids any direct criticism of Agamemnon, but he must engage in delicate rhetorical manoeuvering in order to be able to hold up the son of Atreus as the 'true portrait of the true king'.[62] Even Agamemnon's warriors, who demonstrate on occasion an amazing capacity for exercising prudence, are often misled by pettiness, jealousy, a propensity toward anger and violent behaviour. Homer's warriors are indeed from Mars, but Sponde uses them to construct his vision of a more peaceful planet.

---

[62]   '... Agamemnonis exemplum, in quo Homerus ueram ueri Regis effigiem expressit' (X. 88, p. 178).

9

Éros masqué: figures mythiques de l'homosexualité

Gisèle Mathieu-Castellani

Comme naguère le cinéma américain, soumis aux contraintes du code Hays,[1] usait d'images subliminales et de divers subterfuges pour tromper le regard des censeurs qui traquaient les allusions à la sexualité, et plus encore à l'homosexualité, de même la littérature de la Renaissance et de l'âge baroque a rusé pour représenter par la voie oblique un éros réprimé.[2]

C'est à quelques-unes de ces ruses que je prêterai attention, et en particulier aux divers usages de la référence antique, souvent présente en filigrane pour suggérer ce qui ne pouvait ouvertement se dire, connotant plus que dénotant. Je m'attacherai alors aux figures mythologiques dont la présence discrète permet d'évoquer sans trop de risques un éros hétérodoxe, 'cet autre amour' comme dit Jodelle,[3] bisexuel ou homosexuel. Et je tenterai de préciser la différence entre Éros maniériste et Éros baroque, en suggérant que, comme la peinture maniériste, la poésie maniériste est hantée par les figures de l'inversion.

Les ruses du discours

La Renaissance, découvrant la littérature grecque, a saisi l'occasion, bien souvent, de dire l'indicible en exploitant la voie des références et des allusions aux motifs antiques. C'est en particulier le cas lorsque les écrivains ont voulu dire leur choix d'un autre éros.

C'est ainsi que Socrate a pu devenir *nolens volens* le héros masqué de l'homosexualité. Dans *l'Histoire véritable* de Lucien, qui a ensemencé nombre de romans homosexuels, et dont Perrot d'Ablancourt a donné une version édulcorée, non sans souligner dans ses annotations les diverses

---

[1]   William Hays (1879–1954), homme politique américain, est le co-auteur d'un code de moralité cinématographique (1930) qui porte son nom.
[2]   Voir Guy Poirier, *L'Homosexualité dans l'imaginaire de la Renaissance* (Paris: Champion, 1996).
[3]   Jodelle, 'Contre la Rière Vénus', in *Œuvres complètes*, éd. E. Balmas (Paris: Gallimard, 1968), p. 346.

ÉROS MASQUÉ

omissions et atténuations, l'écrivain présentait Socrate, dans l'Ile des
Bienheureux, en compagnie de ses amants: le voici qui 's'entretient avec
de beaux garçons, comme Narcisse, Hylas, ou Hyacinthe', et 'on dit qu'il
est amoureux du dernier, car il lui fait force caresses'.[4] Les trois héros de-
viendront d'ailleurs les emblèmes de l'autre amour chez les poètes maniéristes.

Le Banquet a été à la Renaissance et au XVIIᵉ siècle soit expurgé,
soit au contraire sollicité. Expurgé par exemple par Le Roy, qui, tradui-
sant le dialogue en 1558, renonce à donner la fin du texte — les propos
d'Alcibiade, présentant Socrate comme amoureux des beaux garçons, et
contant les vains efforts qu'il fit pour coucher avec lui — arguant que 'ces
paroles sont trop sales aux oreilles chrétiennes', 'non convenantes aux
mœurs des Français, ni convenantes à la religion chrétienne'. Sollicité par
exemple par Cyrano, qui, dans les *Etats et Empires du Soleil*, s'autorise du
philosophe pour justifier fort allusivement des mœurs critiquées, en
présentant celui-ci comme le surintendant des mœurs, auquel il appartient
de juger.[5]

Et quelques décennies auparavant, Pontus de Tyard composait une
Ode *Du Socratique*, pour réhabiliter le philosophe accusé de 'mauvaises
mœurs':

> Ainsi les erreurs reprend
> De l'humaine race ingrate,
> Un disciple de Socrate:
> Qui, peu craintif, entreprend
> Des hauts secrets qu'il apprend,
> Comme son Démon l'incite,
> Guerroyer les vicieux,
> Malgré d'Anite, et Melite,
> Le parler calomnieux.[6]

---

[4] Traduction de Perrot d'Ablancourt, in *Voyages aux pays de nulle part*, collection
'Bouquins' (R. Laffont, 1990), p. 25; traduction amendée, comme on sait, et qui évite
les 'saletés': 'Je n'ai pas voulu insister davantage sur cette saleté' (note, p. 26); 'J'ai
ajouté cela pour colorer cette action qui est indécente' (note, p. 30); 'Je ne dis pas [...],
pour ne pas insister sur des saletés' (note, p. 14).
[5] Cyrano de Bergerac, *Les Etats et Empires du Soleil*, in *Libertins du XVIIᵉ s.*, éd.
J. Prévot, Bibliothèque de la Pléiade, (Paris: Gallimard, 1998), p. 1093.
[6] Pontus de Tyard, Ode III, 'Du socratique', in *Œuvres poétiques complètes*, éd.
J. C. Lapp (Paris: Didier, 1966), pp. 174–75, vv. 118–26. Anite et Mélite: accusateurs
de Socrate.

Quand on sait que ces mauvaises mœurs censurées par les accusateurs Anite et Mélite consistaient à corrompre les jeunes gens, prendre sur ce point la défense de Socrate, n'est-ce pas faire de biais l'éloge de la pédérastie?

De la même manière, la littérature homosexuelle emprunte volontiers à la littérature antique l'exemple fameux de la Bande sacrée des combattants thébains , comme le fait Cyrano dans *Les Etats et Empires du Soleil*:

> Cette céleste maladie échauffa leur sang d'une si noble ardeur, que, par l'avis des plus sages, on enrôla pour la guerre cette troupe d'amants dans une même compagnie. On la nomma depuis, à cause des actions héroïques qu'elle exécutait, la 'Bande sacrée'....
>
> (éd. cit., p. 1066)

Jamyn, le Corydon de Ronsard, 'son mignon', selon la rumeur et les pamphlets protestants[7], faisait aussi allusion à la Bande sacrée dans les stances 'A la louange d'Amour', mais prenait soin de la 'normaliser' en feignant de laisser croire que les amants qui la composeraient combattraient pour leurs dames:

> O si des amoureux marchait un exercite,
> Jamais un si beau camp ne tournerait en fuite:
> L'amant pour son aimée entrerait aux combats...[8]

On peut emprunter encore à la fable les fameux couples d'amis célèbres, liés par 'l'amitié réciproque' — tel est alors le nom des amours masculines — pour célébrer l'ami–amant sans craindre les foudres de la censure, au reste plus vigilante dans les premières décennies du XVIIe siècle que dans la seconde moitié du XVIe siècle: Oreste et Pylade, Patrocle et Achille, Hercule et Thésée,[9] et, bien entendu, Nisus et Euryale, figurent dans les 'troupes d'amants' des *Etats du Soleil* de Cyrano (éd. cit., p. 1066). L'intertexte mythologique autorise Cyrano à inventorier et à présenter sous un jour favorable tous les écarts: l'inceste (Myrrha et son père), le transsexualisme (la jeune Iphis devenue homme pour épouser sa belle compagne Yante), l'auto-érotisme (Narcisse), l'hermaphroditisme (Salmacis s'unissant à Hermaphrodite pour former un être double, qui

---

[7]   Voir *Le Temple de Ronsard*, in *La Polémique protestante contre Ronsard*, éd. J. Pineaux (Paris: Didier, 1973), tome II, p. 310 (v. 134), et p. 314 (vv. 204–8 et 212).

[8]   A. Jamyn, *Oriane* (1575), in *Les Œuvres poétiques, livres II, III et IV*, éd. S. Carrington (Genève: Droz, 1978), p. 60.

[9]   C'est Héraclès qui délivra Thésée enchaîné aux Enfers en compagnie de son ami Pirithoos.

ÉROS MASQUÉ

n'est ni homme ni femme mais à la fois l'un et l'autre), la bestialité (Pasi-
phaë éprise d'un taureau), le 'végétalisme' (Artaxerce amoureux fou d'un
platane auquel il s'unit sexuellement[10]); Cyrano ajoute à la liste la sexualité de groupe: au Royaume des Amoureux, où est organisé un séminaire
d'amants, le jeune mâle reçoit pour femmes 'dix, vingt, trente ou quarante
filles de celles qui le chérissent', mais 'le marié cependant ne peut
coucher qu'avec deux à la fois'...

Damon et Pythie, Chéréphon et Socrate, Hoppie et Dimante, Hector
et Nestor, apparaissent dans la curieuse 'Elégie pour une Dame énamou-
rée d'une autre Dame' de Tyard, où la célébration des amours lesbiennes
'vaut pour' un éloge des amours viriles, et où se déclare la rivalité entre
ces deux formes d'amours homosexuelles:

> Notre amour servirait d'éternelle mémoire
> Pour prouver que l'amour de femme à femme épris
> Sur les mâles amours emporterait le prix.
> Un Damon à Pythie, un Enée à Achate,
> Un Hercule à Nestor, Chéréphon à Socrate,
> Un Hoppie à Dimante, ont sûrement montré
> Que l'amour d'homme à homme entier s'est rencontré.[11]

Lorsque Desportes déplore la mort des mignons de Cléophon,[12] il n'omet
évidemment pas d'évoquer les couples d'amants, Achille et Patrocle, Pylade et Oreste, Hercule et Thésée:

> Qu'on ne me vante plus l'amitié vengeresse
> Du preux fils de Thétis, sûr rempart de la Grèce:
> Ni le feu saint et beau dont Pylade est forcé
> Quand il offre à mourir pour Oreste insensé.
> S'éteigne le beau nom d'Hercule et de Thésée...

---

[10]   Le nom du héros amoureux d'un platane est soit Artaxerce, par ex. chez Cyrano,
soit Xerce ou Xercès, par ex. dans *Daphnis et Chloé* (voir *Romans grecs et latins*, trad.
P. Grimal, Bibliothèque de la Pléiade (Paris: Gallimard, 1958), p. 857).
[11]   Éd. cit., p. 246, vv. 56–62. Damon et Pythie (Pythias): deux philosophes liés par
une vive amitié; Chéréphon: compagnon et disciple de Socrate dans *Les Nuées*
d'Aristophane; Hoppie ou Hoplée, et Dimante ou Dimas ou Dymas: amis cités dans *La
Thébaïde* de Stace. Damon et Pythias, Oreste et Pylade sont cités pour leur ardent
amour réciproque dans le *Commentaire du Banquet* de Marsile Ficin, *Oratio secunda*,
éd. R. Marcel (Paris: Les Belles Lettres, 1956), p. 158.
[12]   Desportes, *Adventure Seconde*, in *Elégies*, éd. V. E. Graham, Droz-Minard,
p. 221.

ÉROS MASQUÉ

Damon–Quélus et Lycidas–Maugiron, aimés de Cléophon–Henri III, deviennent ces 'Achilles nouveaux, deux aimables Printemps', qui
s'aimaient 'uniquement':

> ...ce n'était qu'un vouloir,
> En eux un seul esprit deux corps faisait mouvoir.
>
> (vv. 23–24)

Malherbe n'est sans doute pas dupe, qui porte ce commentaire acerbe:
'Voilà deux hommes qui sont deux aimables printemps: jugez si cela est
bien dit.'

Que le choix de certains héros soit l'indice de cet 'autre amour' est
attesté par le curieux sort réservé à Orphée. Celui-ci, selon Ovide, aurait
en effet 'inventé la pédérastie' après la perte de son Eurydice:

> ille [...] fuit auctor amorem
> in teneros transferre mares...
>
> (*Métamorphoses*, X. 83–84)
> (Ce fut lui qui inventa de transférer le désir amoureux sur de jeunes
> garçons...)

Les poètes, les artistes et les érudits de la Renaissance le savent bien,
même si nous l'avons (un peu) oublié: Politien dans sa *Favola d'Orfeo*
fait prononcer au musicien, renonçant à l'amour des femmes, une 'étrange
profession de foi',[13] déclarant vouloir désormais ne plus avoir commerce
amoureux qu'avec des jeunes garçons. Et une gravure de Dürer 'La mort
d'Orphée' porte cette inscription: 'Orphée le premier pédéraste'...

Aussi la référence à Orphée peut devenir un motif satirique, comme
chez Du Bellay qui s'écrie, s'adressant à un ennemi dont il veut se venger:

> Mais j'ai bien quelque chose encore plus mordante,
> Et quoi? l'amour d'Orphée?[14]

Et lorsqu'il se compare aux illustres poètes mythiques, s'il allègue volontiers le nom d'Amphion, il choisit de ne pas citer le nom d'Orphée,
préférant l'antonomase fondée sur la figure de synecdoque, 'la harpe thra-
cienne', de peur sans doute d'être accusé du vice qu'il fustige avec verve.

---

[13] Le mot est de Chamard, citant — sans les traduire! — quelques vers de Politien
pour commenter l'allusion à 'l'amour d'Orphée' dans le sonnet LXV des *Regrets*, cité
ci-dessous.
[14] Du Bellay, *Les Regrets*, éd. Chamard (Paris: Droz, 1934), s. LXV, p. 102.

ÉROS MASQUÉ

L'omission est ainsi parfois aussi éclairante que la mention explicite. Ajoutons que dans les compliments adressés de Rome à l'ami Ronsard qui a le bonheur de jouir de la faveur du roi, se glisse souvent une pointe critique. N'est-ce pas le cas du sonnet en demi-teintes qui lui est consacré?

> Et jà la tourbe épaisse à l'entour de ton flanc
> Ressemble ces esprits, qui là-bas environnent
> Le grand prêtre de Thrace au long sourpeli blanc.
>
> (s. XX, éd. cit., p. 68)

Je serais tentée d'y voir une allusion malicieuse aux mœurs prêtées à Ronsard, par ailleurs accusé aussi de zoophilie, si l'on en croit l'avocat de la défense, Christofle de Beaujeu:

> L'on a blâmé Ronsard d'avoir, vieil sacrilège,
> Un bouc noir immolé, l'ayant voulu aimer.[15]

Dans le discours satirique, la référence à Orphée vaut accusation d'homosexualité. Les écrits polémiques contre Ronsard, reprenant l'accusation de pédérastie et de bisexualité, par deux fois au moins le représentent comme compagnon en vices d'Orphée:

> C'est qu'indifféremment tu aimes la jeunesse,
> Tu aimes autant Bathyl que la folle prêtresse
> La fille de Priam, et as pour compagnon
> L'Orphée Oegrien ...[16]

Ainsi la référence à Orphée est loin d'être toujours innocente! Et tel choisira, comme Tristan ou Théophile (comme Jodelle?), de célébrer le musicien–enchanteur pour dire non seulement son goût pour la poésie lyrique, mais aussi, de biais, ses orientations sexuelles.

On pourrait énoncer ce principe de lecture critique: 'Dis-moi à qui tu empruntes, je te dirai qui tu es!' Les fameuses *Images* de Philostrate com-

---

[15] C. de Beaujeu, *Les Amours* (1589), in *Entouré de silence*, éd. G. Mathieu-Castellani, Coll. Orphée (Paris: éd. La Différence, 1995), p. 91. On sait que Ronsard était accusé par ses adversaires protestants d'athéisme et de pédérastie, mais l'accusation de zoophilie (le crime de 'bestialité' était puni de mort) ne nous est connue, paradoxalement, que par cette allusion d'un défenseur!

[16] 'Seconde Réponse à Messire Pierre de Ronsard' (attribuée à Florent Chrestien), in *La Polémique protestante contre Ronsard,* éd. cit., tome II, p. 339, vv. 137–40 (Bathyl ou Bathylle: l'un des garçons aimés d'Anacréon). Voir aussi '*P. Ronsardo ad ipsius responsum',* ibid., p. 321, vv. 17–22, où sont rappelés le scandaleux choix d'amour que fit Orphée, et le terrible châtiment que lui infligèrent les Bacchantes.

posent, on le sait, un roman rêveur de l'homosexualité: un savant interprète commente devant de jeunes garçons d'une dizaine d'années les fables représentées dans les tableaux d'une galerie napolitaine; le maître,
qui est aussi un séducteur, apprend au jeune fils de son hôte et à ses amis
les diverses voies que choisit Éros, composant ainsi un récit d'initiation
sexuelle: voici en effet que sont illustrées toutes les formes d'un autre
éros, l'homosexualité, le transvestisme, le transsexualisme, la bisexualité... Que les *Images* aient été lues à la Renaissance comme un
'roman homosexuel' est confirmé d'abord par les interventions du savant
traducteur, Blaise de Vigenère, par les diverses corrections qu'il apporte
pour voiler ou gommer les mentions trop explicites. Mais aussi par la
postérité du texte du sophiste: qui fait référence avec prédilection aux
Images? Ce sont précisément ces écrivains hantés par les figures de
l'inversion qui allèguent volontiers Philostrate, comme Muret dans ses
Commentaires aux *Amours* de Ronsard, Tristan l'Hermite dans ses
Annotations aux *Plaintes d'Acante*, ou Pontus de Tyard dans ses *Douze
Fables*; Tyard compose, en effet, une espèce de suite aux *Images,* un autre
roman rêveur de l'homosexualité, ou plutôt de la bisexualité: Narcisse,
Hermaphrodite, disent assez clairement, sous le voile de la fable, les goûts
du poète.

Il faut aussi observer que la traduction — ou la réécriture — autorise
sans trop de risque la représentation d'amours homosexuelles, comme
celle que donnent les graves humanistes des poésies d'Anacréon:[17] le seul
nom de Bathylle suffit d'ailleurs à connoter la pédérastie.

D'autres ruses sont également intéressantes. Il suffit en effet à un
poète–amant de feindre d'écrire 'au nom d'une dame' pour se donner le
plaisir de célébrer à loisir les charmes d'un beau garçon. C'est ce que fait
Théophile, non sans complication parfois. Sous couvert de laisser la parole à Thisbé, demandant à un peintre le portrait de Pyrame son amant, il
se donne loisir de vanter les charmes d'un jeune garçon, mais d'un garçon
présenté sous une figure féminine; pour peindre Pyrame, en effet,

> Il ne faut que peindre l'Aurore
> Sous l'habit d'un jeune garçon.[18]

Double travestissement: le garçon se présente sous les traits de l'Aurore,
mais d'une Aurore en habit masculin. Comme si la féminité n'était adorable que sous les traits d'un éphèbe. Et si l'amante propose ensuite

17 Voir G. Poirier, op. cit., pp. 168–75.
18 Théophile de Viau, *Œuvres poétiques*, éd. G. Saba (Paris: Bordas, 1990), p. 243.

l'amant pour modèle de beauté masculine, encore est-ce pour peindre Hyacinthe, un héros bien peu viril, aimé tendrement d'Apollon, le dieu Soleil:

> Si tu voulais peindre Hyacinthe
> Pour le faire voir au Soleil,
> . . . .
> Tu peindrais Pyrame...

Voici que Pyrame pourrait susciter le désir du dieu, comme le bel Hyacinthe!

Et nommer l'ami Damon, Corydon, ou Tircis, comme le fait Théophile, est évidemment un choix qui manifeste le goût des 'amitiés viriles' à la grecque.

Il faudrait encore, dans cette revue sans exhaustivité, examiner le cas plus douteux de certaines satires de la sodomie, que les contemporains, plus avisés que nous sans doute, ont pu lire comme des éloges masqués. Deux exemples, fort différents.

Jodelle a écrit dans ses derniers jours un poème 'Contre la Rière Vénus', qui explicitement condamne les mœurs abhorrées. Et pourtant... Si l'on en croit le témoignage de L'Estoile, ce poème a été lu comme une célébration de la sodomie, un éloge à l'envers, si j'ose dire...:

> Finalement il fut employé par le feu Roi Charles, comme le plus vilain et le plus lascif de tous, à écrire l'arrière hilme [hymne] que le feu roi appelait la Sodomie de son prévôt de Nantouillet...[19]

Le curieux texte d'Artus Thomas ou Thomas Artus, *L'Ile des Hermaphrodites*, publié au tout début du XVIIe siècle (vers 1605) sans nom d'auteur, est en réalité, sous couvert de satire, une description émerveillée du monde de l'inversion généralisée, une espèce d'utopie bisexuelle, où est présenté un monde à l'envers, et les censeurs ne s'y sont pas trompés.[20] Le même Artus Thomas, d'ailleurs, avait composé des épigrammes

---

[19]   'Fragments du recueil de L'Estoile relatif aux événements antérieurs à 1574', in *Journal de L'Estoile pour le règne de Henri III*, éd. L. R. Lefèvre (Paris: Gallimard, 1943), n. 86, p. 680.

[20]   L'avis de condamnation par l'Inquisition espagnole en 1727 est reproduit dans l'édition de *L'Isle des Hermaphrodites* procurée par C. G. Dubois (Genève: Droz, 1996), pp. 191–94. Sur les aspects ambigus de cette 'satire', voir mon article 'L'Autre Monde ou l'utopie sexuelle', in *La Découverte de nouveaux mondes* (Turin: Schena Ed., 1994).

pour l'édition française illustrée des *Images* de Philostrate, prétendant
'moraliser' ce que les fables avaient de choquant...

Ces ruses sont certes fort diverses; il me suffit pour l'heure de noter
brièvement qu'il suffit parfois d'une simple référence, d'une fugitive allusion à l'intertexte fabuleux ou littéraire, pour que se dise par un biais ce
qui autrement ne saurait se dire.

Les figures mythiques

J'en viens maintenant à cet usage des figures de la fable antique devenues
des mythes de l'éros homosexuel: 'Dis moi quelles figures mythologiques
tu choisis, je te dirai qui tu es, quel est ton désir.' Ici encore, la littérature
grecque est mise à contribution, ne laissant, il est vrai, que l'embarras du
choix: combien d'adolescents aimés des dieux et des héros dans la fable!
Parmi eux, Ganymède aux beaux yeux, le délicat Hyacinthe, et le char-
mant Hylas sont sans doute les favoris des poètes qui choisissent de déclarer obliquement leurs goûts. Ces trois héros sont d'ailleurs associés
dans l'*Orfeo* de Politien, lorsque le musicien, pour justifier son choix de
nouveaux objets amoureux, 'fuyant le commerce des femmes', allègue les
exemples de Jupiter jouissant au ciel du bel Ganymède, de Phébus jouissant sur terre d'Hyacinthe, et d'Hercule, vainqueur du monde, vaincu par
le bel Hylas.[21]

Ganymède devient par exemple la référence pour dire non seulement
la qualité d'un breuvage exquis, mais la sorte de bonheur recherché; ainsi
chez Théophile, adressant sa prière à la 'barbare saison', l'hiver:

> Ta neige fonde sur son toit
> Un sacré nectar qui ne soit
> Ni brûlant, ni glacé, ni tiède,
> Mais tel que Jupiter le boit
> Dans la coupe de Ganymède.
> Si tu m'accordes ce bonheur...
>
> ('Contre l'Hiver', éd. cit., p. 49)

Ou adressant un délicat compliment au médecin Charles de Lorme,
nommé Chiron, du nom du Centaure éducateur d'Hercule et d'Achille:

> Toi qui fais un breuvage d'eau
> Mille fois meilleur et plus beau

---

[21]   'Fanne di questo Giove intera fede, / Che dal dolce amoroso nodo avvinto / Si
gode in cielo il suo bel Ganimede; / E Febo in terra si godea Iacinto; / A questo santo
amore Ercole cede, / Che vinse il mondo e dal bell'Ila è vinto...' (vv. 346–53).

ÉROS MASQUÉ

Que celui du beau Ganymède…
('Théophile à son ami Chiron', éd. cit., p. 288)

Fort allusivement, s'inscrit ainsi dans le texte la référence à un Éros non-dit, suggéré par le rappel discret des amours de Jupiter et de ses goûts, de sa tendre relation avec son échanson favori, réputé 'le plus beau des mortels', qu'il avait ravi et transporté sur l'Olympe pour satisfaire ses désirs.

La triste aventure de l'adolescent aimé et éduqué par Hercule, le bel Hylas, dont l'écho porte le nom, après sa mort, était chantée par Apollonios de Rhodes dans le livre I des *Argonautiques* et par Théocrite dans l'une de ses *Idylles* (XIII), puis par Virgile dans la sixième *Bucolique*. La seule évocation de son nom est l'indice d'un goût pour les beaux adolescents: Hylas est présent chez Ronsard, qui lui consacre un long poème,[22] comme chez Jodelle, chez Jamyn comme chez Desportes. Ce dernier, composant un poème pour Henri III, feint de chanter la femme aimée du souverain, mais à quels modèles la compare-t-il?

…vous nous représentez
D'Hylas ou d'Adonis les célestes beautés.
(*Elégie* VII, éd. cit., p. 58)

Sans doute la femme n'est-elle en effet 'adorable' que si elle ressemble au bel adolescent.

Quant à Hyacinthe, dont les vents Borée et Zéphyr auraient disputé les faveurs à son amant Apollon, sa métamorphose en fleur, comme celle d'Ajax ou de Narcisse, n'a guère cessé de fasciner les maniéristes. Ce serait pour lui que, selon la fable rapportée par Apollodore dans sa *Bibliothèque*, le musicien Thamyris aurait 'inventé' la pédérastie. Rêver de devenir fleur, fleur languissante et penchée, n'est-ce pas rêver d'une métamorphose qui efface la virilité au profit de la tendre féminité?

Quel est au juste le sexe d'Hyacinthe dans ce poème de Jamyn?

Digne d'amour, ô belle fleur éclose,
Bel Hyacinthe, heureux est ton malheur:
Si tu n'étais en l'être d'une fleur,
Tu n'aurais l'heur qui passe toute chose.

Voici une belle fleur, un amant qui eut le singulier privilège d'être aimé…du frère et de la sœur, des jumeaux Apollon et Artémis:

---

[22] Un poème de 430 vers, *Hylas*, in *Septième Livre des Poèmes* (1569), *Œuvres complètes*, éd. Laumonier, tome XV–2 (Paris: Didier, 1957), pp. 234–53.

ÉROS MASQUÉ

> En ton vivant tu fus aimé d'un dieu,
> Après ta mort d'une sage Immortelle,
> Qui est sa sœur et qui règne en son lieu.[23]

La référence à Hermaphrodite, qui a les deux sexes ensemble, ne saurait évidemment surprendre chez Pontus de Tyard qui lui consacre l'une de ses *Douze Fables*. Le rêve d'idéale bisexualité ne saurait mieux se dire. L'épigramme s'achève sur l'heureuse promesse faite par la déesse de l'amour:

> Soit ainsi (dit Vénus) mais aussi vrai sera
> Que quiconque en ton fleuve, ô Salmace, entrera,
> Aura, comme vous deux, les deux sexes ensemble.
>
> (éd. cit., p. 272)

De même, l'éloge de l'ancien Androgyne, qui était 'Ensemble mâle et ensemble femelle', est l'occasion de célébrer les privilèges de la bisexualité, comme le fait Jamyn dans les *Stances de l'Androgyne figuré par la danse des voltes*:

> Sur quatre pieds elle pouvait marcher,
> Et de quatre yeux voyait ce qui s'oppose:
> De quatre mains elle pouvait toucher,
> De quatre oreill' écouter toute chose.
> Rien ne manquait à la perfection
> De ces deux un...
>
> (éd. cit., p. 126 , vv. 29–34)

Quant au héros de l'auto-érotisme, le malheureux Narcisse abusé par l'image de sa beauté reflétée par le miroir des eaux, il séduit le poète attiré par cette forme d'éros, comme Jamyn, un nouveau Narcisse:

> L'eau vive me semblait et de braise et de feu,
> Et ma soif s'augmentait tant plus j'en avais bu.
> Ainsi le beau Narcisse, amoureux de soi-même,
> Pour étancher sa soif, en sentit une extrême,
> Une soif amoureuse...
>
> (*Elégie*, III, p. 135, vv. 125–29)

Et il est intéressant de constater que Tyard choisit, de préférence à celle d'Ovide, la version du mythe donnée par Pausanias, qui prête au héros une sœur jumelle, pour 'rationaliser' la fable:

---

[23]   *Œuvres poétiques*, livre IV, éd. cit, s. XCV, pp. 238–39.

191

ÉROS MASQUÉ

> Narcisse aime sa sœur, sa chère sœur jumelle;
> Sa sœur aussi pour lui brûle d'ardeur extrême:
> L'un en l'autre se sent être un second soi-même:
> Ce qu'elle veut pour lui, il veut aussi pour elle.
> De semblable beauté est cette couple belle,
> Et semblable est le feu qui fait que l'un l'autre aime,
> Mais la sœur est première à qui la Parque belle
> Ferme les jeunes yeux d'une nuit éternelle.
> Narcisse en l'eau se voit, y pensant voir sa sœur...[24]

Étrange façon de 'rationaliser' la fable! La gémellité rêvée dit le fantasme de bisexualité: tout pareil à une fille, Narcisse tombe amoureux de lui-même, d'un lui-même qui est son double féminin. On sait que le fantasme de gémellité est l'un des traits d'une forme d'homosexualité, comme on le voit, par exemple, dans le cas de Thomas Mann et de Klaus Mann, ou de Robert Musil.[25]

Devenir Narcisse, c'est rêver de se voir transformer en fleur, symbole de féminité, en fleur porte-nom, comme chez Ronsard:

> Je veux encor de ma pâle couleur
> Dessus le Loir enfanter une fleur
> Qui de mon nom et de mon mal soit peinte.[26]

C'est aussi nourrir un désir d'enfantement, et il est remarquable que Ronsard ait choisi dans l'édition de 1560 de corriger 'enfante', qui laisse trop apparaître le fantasme de féminité,[27] pour tenter d'assurer le caractère viril de cette procréation, un engendrement:

> Je veux du teint de ma pâle couleur
> Aux bords du Loir *faire naître* une fleur...

---

[24] Pontus de Tyard, éd. cit., 'Huitième Fable de la Fontaine de Narcisse...', pp. 270–71.
[25] Voir de Thomas Mann la nouvelle *Sang réservé*; Klaus Mann, qui a assumé son homosexualité un peu plus hardiment que son père, se plaît à voir dans sa sœur d'un an plus âgée que lui sa jumelle, et c'est sous le nom des 'Literary Mann Twins' qu'ils ont fait une partie de leur carrière aux États-Unis... Voir également de Robert Musil *L'Homme sans qualités*, où le couple fraternel d'Ulrich et d'Agathe (qui ne sont pas jumeaux) déclare un fantasme de gémellité, et de surcroît de gémellité 'siamoise'.
[26] Ronsard, *Les Amours*, s. XVI, in *Œuvres complètes*, éd. cit., VI, p. 21.
[27] En effet, si la femme *enfante*, l'homme *engendre*: nuance! Lou Andréas Salomé mettait en évidence ce fantasme de féminité chez l'homme–écrivain, 'gros' de son œuvre.

Bref, sans multiplier les exemples, on peut assurer, il me semble, que le recours à la fable permet de déclarer allusivement un choix d'éros, sans offenser les bonnes mœurs...

Éros maniériste

L'éros maniériste me semble bien différent de l'éros baroque, et l'objet amoureux y est, dirait-on, le produit d'un autre 'étayage': ne pourrait-on opposer l'hétérosexualité de l'un à la bisexualité ou à l'homosexualité de l'autre?

L'amant baroque, Sponde, Aubigné, Habert, trouve en Actéon, l'imprudent ou l'impudent chasseur dévoré par sa propre meute, l'image idéale de son martyre, alors que le gracile Sébastien percé de flèches fascine l'homosexuel, comme le souligne justement Mishima. L'amant maniériste, incertain de lui-même et de son sexe, androgyne, n'est épris que de lui-même, d'une sœur jumelle qui porte ses traits, d'une dame déguisée sous l'habit d'un garçon. Il est séduit par le travesti, comme Tristan, disant bien curieusement à sa dame:

> Bien que ta froideur soit extrême,
> Si dessous l'habit d'un garçon
> Tu te voyais de la façon,
> Tu mourrais d'amour pour toi-même.[28]

Qui parle ici? Un amant fasciné par un homme–femme, aimant le déguisement qui trouble les identités sexuelles.

Narcisse mélancolique est un héros maniériste; comme on peut lire Narcisse à la lumière du maniérisme, on peut lire le maniérisme à la lumière de Narcisse: ce héros de l'erreur, de la semblance, de la vaine semblance, est aussi le héros du *vano desio*, du désir vain, que seule satisfait l'illusion. Il hante les textes des maniéristes, de Ronsard à Théophile, de Desportes à Tristan. Ainsi, chantant sa dame nommée Narcize, Siméon-Guillaume de La Roque voit en elle une figure féminine de Narcisse, tandis que lui-même se transforme en Écho dolente:

> Vous semblez un Narcis de grâce et de rigueur,
> Il avait comme vous l'apparence divine...
> De moi, je suis Echo dolente forestière...[29]

---

[28] Tristan l'Hermite, 'Le Promenoir des deux amans', in *Les Plaintes d'Acante et autres œuvres*, éd. J. Madeleine (Paris: Cornély Éd., 1909), p. 60.

[29] Siméon-Guillaume de La Roque, *Amours de Phyllis*, éd. G. Mathieu-Castellani (Paris: Nizet, 1983), s. XI, p. 25; ou *Anthologie de la poésie amoureuse baroque*

ÉROS MASQUÉ

En Écho piteuse:

> Eloigné de mon bien, je me vois transformer
> En voix d'Echo piteuse, en amère fontaine...[30]

Curieuse inversion sexuelle! Voici que l'amant se représente volontiers sous une figure féminine, celle de la plaintive Clytie, tandis que l'amante devient la figure mâle du Soleil ardent:

> Je suis en ces déserts l'amoureuse Clytie
> Qui suis jusques au soir mon Soleil radieux,
> Dont la jalouse ardeur d'un amour furieux
> Fut cause que je suis en souci convertie.[31]

De même Desportes, contant les métamorphoses qu'Amour lui infligea, choisit des figures qui révèlent sa féminité langoureuse, une fleur comme Hyacinthe, une fontaine comme celle où mourut le joli Narcisse, une piteuse voix comme celle d'Écho:

> Après je devins fleur languissante et penchée,
> Puis, je fus fait fontaine aussi soudain séchée,
> Epuisant par mes yeux toute l'eau que j'avais;
> Or je suis salamandre et vis dedans la flamme;
> Mais j'espère bientôt me voir changer en Voix...[32]

Voilà, on en conviendra, des emblèmes bien peu virils...

Pygmalion, Actéon, Ixion, sont les figures mythiques privilégiées de l'éros baroque, qui voit l'autre comme autre, tandis que Narcisse, Hermaphrodite, Hyacinthe, Hylas, sont les figures privilégiées de l'éros maniériste, et de son indécision, de son trouble.

De même, la Diane chasseresse éprise de sang, la terrible Tauroscytienne qui exige des sacrifices humains, devient dans la poésie maniériste l'image de la féminité sans attraits, tandis que l'amant se voit volontiers sous la figure d'Endymion, que Diane posséda malgré lui, et dont le long sommeil dit le refus du commerce sexuel avec la déesse, cet Endymion qui, chez Théophile,

---

(Paris: Hachette, 1990), p. 274.

[30] Id., *Amours de Narcize*, in *Œuvres* (1609), s. XCI, p. 193.

[31] Id., *Amours de Phyllis*, éd. cit., s. XXXVII, p. 57, ou *Anthologie*, p. 275.

[32] Desportes, *Les Amours de Diane*, éd. V. E. Graham (Genève: Droz-Minard, 1959), s. XXXIV, p. 75.

ÉROS MASQUÉ

Vaincu du froid et du sommeil
Ne peut tenir parole à la sœur du Soleil.

(*Elégie*, XXIII, p. 246)

Il ne *peut* tenir parole, ou il ne *veut*? Le meilleur exemple d'un Éros masqué se voit dans la poésie de Théophile, ce maniériste dont la poétique explicite revendique la liberté et la franchise, tandis que se déclare de biais le choix du déguisement:

Si pour un beau dessein il se faut déguiser,
Si le secret d'amour a besoin qu'on le couvre,
On ne me saurait accuser
D'être aujourd'hui le seul qui dissimule au Louvre.[33]

Tout est en effet ici à double entente: quelle est la nature de cette amitié sainte qui le lie à Tircis (Des Barreaux)?[34] Qu'est-ce que ce 'plaisir naturel' qui ne laisse 'point de place à des désirs malins'?[35] Ce 'divertissement qu'on doit permettre à l'homme',

Ce que sa Sainteté ne punit pas à Rome

(v. 78)

n'est-il pas la sodomie? Le texte dans ses premières éditions portait *permet* au lieu de *punit*; et le père Garasse voyait dans ce plaisir naturel un plaisir contre nature: corrigeant le texte, Théophile feint de 'normaliser' son discours, mais on peut comprendre autrement la nature de ce 'divertissement' autorisé par le pape si l'on se rappelle que de malicieux pamphlets protestants[36] assuraient que la sodomie avait été tolérée... en été, par une bulle papale! Et A. d'Aubigné le rappelait dans *Les Tragiques*:

---

[33] *Le Déguisé pour Monsieur le Premier*, éd. cit., p. 242, vv. 21–24.
[34] Appelé, selon la plaisante anecdote rapportée par Tallemant des Réaux, 'la veuve de Théophile': 'Quelque temps après la mort de ce poète [Théophile de Viau], en une débauche où était le feu comte du Lude, des Barreaux se mit à criailler [...]; le Comte lui dit en riant: "Oy! pour la veuve de Théophile, il me semble que vous faites un peu bien du bruit"' (*Historiettes*, éd. A. Adam (Paris: Gallimard, 1970), p. 29).
[35] *La Plainte de Théophile, A son ami Tircis*, p. 257, vv. 75–76.
[36] Henri Estienne assure dans son *Apologie pour Hérodote* que Sixte IV 'octroya à toute la famille du cardinal de S. Luce d'avoir la compagnie charnelle des mâles, durant les trois mois les plus chauds de l'année' (éd. Ristelhuber (Paris: I. Liseux, 1879), tome II, p. 383). Philippe Duplessis-Mornay dira à son tour dans son *Mystère d'Iniquité* (1607) que le pape Sixte IV aurait répondu favorablement par une bulle à une requête lui demandant d'autoriser la sodomie durant les trois mois les plus chauds de l'année...

ÉROS MASQUÉ

Voici donc, Antéchrist, l'extrait des faits et gestes:
Tes fornications, adultères, incestes,
Les péchés où nature est tournée à l'envers,
La bestialité, les grands bourdeaux ouverts,
Le tribut exigé, la bulle demandée
Qui a la sodomie en été concédée...

(Jugement, vv. 811–15)

La correction donnerait ainsi, en fait, un texte plus décisivement libertin, du moins pour qui peut déchiffrer l'allusion.

Dans *La Maison de Sylvie*, c'est par le biais du rappel des fables que se dit l'autre éros. Ainsi dans l'ode III, Cycnos, l'amant de Phaéton, lié à lui par 'une amitié si sainte' (v. 87), cherche 'l'objet de sa plainte':

Ainsi pour flatter son ennui
Il demande au dieu Mélicerte
Si chaque dieu n'est pas celui
Dont il soupira tant la perte...

(éd. cit., p. 308, vv. 91–94)

Et l'*Ode* IV, sous couleur de chanter le 'chaste oiseau', fait l'éloge des amours viriles tout en niant qu'elles puissent être un crime:

Pour avoir aimé ce garçon
Encore après la sépulture,
Ne crains pas le mauvais soupçon
Qui peut blâmer ton aventure.
Les courages des vertueux
Peuvent d'un vœu respectueux
Aimer toutes beautés sans crime...

(p. 310, vv. 21–27)

Qui parle ici? Évidemment un autre Cycnos, lié à son Tircis par une 'amitié chaste et fidèle', qui réclame obliquement le droit d'aimer 'toutes beautés', sans craindre quelque 'mauvais soupçon':

Ainsi malgré ces tristes bruits
   Et leur imposture cruelle,
   Tircis et moi goûtons les fruits
D'une amitié chaste et fidèle.

Rien ne sépare nos désirs...

(vv. 61–65)

Bien différent en effet de l'éros baroque, qui tient l'autre pour autre, et s'efforce de le posséder, l'éros maniériste rêve en effet d'une idéale indifférence sexuelle, que l'amant soit *neuter* ou *uterque*, d'une idéale androgynie...

* * *

Lorsque l'amant–poète choisit comme comparants Hyacinthe de préférence à Actéon, Narcisse plutôt que Pygmalion, Endymion au lieu de Tantale, il déclare sous le masque transparent de la référence mythologique ses goûts et son désir. Comme le montrait Hocke dans *Le Labyrinthe de l'art fantastique*, l'artiste maniériste est hanté par l'inversion, et représente le sexe comme 'énigme'; et le critique soulignait l'importance des mythes de la bisexualité, proposant de voir en l'hermaphrodite et en l'androgyne des 'emblèmes' du maniérisme.[37]

Le poète maniériste, hanté en effet par les figures de la bisexualité ou de l'homosexualité, nouvel Hermaphrodite ou nouvel Androgyne, nourrit un rêve d'inversion, que les héros mythologiques lui permettent de déclarer allusivement, mais de façon insistante... Le recours au régime de l'allusion est d'ailleurs d'autant plus nécessaire que, si l'homosexualité semble tolérée à condition qu'elle se masque dans la seconde moitié du XVIᵉ siècle, on assiste à un 'tour d'écrou' dans les premières décennies du XVIIᵉ; la censure se montre beaucoup plus vigilante, comme on le voit évidemment dans le cas tragique de Théophile, qui osa déclarer faire 'vœu désormais de ne foutre qu'en cul',[38] de ce libertin dont les mœurs faisaient condamner les textes, dont les textes faisaient condamner les mœurs.

Si les références à la mythologie apparaissent d'abord comme un indice de culture (classique), elles peuvent être également le signe discret des préférences sexuelles... Et la poésie maniériste, de Ronsard, Tyard ou Desportes, à Théophile et Tristan, a privilégié un autre éros, où les fantasmes de bisexualité se déclarent obliquement par le recours à la fable et à ses figures emblématiques.

---

[37] G. R. Hocke, *Labyrinthe de l'art fantastique* (*Die Welt als Labyrinth*), trad. fr. C. Heim (Paris: Éditions Gonthier, 1967), p. 209 et p. 196.
[38] Sonnet XII, éd. cit., p. 358 (paru dans le *Parnasse satyrique* de 1620 sous son nom).

INDEX

Achilles, 28, 30–32, 39, 167–79, 189
— and Patroclus, 114, 183–5
adultery, 3–4, 113–14, 196
Agamemnon, 167–79
Agricola, Rudolph, 65
Ailly, Pierre d', 2, 7, 10
Alacoque, Margaret Mary, 20
Alcibiades, 122, 182
Alençon, duc d', 148
Anacreon, 186–7
Androgyne myth/figure, 32–3, 42, 104–5, 108, 161, 191, 193, 197
— François Ier portrayed as, 44, 134, 137
Anne of Brittany, 23
Apollo, 31–33, 38, 43, 71–2, 90, 175, 188, 190
Apollonius of Rhodes, 99–100, 190
Aristophanes, 184
Aristotle, 3, 82, 109
Attis, 34–6
Aubigné, Agrippa d', 132, 134, 142, 154, 159–64, 193, 195–6

Baïf, Jean-Antoine de, 61, 89, 122
Baroque poetry, 181, 193–4, 197
Barry, Paul de, 1–2, 5–8, 18, 19
beards, 25, 128
Beaujeu, Christofle de, 186
Bernard of Clairvaux, 7
bestiality, 35, 184, 186, 196
Billon, François, 90
birthing, male fantasy of, 115–17, 192
bisexuality, 181, 186–8, 191–3, 197

Blanchon, Joachim, 154–5
Bourdichon, Jean, 23
Bovelles, Charles de, 65–6
Brantôme, Pierre de Bourdeille, seigneur de, 25
Budé, Guillaume, 23, 31–3, 36, 39, 41–2, 44
Butler, Judith, 104

Calchas, 175–6, 178
Castiglione, Baldassare, 24
castration, 35–6, 159
Catherine de Médicis, 132, 140, 147–8, 160, 165
Catullus, 85, 87–93, 95, 97–8
Champier, Symphorien, 64
Chappuis, Claude, 28
Charles IX, king of France, 160
Charles V, Emperor, 36, 38, 41
Cheffontaines, Christophe de, 4, 6
Chicot, Henri, 5, 11
Christine de Pisan, 11, 16
Colin, Jacques, 24, 27–8
Conrard, Olivier, 3–8, 19
cosmetics, 161
cuckoldry, 3, 27
Cyrano de Bergerac, 182–4

Dacier, Anne, 171–3
Davent, Léon, 27, 36
Descartes, René, 63, 77, 81–4
Desportes, Philippe, 184–5, 190, 193–4, 197
Diogenes, 118
Doré, Pierre, 5
Du Bartas, Guillaume de Saluste, seigneur, 61, 74–5, 134
Du Bellay, Guillaume, 25, 40
Du Bellay, Jean, 25

Du Bellay, Joachim, 70, 85, 185
Du Ferron, Arnould, 45
Du Haillan, Bernard Giraud,
136–40
Du Monin, Jean-Édouard, 75
Durant, Denis, 97
Dürer, Albrecht, 185
Du Tilh, Arnaud, 130, 141
Duval, Jacques, 129–31
Du Verdier, Antoine, 130, 134

Ebreo, Leone, 61, 63–6, 69, 72–3,
75, 77–80
effeminacy, 26, 88–9, 92, 96,
104, 132–4, 137, 142, 158, 160
Epimenides, 141
Erasmus, 4, 6, 15, 25, 31, 33
Estienne, Henri, 106, 112–13,
120, 195

Ficino, Marsilio, 26, 32–3, 63–
78, 82–3, 104–6, 122, 184
Fontaine, Charles, 87–8
Foucault, Michel, 103
François Iᵉʳ, king of France, 26–8,
30, 38, 40–1, 43–5, 134, 137,
147

Gaguin, Robert, 26
Ganymede, 108, 189–90
Gaspar de Bono, 2
Gerson, Jean, 2–12, 16–21
Greek Anthology, 92
Guise, Henri de, 135–41

Henri II, king of France, 43, 88,
95
Henri III, king of France, 10, 119,
131–41, 147–65, 185, 190
— mignons of, 152–7, 162–5
Henri IV (Henri de Navarre) 132,
135–7, 167–8, 178
Heraclitus, 108

Hercules, 26–7, 29, 159
— and Hylas, 189–90
— and Theseus, 183–4
Hermaphroditus,
hermaphroditism, 86, 127–43,
183–4, 187, 191, 194, 197
Héroët, Antoine, 32–3
Homer, 105, 110, 167–79
homosexuality, 29, 34, 89, 103–
126, 181–97
Hyacinthus, 182, 188–90, 194,
197

impotence, 133, 135, 139, 148–53
incest, 35, 183, 196

Jacquinot, Jean, 2, 5, 8, 14
Jamyn, Amadis, 183, 190–1
Jeremiah, 4
Jesuits, 1, 10, 14, 18–19
Jodelle, Étienne, 163, 181, 186,
188, 190
John the Baptist, 4
Joyeuse, duc de, 154–5, 162
Juvenal, 161–2

Labé, Louise, 90
Lacan, Jacques, 81–4
La Roque, Siméon-Guillaume de,
193, 197
Lefèvre d'Étaples, Jacques, 4
Le Roy, Louis, 108
lesbianism, 86, 184
L'Estoile, Pierre de, 149, 151–7,
164, 188
Liebault, Jean, 150
Loarte, Gaspar, 10
Lorme, Charles de, 189
Louis XII, king of France, 23
Louis XIV, king of France, 10
Louise de Lorraine, 148, 151–4,
164
Louise de Savoie, 33, 38, 40

Lucian, 181

Magny, Olivier de, 87–8, 98
Maillard, André, 137
Malherbe, François de, 185
Mannerism, 164
— in poetry, 93, 181–2, 190,
  193–7
Marguerite de Navarre, 23, 32–3,
  39–40, 44, 65, 105
Marie Germain, 127–30, 141
Marin le Marcis, 129–31, 134,
  141
Marot, Clément, 37, 87, 92, 97
Marquets, Anne de, 5
Martial, 94
masculine love opposed to
  feminine love, 66, 68, 78–80
masculine rhetoric, 98
masculine women, 67, 69
masculinity
— military prowess as measure
  of, 95–6
— noble ideal of, 29, 34, 168
— warrior ideal of, 23–5, 135,
  139, 167
masturbation, 118
Matthieu, Pierre, 136–7, 138–9
melancholy, 82–3
Mireurs, Pierre des, 87–8
Montaigne, Michel de, 26, 62–3,
  92, 127–9, 133, 137, 140–2,
  171
— Apologie de Raimond
  Sebond, 103–126
— Journal de voyage, 127–30
Montmorency, Anne de, 24, 43–4
Morel, Jean de, 98, 100–1
Muret, Marc-Antoine, 27, 187

Narcissus, narcissism, 66–70, 73–
  4, 76, 80–3, 182–3, 187, 190–4,
  197

neo-Platonism, 26, 28, 32, 39, 42,
  65–6, 69, 73–5, 77–83, 105–6,
  108, 155
Nestor, 31, 167, 170–6, 178, 184
Nicholas of Cusa, 65

Odysseus (Ulysses), 28, 31, 167,
  169–72, 174
Olimpo degli Alessandri,
  Baldassari, 97–8
Orpheus, 185–6
Ovid, 92
— Fasti, 26–7
— Metamorphoses, 28–9, 31,
  37, 40, 45, 69, 185, 191

Paré, Ambroise, 129, 149–50
Pascal, Blaise, 63, 83–4, 143
paterfamilias, role of, 12–13
Pausanias, 191
pederasty, 106, 113, 118, 183,
  185–7, 190
Peletier du Mans, Jacques, 70
Perrot d'Ablancourt, Nicolas,
  181–2
Petrarchan motifs, 72, 78, 81, 98
Petronius, 133
Philostratus, 186–7, 188–9
Pindar, 99
Plato
— Laws, 108–9
— Republic, 178
— Symposium, 32, 63, 104,
  108–9, 122–4, 182
Pléiade, 82–3
Pliny the Elder, 6
Plutarch, 31, 136, 174
Poliziano, Angelo, 185, 189
Primaticcio, Francesco, 24, 26–7,
  36–7, 43–4
prudence, 41, 155 (prudentia)
  168–79

INDEX

Rabelais, François, 32, 62, 87
Rabineau, Quentin, 4–5, 7
Raulin, Jean, 3–4
Robertet, Florimond, 25
Romieu, Jacques de, 155
Ronsard, Pierre de, 26–7, 69,
    183, 186, 190, 192–3, 197
— Amours, 85–6, 99, 187, 192
— Folastries, 85–101
— Odes, 85, 96
Rosso Fiorentino, 24–5, 28–34,
    37

Sadoleto, Jacopo, 40
Saint-Gelais, Mellin de, 85
Saint-Luc, 148, 156, 162
Sales, François de, 2–9, 14, 18–
    19
Salic Law, 11
Sauvage, Denys, 64
Scepticism, 105, 111–121, 124–6,
    142
Scève, Maurice, 61–84
Secundus, Johannes, 85, 93
Serres, Jean de, 140–1
Sextus Empiricus, 112–15, 118–
    20, 124
Socrates, 104, 106, 117–8, 122–3,
    178, 181–4
sodomy, 35, 88–9, 103–5, 114,
    120, 125, 188, 195–6
Sorel, Charles, 87
Speroni, Sperone, 65
Sponde, Jean de, 167–79, 193

Statius, 184
sterility, 117, 147–65
Stoicism, 178
Sun
— as female, 70–3
— as male, 43, 61, 66, 68, 194
Sylvius, Symon, 64

Teresa of Avila, 2, 19
Theocritus, 190
Thomas, Artus, 133, 188
transvestism, 26–7, 128, 157,
    160, 187, 193
Tristan L'Hermite, 186–7, 193,
    197
Tyard, Pontus de, 64, 182, 184,
    187, 191–2, 197

Valour (fortitudo), 168–9, 172,
    179
venereal disease, 35, 148, 150,
    162
Verville, Béroalde de, 62
Viau, Théophile de, 186–9, 193,
    195, 197

Vigenère, Blaise de, 187
Virgil, 190
virginity, male, 5–6
virtus, 98, 168, 172
Voragine, Jacobus de, 5

Wars of Religion, 45, 167